ORGANIZATIONS THAT MAY EXEMPLIFY THE CATEGORY	PERIOD OF THIS SYSTEM'S PROMINENCE IN SOCIETY	CAPACITY TO PRODUCE VALUE	ABILITY TO ADOPT TECHNOLOGY AND SYSTEMS ADVANCES	ABILITY TO ALTER OWN ORGANIZATION STRUCTURE	MULTINATIONAL POTENTIAL
Leader/tribe model, Napoleon's army, Hitler's Germany, Mao's China, Chiang's Taiwan, most R&D groups, performing arts companies, the military squad	5.5 million BC to today	High, but eroding rapidly except in emergencies	Low	Almost none	None
Holy Roman Empire, United Nations, NATO, SEATO, European Common Market, urban communities, voluntary associations, IGY, ILO, tribal nations, medical groups, law partnerships, colleges	9000 BC to today	Low, but excellent for single-interest cooperation	Low	Low	Low
U.S. government departments (HEW, Agriculture, etc.), unions, utilities, banks, transportation companies, public education system, religions, foundations, public corporations like N.J. Turnpike Authority	1000 BC to today	Medium to low	Almost none except in phoenix process	None	Low
Military establishments, organized churches, courts of law, political parties, governments in general, most small and middle-size businesses	2600 BC to today	Medium and fading due to rising expectations	Low	Fair	Fair
The 1900 trusts in the United States, the 1929 holding companies, European cartels, the modern LTV, Litton Industries, Sperry Rand, Monogram, Glen Alden, Gulf + Western, Allied General, City Investing, Marcor, Boise-Cascade, ITT, the Pentagon	AD 1000 to today	Low; at times a historically destructive device	Moderate	Fair	High, but has limiting goals
General Electric, Eastman Kodak, Sony, Du Pont, International Harvester, Shell, U.S. Steel, Unilever, Philips, Nestlé, Alcoa	AD 1800 to 2500 (est.)	High; results-oriented	High with diminishing potential	High with slowing rates of change due to excessive growth	High with encouragement of other cultures
Possibly IBM, Xerox, NASA, Texas Instruments, Volvo, Battelle, and CSIRO (Australia); and unknown forms yet to be developed	AD 1950 to 3050 (est.)	Highest future potential; creates futures	High with unusual potential	Highest with capacities for complete metamorphosis	High and globally wholesome

CORPORATE CITIZENSHIP   the notion that any employee can be equal to any other in the exercise of certain rights of organization membership (job development, self-development, goal setting, future creating, decision making, and others) in contrast to the notion that an employee is an adjunct to a machine or a desk (a second-class citizen)

Organizational Evolution

Organizational Evolution

A Program for
Managing Radical Change

GERALD J. SKIBBINS

amacom

A Division of American Management Associations

Library of Congress Cataloging in Publication Data

Skibbins, Gerald J
   Organizational evolution.

   Bibliography: p.
     1. Organizational change. 2. Management.
I. Title.
HD38.S578   658.4'06   73-88390
ISBN 0-8144-5353-8

© 1974 AMACOM
A division of
American Management Associations, New York.

International standard book number: 0-8144-5353-8
Library of Congress catalog card number: 73-88390

First printing

Contents

Foreword

If business is to be more than a government-subsidized employment agency in the future—as Skibbins sees it—it must meet the radical changes now going on in society with radical changes of its own in motivation, organization, and management. In other words, MOM needs to be reinvented. To business managers who like their MOM as usual, that can be a disturbing thought, if not a downright sacrilege.

Assuming that profit is society's reward to business for services rendered, if business is to be profitable—that is, to survive—in this technological era of unprecedented change, something more remarkable than business as usual is to be expected from the managers of all economic organizations. Business too will have to change—radically. (Kelso, for instance, asks why, if American capitalism is so great, only 5 percent of the people are capitalists.)

This book uses a provocative analogy. The butterfly. Once it was a caterpillar. *Now* it's a butterfly. That's radical change. And it is *natural*. But how does a caterpillar decide it wants to become a butterfly? *That's management's problem*. Just how does management become aware that it needs and can actually achieve a radical change in its totality?

Until managers recognize the radical changes industrialized societies are already into and can see for themselves the really potent sources of social and economic profits which radical change might give them, they probably won't try to change their organizations other than in minor ways. Why should they?

Skibbins is aware that we are already into a fluid technological era, and he has prepared for it; but do most managers really understand that we are living in a time of major societal transition? Harried as we are with daily concerns, here we sit with the levers of decision in our grasp, unable to attend to the sort of alien future that we fear lies immediately ahead of us. Many leaders try to push the entire subject aside. (It is interesting that their wives and young people seem to have a more accurate understanding of the new values people are adopting and the new demands for wholesale change in all our institutions.)

The trouble is that most managers of business (or government or other organizations) cope with the future in small here-and-now increments. They adapt. The management styles they assume for day-to-day operations all too often dominate their dealings with the future too. For many managers ten or fifteen years spent in the Skinner boxes of management, while slowly finding their way to decision-making levers, results in a lobotomy of that part of the brain where original, innovative, or radical thoughts may once have occurred. In time, within the walls of most institutions, the ambitious manager learns what thoughts aren't smart or safe to hold. The result is that he doesn't think them anymore. As the Watergate affair so clearly demonstrated, in every organization key people do not raise fundamental questions because they have been conditioned to "know" what works and what doesn't work.

Now comes this book to reopen inquiry into the fundamentals of organization life, especially in business and industry. (How many will attempt this after they have taken ten to fifteen years to master the lore of the place in which they work? Won't most conclude there's quite enough to do just to keep up with hectic daily operations?) Despite these hurdles to change in men's minds, Skibbins believes that most managers are responsible, adult human beings who can and will take on the tasks of managing radical change in their organizations when they fully appreciate what great new opportunities are hidden in that process.

I agree that this is a time when we can do anything we want to but not everything we want to. Choices have to be made. Yet most institutions, whether business or government, move toward their future by making today's choices on the basis of what they've learned in the past. That's considered practical. And, in fact, it is true that, in bygone eras of much slower and far fewer changes in the world, it *was* practical. But not now. Skibbins hopes to alert business managers to lead their organizations, and indeed the whole society, into a radically different and better future. He provides for backup to such leaders in the form of outside expertise, interdisciplinary approaches, systematic procedures, and widespread participation by organization members. But what concerns me is what will motivate top managers to pick up this new and exciting tool.

It will probably take what de Tocqueville recognized as the core of American genius—the voluntary association—revitalized and put into new form for this technological era and commissioned to establish generally within the society both the immediate necessity for radical change and the means to accomplish it.

Aside from that thought, it seems to me that Jer Skibbins' book is an opening wedge that will prove immediately useful to those exceptional managers who are already aware of the meaning of our times and have distinguished the great opportunities presented by the ongoing technological and social explosion. But for most managers, a clearer comprehension of the demand for change will first have to be built nationally, regionally, and within various functions of society. The bicentennial celebration of the founding of the United States of America *could* take on this task. It could adapt the core revolutionary dynamics of democracy and capitalism into new innovative organizations that can create better futures for people in the free societies. Alas, there's no sign yet that the bicentennial's way of looking backward will produce anything so bold. In contrast to such safe preoccupation with the past, this book opens wide the door to our future as a free people and insists that radical change is an option whose time has come for every manager of a value-producing organization.

WILLIAM R. EWALD, JR.
Development Consultant
Author and Editor

Introduction

The Trouble with Jer Is Jill

The man who wrote this book is called Jer by his friends, and there are many of them. He leads a tough, California life, spending much of his time at The Sea Ranch in a beautiful house overlooking the surf breaking up over the rocks of the Sonoma Coast. At other times you can see him in a business suit, tootling along on his ten-speed bicycle from his Fisherman's Wharf apartment to work in an old wharfinger's office on The Embarcadero, the San Francisco waterfront; but that's another tale.

For now, you are with him at The Sea Ranch. He has a dog, an enormous golden retriever. Her name is Jill. Like any dog, anywhere, she has to go for a walk in the morning. Waves high, gulls screaming, hawks circling, Jill lets you know when she wants to go. She leans on you until the pressure is too great to bear.

Now follow this closely. There is a path through the meadow, leading down to the sea cliff. The meadow is glowing with wild flowers, gleaming with grass, knee high. The surf is a foamy thunder.

Jill leads the way. Jer stumbles after her, still half asleep. The trail branches at the high cliff's edge—right, up toward Alaska; left, toward Mexico. Jill makes her choice; it's an either/or Aristotelian kind of thing. Left or right? Some doggy instinct or intuition, or whatever it is dogs have, triggers the direction. It's a go/no-go system. Jill bounds away toward Mexico, stopping only to glance back once in a while to make sure Jer is following. Doggone!

This is, of course, the pattern of most management decisions. Does one go ahead, and if so, in what direction? Jill's choice is a relatively predictable one with a probability of 50 percent. Left or right?

Management decisions in an institutionalized society are not all that simple.

Watch Jill. She's at the end of her run. She wants to go home again. The simplest way would be to retrace her steps. That's what most institutions do. But there are other ways to her goal, which is familiar territory: a pan of water and a dog biscuit tossed high in the air. Which is her profit. Being a born retriever, she will probably miss the biscuit; that's the way it sometimes goes.

But her choices at this moment as to how to get home—a sort of doggy Utopia—are manifold.

Squatting there on the path, Jill can either just retrace her steps or come bounding back through the meadows, sniffing flowers, chasing bees, digging for gophers, chasing butterflies, slopping through muddy water from the springs that flow like liquid crystal from the rocks on the hillside.

She also can jump over the cliff into the boiling seas bursting over the rocks below or head for the high timbers that line the ridge; these too are choices that she can make. One of her doggy-like errors is that she has forgotten (if she ever knew) about the possibility of an avalanche, or a tidal wave, or an earthquake. They are not among her choices. These natural cataclysms are analogous to the great political, economic, and social forces that may build up around a human organization. Those are the ones *we* forget. But that is *not* the kind of inadvertent change Jer is thinking about; he is contemplating how men might themselves control the radical change process.

Well, Jer is standing there, contemplating Jill, and he knows that she is much more complex than any institutional organization he has ever studied. He also has a pretty good idea of the number of alternatives available to Jill. Jer is, in essence, scanning an array of probabilities and assigning a value to them.

Being a little tired now, Jer sits down, stares at Jill, and wonders what course she may take among the alternatives open to her. He thinks up an idea for his book: "We can deliberately form the future."

Could Jill? Could she come up with something really new?

He thinks: "Radical change? When a caterpillar metamorphoses into a butterfly, it has the same identity, but it is almost wholly different."

Can any organization transcend its nature? He remembers the many devices most organizations adopt to resist change. He thinks: "The winds of change blow far too hard for these fragile, wishful kites."

See what is happening to Jer, writing his book while he is caught up in the same space/time frame as Jill? He is drawing upon those organic processes that are within the scan of his attention. Bugs. Wind. Forks in the paths we choose.

He thinks: "Let's face it, a cabbage plant in the ground is an infinitely more complex and more efficient system than a computer assembly plant on top of the ground. A tree is a much more complex system than the lumber company that chops it down. Your dog is a far more sophisticated system than is your government. A firefly gets more light efficiency from its resources than Con Edison ever could, and an ordinary river has more identity than ITT."

Why do you suppose he chose a dog for his analogy instead of some other equally complex animal? Jill, of course.

He thinks: "If we ranked all the organisms alive on this planet on the basis of the sophistication of their internal organization, then our companies, schools, governments, and institutions would rank somewhere down among the algae." He thinks about what people want when they organize enterprises: "Who wants anything but a quietly humming, completely automated company with no employees but huge profits?"

Here the bees servicing the wildflowers contributed the humming. They were above the meadow, atop the sea cliff, in the presence of Jill. These subsystems—as they are for any institution—are a part of the total context in which Jill must make her choice. Systems within systems within systems. Fields within fields within fields.

He thinks: "Perhaps the most awful thought to contemplate about the future is that we are afraid we already know what it will be like. Aren't most of the people irrelevant to the enterprise already?"

A little depressed now, he looks out over the cliffs to the seas breaking up over the rocks below. The conflict speaks of change and stability. "True stability today is symbolized by the surfer mastering a giant wave. It cannot come from a rotten little rigid organization whose leaders myopically peer out at an unfriendly world."

He thinks about bureaucracies: "We seem to be afflicted with thousands of government agency programs which have never been anything but total failures but which continue to exist like ticks on a dog."

So Jer thinks about controlling radical change in this organic environment he shares with Jill and comes up with what you are going to read in the following pages.

And what did Jill do, after all? She followed him home. If you read him carefully, you will follow him home, too.

DON FABUN
Author and Editor

Preface

The flood of communication about management, organization, and systems may never ebb. Its current level marks the intensive search which is now going on for ways to make life inside organizations more rewarding and to make the multifold outside effects of organizations more benign. Anyone attempting to add to this exploding literature is humbled by its size and complexity. The author is not immune to that mood.

The main body of this book differs from most of this literature in that it provides the rationale and the how-to-do-it techniques which managers can use now to deliver large-scale, socially positive, economically buoyant radical change to their own organizations. The appendix reviews major contributions to the literature of organization and describes the change system model for the management scientist.

Many people have helped me through this intensive fifteen-year investigation of the many literatures affecting change management. As to seminal concepts, I think of acknowledging debts to Don Fabun, William R. Ewald, Jr., Eric Hoffer, Abraham Maslow, Stafford Beer, Robert R. Blake, James V. Clark, Warren Bennis, Chris Argyris, Ludwig von Bertalanffy, Robert Guest, and Jay Forrester, among many others. Direct stimulation and personal assistance came from Roger Warner, Jr., Gary Chism, Stephen Barker, William Brickner, and Penelope Wong-Berner; manuscript help came from Lynne Bartholomew and Helen Grann. Ernest C. Miller of American Management Associations provided unusually accurate editorial counsel which improved the entire work. My mother's lifelong encouragement and the unfailing trust, love, and care of my wife, Sara Lee, made it possible to arrange my life so that I could complete the job.

If mistakes of comprehension appear in the book, blame should come to me. Like any other manager or student of organization, I am painfully aware that organizations are extremely complex environments in which our personal observations can be quite erroneous; yet the option every day is the same: We must move ahead. Hopefully, this work will help managers move toward a future that will be unusually rewarding.

GERALD J. SKIBBINS

PART ONE

Organizations Today

CHAPTER ONE

The Demand for Radical Change

Many of today's problems arise partly because the technological advances which have so greatly affected our social
environment have occurred much faster than the
normal rate at which adaptive changes in social behavior
can accommodate to them.

J. H. MILSUM

The behavior of the community is largely determined
by the business mind.

ALFRED NORTH WHITEHEAD

The attack on business takes the form of a demand for
change—rapid, radical, revolutionary change.

GEORGE CABOT LODGE

Change proceeds at one rate or another in all things. If we evaluate a substantial part of the life cycle of any human organization—such as a business organization—we can distinguish three large categories of change:

A minimum rate of change　which occurs in what is called homeostasis.

A modest rate of change　which occurs in adaptation.

A high rate of change　which occurs in continuous radical change, continuous metamorphosis, continuous transformation, or rapid evolution.

A characteristic of these rates of change in organizations is that they can be positive or negative. Through *negative* change processes, for example, a company or other organization can lose ground grudgingly, steadily, or at disastrous rates. Similarly a company can, if it will, create *positive* change processes that operate at slow, medium, or fast rates, depending upon its management's ambitions, skills, resources, and environment.

Looking back through the history of management practice to about 1900, Taylor, Fayol, Weber, and others taught managers how to design and control what we would now call homeostatic organizations which ran by the book and made changes relatively slowly. In their day, these practices turned out to be innovative, efficient, and highly profitable. The next major advance in management practice was developed from about 1920 to 1950. In this era a much larger group of innovative managers and management scientists created the bulk of what we now regard as modern management technique, classified here as adaptive management. It has the capacity to maintain medium rates of change. As revealed in the bottom-line performance of today's more advanced business and industry managers, adaptive management is now generally more profitable than running companies by the book.

We are now approaching another great revolutionary phase in American management practice, wherein managers of organizations large and small will learn how to live with, control, and profit from much higher rates of change. Most advanced managers and management scientists are already aware that it is possible to break through the medium-rate-of-change sound barriers in their organizations. They are pushing hard for experimentation in this field. They recognize the possibility of creating far more valuable, rewarding, and profitable organizations by altering the objective, the form, the technology, and the function of their present organizations. Such thinking among the most skilled managers brings up the problem of how to manage the process of radical change. The change systems described in this work were designed to meet that problem.

Managers can now transform their present organizations. Managers can remove the many obstinate conditions which block them every day as they try to raise performance and create constructive growth. In any poorly performing operation, they can introduce basic factors of organization dynamics which will deliver new and better organization behaviors. Among these potential benefits are:

1. The overall profitability of operations will leap upward.
2. Both employees and managers will experience new and much more rewarding careers.
3. Innovations will be created in greater volume and will be adopted more readily throughout the organization.
4. Life in the organization will experience a fundamental change of identity, a revolution or metamorphosis to levels which are more humane, more considerate of individuals and of greater interest to people, more adaptive to the higher technologies, and more benign to society and to the natural environment.

Certainly no system proposal could deliver all these qualities to all kinds of organizations in all circumstances; but just as the homeostatic style gradually turned America's job shops into production lines that hummed with efficiency and profit and just as adaptive modern management tripled our gross national product and expanded American businesses all over the world to a position of dominance, so too will the next American management revolution—the one in which managers will learn how to live with high rates of change—offer to most organizations a large, new field of opportunity that has rarely been plowed.

To begin answering the questions which experienced managers must have at this stage, let's reconsider the three basic conditions which characterize organizations:

1. *Homeostasis* (or stasis) describes a system in which internal and external forces are nearly in equilibrium. Managers of homeostatic organizations operate with limited short-range goals and tend to run such systems pretty much as they are. Most organizations and institutions of which men are components now operate in stasis. They make few changes from year to year, use old-fashioned authoritative management styles, and run by the book until their organizations run out of energy, resources, or market demand. Some examples are:

— The mature company using established and orderly techniques to produce basic products or services which are in demand
— A government agency operating with hundred-year-old guidelines despite the evaporation of public need for its output

— A publicly supported school routinely equipping young people with
the skills needed in a bygone era
This general organization condition works as long as the environment and the economy are stable and permissive. In a time of transition
—such as the one we now live in—when the societies and economies
of the world are in turbulence and new demands spring up every day,
homeostatic organizations are in extreme danger of extinction by outside forces. Under these conditions they can be rescued only if they
set aside their traditional, limited goals and seek new organization structures, purposes, and technologies and a distinctly new environmental ac-
commodation.

Due to the remarkable work of Rensis Likert [1] and other management researchers at the University of Michigan's Institute for Social
Research, there is no longer much doubt that, in all but the best-run
companies, managers continue to rely upon these old homeostatic management systems, which produce short-term gains but now risk long-
term losses. Likert defines management styles with his systems one to
four: exploitive authoritative, benevolent authoritative, consultative,
and participative group. These systems have been measured in many
U.S. companies. Most of the high-profit, high-productivity, low-labor-
trouble companies check out as reflecting system three or four, and the
bulk of the low-profit, low-productivity, high-labor-trouble companies
turn out to be system one or two.

These definitive data have removed any doubt that a large majority
of managements have retained the management systems least likely to
accomplish their objectives under current conditions. Likert's findings
are likely to prevail over unscientific attitudes about management systems. Lean bottom-line performance for many years will eventually
encourage a great many companies to consider whether their present
management system needs replacement by at least the adaptive model.

2. *Adaptation* is the second condition of organizations, wherein
managers maintain medium rates of change. This is a common trait of
human beings, but only the more advanced business and industrial organizations in the United States consistently demonstrate this trait. They
have this characteristic because they must and do face up to rapidly
changing conditions in an open, high-technology, high-competition market. In contrast to such enterprises, few of the other institutions of
industrial societies display much adaptation. Our schools, governments,
religions, cultural organizations, and settlements change far more slowly
than business organizations do. Even within the field of business enterprise, as stated earlier, most organizations cling to turn-of-the-century
homeostatic concepts and are slow to accept the adaptation techniques

developed over the last 50 years. Chapters 2 and 3 describe how and why this steadfast rejection of modest rates of change limits most organizations. Chapters 4 to 7 explain how to circumvent these obstacles and move on to the higher rates of change.

3. *Radical change* refers to the kind of high-speed, large-scale process that occurs within a single organism when caterpillars metamorphose into butterflies, tadpoles into frogs, or mycelia into mushrooms. It also occurs over generations in the process of evolution described by biologists. The organism retains the same identity, yet it is transformed into something wholly different. In these cases, the organism moves from state A to state B, which is a first step in defining radical change. The rest of the definition is that we are really seeking *continuous* radical change in which the organization will move from state A to states B, C, D, E, F, and so on.

Modern organizations with men as components do not yet possess this continuous-change capacity, although we know it is displayed as a system capacity of the long evolutionary cycles of nature. Within reason, whatever nature thus displays, men can unravel. When the systemic sources of radical change are thus completely revealed, it is predicted here that the managers who use these skills will uncover enormous social and economic profits from within their own organizations. This great profit potential, the sheer newness of the venture, and the scope of the social challenge make understanding how to manage radical change the biggest game in town—*the next American management revolution.*

By rejecting stasis as a goal and by recognizing adaptation as a way station, we can now concentrate upon continuous radical change as the true organizational mode for the future of most ambitious organizations. This sweeps away the muddled thinking which forces today's organizations into painful, go-nowhere adjustments to the pressures of our times. Instead, managers can propel their organizations forward into a future they design. Instead of being buffeted unmercifully, as they now are, by the storm waves of change, they can ride them, like skilled surfers, with exhilaration and enjoyment and with personal, economic, and societal profits well beyond any levels they could reasonably expect from their present organizations.

To add the manager's personal perspective and knowledge to this discussion of the three general conditions of organizations—homeostasis, adaptation, and radical change—Test 1 was designed. At this stage we are not defining organizations or their variables with any precision. That process begins in Chapter 2 and is pursued in detail for the management scientist in the appendix. At this point, each manager can gain a sharper

TEST 1

Checklist of Organization States

Circle those items in any column that describe your organization.

IN HOMEOSTASIS Managers Tend to:	IN ADAPTATION Managers Tend to:	IN RADICAL CHANGE Managers Tend to:
Tighten the system	Improve the system	Replace the system
Control variances	Adapt to market changes	Create new markets
Retain top manager authority and control	Decentralize authority	Allow authority and control to follow operational needs
Write more detailed operating manuals	Install job enlargement programs	Expand individual rights to commit the organization
Limit employee education	Expand lower-level training	Commit and encourage people at all levels to continuous education programs
Avoid and reject outside forces	Focus on and adapt to the most pressing environmental demands of the organization	Regard the exterior world as equal in importance to the world inside the organization's boundaries
Rely on and exploit an old technology	Adapt to new technologies mostly by creating new divisions or subsidiaries	Develop procedures which often replace technologies in operations and develop new ones in R&D
Expand mechanical and automatic systems to reduce employment	Use automation to cut out drudgery and make jobs more interesting	Explode automation, free people from machines, and use them as human beings
Set up a class structure	Speed the process of moving people up in status	Have only one status— human
Concentrate on better ways to run the system faster	Concentrate on loosening up the system in many ways	Concentrate on designing deliberately open-ended systems

TEST 1 (Continued)

IN HOMEOSTASIS Managers Tend to:	IN ADAPTATION Managers Tend to:	IN RADICAL CHANGE Managers Tend to:
Regard power and authority as a given	Regard power and authority as privileges to distribute gradually	Regard power and authority as products of a changing consensus of all participants
Exploit and manipulate markets	Educate and sell markets	Tune into and create markets
Regard outside experts as threats	Periodically appraise any activity through outside eyes	Be an experienced and regular buyer of outside expertise
Regard profit as a cyclical result of external forces	Adapt operations and expansion to maintain a profit level above average	Regularly invest in and concentrate on high-profit opportunities
Rely on rigid, vertical communications	Develop some horizontal communications	Establish open and uncontrolled communication
Pursue traditional goals	Adapt goals to current conditions	Develop wholly new goals to adopt for the future
Total	Total	Total

perspective of these three conditions as he evaluates his own organization realities.

Read down each column in Test 1 to decide at which rate of change your organization is now operating. Circle each characteristic which you feel is now true of your organization. You may wish to evaluate your organization headquarters group or a division or subsidiary you know well. After you have circled all those items which describe how managers in your organization operate, a simple total of each column will tend to generally classify your organization in your own experience. If the entire group of managers in any one management system goes through this appraisal, of course the totals reflecting their perceptions will be more definitive.

As Test 1 is likely to demonstrate to the individual manager, most organizations and institutions can now consider radical change as a strong candidate for future profit expansion and constructive growth. A great exciting adventure over uncharted territory awaits management. The art of managing change is now in such state that it is ready for application to business, industry, and other organizations of society. We are on the threshold of a revolution, an era of vast transformations in the structures of business, government, education, and all the social instruments of mankind. If we will deliberately raise our sights to this target, human society and the earth's ecology can be a good deal more in our control than they ever have been in our long journey from the primeval seas. We can decide what will happen to us all. We can deliberately form a better future, and, as we will see later, some organizations are already doing just that.

This book explains why our greatest opportunities as managers will come from the deliberate fostering of radical change in our organizations. It explains where and why radical change is in demand, how much is available today, what the obstacles to change are, and how a manager can radically change his own organization starting Monday morning.

The General Demand for Radical Change

Thoughtful managers around the globe sense an increasing tempo in the demand for radical change from those who are upset by the deteriorating quality of our daily lives. Many young people, employees, supervisors, stockholders, governments, communities, minority groups, undeveloped countries, professionals, and scientists demand that our companies and our institutions wake up to our needs for large-scale change throughout human society. This mounting pile of unresolved issues cannot be ignored much longer. People are weary of expecting their politicians to do anything about it and are seeking other leaderships. In the public mind, business and industry managers are the prime candidates to satisfy this search; but more importantly to business itself, these great demands can be turned into profits if they are met in economic as well as social arenas.

Chapter 2 demonstrates that these demands for change far exceed the supply now available from the managers of companies and other institutions of society. As a result, the day-to-day security of every business organization and social institution is threatened. We have allowed a great, ravening demand for change to arise in our midst without providing any way to slake its thirst. Who can afford such risks?

Besides these demands for business managers to lead this society, we also face massive challenge from the broader social, economic, physical, and technological forces we have inadvertently set loose on this planet. Some of these are crippling labor costs, heavy taxation, resentment of multinational corporations, pollution, inflation, urbanization, crime, a still-potential nuclear holocaust, overpopulation, excessive government overlap, choking traffic, alienation, shoddy products, and the depletion of natural resources and the beauty of nature. For the most part we have not yet figured out what to do about these large-scale problems. Despite our best efforts, they continue to get worse. What is more, most of our present organizations are constitutionally unable to deal with them, as Chapter 2 will demonstrate.

The greatest challenge of all comes from the recent scientific and technological advances which made space travel a reality. The first human footprint left on the soft surface of the moon was a symbolic message to every man alive: Prepare yourself for a wholly new existence. *We are headed for the stars.* There is no room among star travelers for ancient hates, prejudices, and blood loyalties to some particular piece of dirt or to any one genetic strain. Now we are one, one people, the people of earth. Some of us may find this idea uncomfortable and embarrassing, but when we saw our beautiful planet on the TV screen, being photographed in the void of space by men we sent to the moon, we knew in our hearts we were one people at last.

Whose System Will Prevail?

If we think ahead to the days when space travel will be much more common, an essential quality of humankind's journeys among the stars will be our ability to evaluate other systems, that is, other organizations. An enriched vocabulary of systems concepts and an understanding of organization types will help us to understand and deal with the alien animate and inanimate systems we will find in our galaxy. When and if we meet other thinking-being cultures out in space, the issues of who will govern and who will dominate are likely to arise between us. Whether we deal with such systems on an interplanetary or galactic basis and whether our designs are benign or evil, all such interstellar relations depend upon the participants' systems sophistication and wisdom. In space or on earth, the society which has mastered the art of managing systems of which humans or other thinking beings are component will master all.

Let's narrow our focus from the stars to life on this planet. Despite many contrary and discouraging events in man's history, it is now likely that societies which develop plural, open, and accepting cultures will prosper and grow, whereas those which continue primitive organization methods to shackle their people with control, futility, oppression, terror, ignorance, or demands for conformance are more likely to remain static or die out. The rigid societies, as well as those business or social organizations which persist in imitating their methods, have placed limits on their own survival. They also tend to be less profitable and less socially useful ways to manage people.

Whether we appraise life systems on Mars, the planets of Arcturus, or our own organization here on earth, as managers we need new and more effective ways to evaluate systems and lead them to the more free and open, pluralistic arrangements that are possible.

Very few organizations, however, will change themselves in the direction of openness or plurality as a public duty or a social responsibility. If radical change did not hold up the real prospect of inordinate profits—which it does—it would have no more chance of widespread acceptance than any other do-good policy. The point to be made throughout this book is that radical change opens the door to a much higher level of profitability and reward and that every manager can ascertain this to his own satisfaction.

Must We Change Radically?

When top managers contemplate the complexity and the cost of the radical change process, some are bound to ask: "How can our organization survive while all this is going on? Can our stability and profits performance be maintained for three, five, or ten years while the main focus is elsewhere?" Concern over this issue can overwhelm any management's interest in radical change. An effective argument to kill the radical change option often goes like this:

"We are extended to the limits of our present abilities to deliver a minimum level of profits performance. How can we pile on the considerable costs of a change system and endure the lowered performance which this internal disruption will create in all our operations?"

Another telling argument is: "The gamble is too great. We *know* we can survive as we are now, even though any major growth in profitability seems remote. If we try to change, we lose what we have and gamble that we won't go broke. It's too great a risk."

Or retreat can be made to old canards: "We're not farming as well as we know how now; why fool with something new?" "We better wait and see what happens at the next board meeting." "When the international monetary [or inflation, labor union, political, or interest rate] situation clears up, we'll take a look at it."

All these management attitudes are based upon very real concerns. Management sees hundreds of options come down the pike. Most of them are of poor quality. Some are even suicidal. Good common sense requires managers to see their way clear before embarking upon new courses. Thus we are brought back to the issue: *Can an organization survive while undergoing radical change?*

As we will see later, it is unlikely that any but reasonably healthy and prosperous organizations can endure the individual, economic, and systemic stress costs of a radical change program. While it may be true that most organizations need to make radical changes today, those that have already dissipated most of their inner resources are doomed to fade out quietly or be swallowed up by more vital institutions. Only the healthy organization will be able to survive the long journey through the valley of radical change.

The Gap

Obviously, change occurs everywhere to all things at all times. The basic question really is, *at what rates?* Over the last few thousand years, changes took place slowly in most human affairs. Feudalism took a few hundred years to die out. Rome, like the opera singer, seemed to be dying forever. In these slow movements, people, organizations, social forms, and environments had time to adjust. Each generation had to endure only a very small part of the total adjustment that took place when men moved from agriculture to commerce to industry. There was time and ample room for rebels and people who refused to give up traditional and habitual behaviors. Now we have stepped up the speed of human society and, by bringing it into everyone's living room through television, we have narrowed the space, with the result that we have run out of both time and space to adjust slowly.

Figure 1-1 demonstrates the gap that exists between the major adverse conditions in society that man has inadvertently created—pollution, gross inequality of gain, inflation, urbanization, overpopulation, moral erosion, rejections by youth, meaningless wars, outsized defense systems, environmental decay—and the low response rate of human organizations. Figure 1-1 is based on judgment; quantifiable data have not yet been produced in this area. But the point is simple. We have speeded up some sectors of our society but have not yet created matching speeds in many of our basic and most important social organizations. Large-scale dislocations or rips are apparent in the fabric of business and the fabric of modern society. Many organizations are more out of touch, more inadequate, more primitive, and more of a drag on society every day they operate. We can measure the gap between the current rate of organizational change and the exponential rate of change demand let loose in the world, and every day the gap grows. We let this happen to us when we kept our organization's attention on small, gradual improvements but shrank from the risk and the challenge of large-scale, high-speed radical change.

This entire book is aimed at reducing the gap by speeding up the rate of large-scale organizational change. While it is natural for managers to recognize the value of small organizational adjustments in their daily work experiences, they must also realize that the basis for even greater achievements and profit potential is in the large-scale radical change process.

To me, the gap is reason enough for many organizations to seek out radical change as fast as possible. History records many instances in which sectors of a society leap ahead while more stable institutions drag their heels. At times this drag is normal and necessary, but in today's era of transition this policy could be the most dangerous any organiza-

FIGURE 1-1.   The gap between demands for change and organization response.

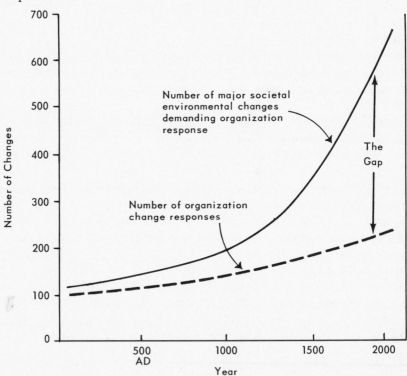

tion's management could follow. Too often the only way to adjust large-scale societal dislocation—such as we experienced in the case of black Americans recently or some time ago in the case of the Luddites *—is to resort to violent revolution. Revolution is not a very intelligent or effective procedure most of the time. Far too many people, as well as constructive organizations of society, get smashed in the process. Kindly minds recoil from the carnage, and wise heads seek to prevent it by attacking its causes. We can do better than to leave our own society wide open to revolutionary attack.

Men who value the rights of the individual, the great humanitarian ideals, and the social structures that enhance life and human liberty more than they value narrow self-interests and tradition will recognize that the future of what they hold dear depends on their reducing the gap before it produces a holocaust. It might be useful to reflect upon many other aspects of man's past and present as we decide whether radical change—closing the gap—is truly necessary for our own organization.

The Deep Past and Radical Change

The best way to get what we want out of the deep past is to spin the dials of a TV time machine back to 4.5 billion years ago, when one-celled life began to wiggle in the primordial seas. The action under water is still too slow to get a rating on NBC–TV, so let's skip forward another billion years, then another, then a few hundred million more to about 800 million years ago, when the first simple oxygen-breathing animals appeared. More slow changes went on under water in building backbones and differentiated organs, but about 400 million years ago the first amphibians stuck their noses out of the wet and looked around.

The whole scene is still of interest mostly to a paleontologist, but about 200 million years ago it was obvious that the dinosaurs dominated the planet. A million dinosaurs don't do much more than munch and lumber around, however, and about 100 million years ago, luckily, something went phut! Now, at last, there was room for the mammals, and they got going. After a while the earliest primates, the prosimians, could be seen peeking out of the trees. Soon lots of animals, birds, insects, and lizards speeded up the action, swallowing each other or the lush vegetation.

Skipping forward again on the dials to about 5.5 million years ago, we can see a character we now call *Australopithecus,* who might be one

---

* In the early 1800s the Luddites saw their way of life vanishing due to the introduction of textile machinery. Their reaction was to riot and smash the machines.

of our ancestors, doing manlike things.* *Homo erectus,* another variety, soon appears on our screen in the role of a more likely and better-looking ancestor of *Homo sapiens.* At any rate, various kinds of men and women and children can be seen all over the planet—hunting, fishing, and cooperating simply in the tasks of basic survival. They don't live long and there are not a lot of them, but they have one overwhelming thing going for them. They can think, reason, generalize, and apply thought to real life problems. No other animal comes close to these critters in this characteristic.

It must have taken some pretty careful organization to set up a large-scale woolly mammoth hunt in Europe 100,000 years ago. Recently enough bones were found to indicate that cavemen were pretty good at it. As they slogged through the Stone Age, the Copper Age, the Bronze Age, and the Iron Age, they got better and better at organizing control of their environment, using tools, and feeding their hairy faces.

Nine thousand years ago, Jericho was perhaps the first town. It must have been fed by new developments in an agriculture that gradually superseded the nomadic care of herds of domesticated animals. By this time the glory that was Greece was glorying and our time machine rolls up to about 1 B.C. on the calendar we now use in Western society. After the rise and fall of Rome and a lot of inventions resulting in wheeled vehicles, architecture, city design, laws, and military organizations, things went to pot in the Middle Ages while everyone concentrated on religion. The Renaissance, Martin Luther, and Calvin bounced us out of that holding pattern, as did the Crusades, the Great Explorations, and the Galileos and Newtons among us. We had now replaced the dinosaurs as the dominant predator, and we covered the earth. Let's hope nothing goes phut! for us.

So the world began getting smaller and a lot of processes began to speed up in a giant crescendo that is roaring in our ears today. Once man could move no more than a few miles an hour; now on our TV screen we tune in a picture of him rocketing along at escape velocity, 25,000 miles an hour. He used to move no more than a few miles from home; now he steps on the moon. He once knew no more than a few people; now, through electronic broadcasting from space platforms, this world and the farthest galaxies are in his acquaintance. A few traditional facts and principles once guided his conduct; now a library crams his brain. It has all speeded up to a blur on our time machine screen as we move

---

* In addition to other sources, much of this section on the deep past was drawn from *Life Before Man,* Time-Life Series, 1972, and *Anthropology Today* (Del Mar, Calif.: CMR Press, 1972).

through the first industrial revolution, the second, and then the third just completed. It makes one's head hurt just to think of it.

If we flip the dial back a billion years, the screen shows green plants, tall trees, slow-moving animals, and really not much activity. But flip forward to 1960 or 1970 and the kaleidoscope of organized life flashes by until we're dizzy with its input. So much is going on! Our consciousness is overladen with the sheer quantity of people and events around the world. And in a very short time the world has become almost impossibly complex except for one very important part of life: our organizations. In the long sweep of life's history both man and evolution have perfected many sophisticated and complex systems to make up the web of life, but our organizations are still primitive, a long way behind the rest of life.

Let's face it, a cabbage plant in the ground is an infinitely more complex and more efficient system than a computer assembly plant on top of the ground. A tree is a much more complex system than the lumber company that chops it down. Your dog is a far more sophisticated system than is your government. A firefly gets more light efficiency from its resources than Con Edison ever could, and an ordinary river has more identity than ITT. These systems, these organizations of ours are too simple. Maybe their time has come. Maybe a great many of the ills of civilization stem from the inefficient simplemindedness of the organizations we use to get the work of the world done.

If we ranked all the organisms alive on this planet by the sophistication of their internal organization, then our companies, schools, governments, and institutions would rank somewhere down among the algae. The point is that paleontology gives us a very good argument for radical change in the organizations man has created. Among nature's systems, the ones man has created for his institutions are primitive, too primitive.

People and Radical Change

When World War II Japanese army corporal Shoichi Yokoi recently came out of the Guam jungle after 28 years of hiding, he was baffled and confused. "Practically everything I encounter is tough to accept," he said. "I am having trouble preparing my mind to cope with all these changes that have happened in my country." He was glad to see the end of "the old kind of poverty," but, he exclaimed, "what a price to pay! The glories of nature that I used to know have all disappeared. Instead, up in the sky we have this thing called smog. On earth, cars are killing people even faster than war." He concluded, "The jungle of Guam may be the most reposeful place there is."

The impact of our times on us is clear enough. Despite the goodies distributed by our organizations, quite a few of us would run if we had a place to run to. Vance Packard says a lot of us are trying to run these days: Forty million Americans change their addresses at least once a year; the average American moves about fourteen times in his lifetime; many managers' wives have moved some twenty times during their marriages; and over six million Americans live in so-called mobile homes, perhaps ready to move from one shopping mall to another. These rootless people are in addition to the footloose airlines and steamship personnel, bus drivers, and other segments of the population who belong nowhere. What is worse, as we consider this dislocation of men from place, we realize that we are giving ourselves more and more time to run, to cut loose.

In his *Future of the Future*,[2] John McHale says that primitive man's eighteen years of life expectancy had about three years of leisure and creative time (including childhood play), six years of work, some eating time, and about eight years of sleeping. Not much to work with there. Agricultural man doubled this to thirty-five years of life expectancy divided into eight years of leisure, ten of work, one of education, two of miscellaneous activity, one of eating, and thirteen of sleeping. Industrial man, however, has doubled that span to seventy years and doubled virtually every other category while he reduced work from ten to seven and a quarter years. What's next on the curve? 150 years for postindustrial man with 100 years for leisure and three and a half for work? Or, as some biologists suggest, will babies born after the year 2000 have the option of eternal life? Then what do they do with it? Why do the organizations in our lives demand less and less work from the individual yet allow him decades for amusement and leisure when they provide him with so little to choose from? What is man to do with himself?

One answer may reside in man's inner space. Many philosophers and religious leaders have extolled introspection, trance states, contemplation, and the development of inner verities since the dawn of time. One can spend a lot of time exploring inner space. Partly because young people and others reject the outer world they find so bewildering, they now seek to turn on internally by a variety of means. A strong advocate for the value of the inner life, for new consciousness, and for new awareness is George Leonard. His recent book *The Transformation* [3] seeks to open men's minds to inner channels of growth as being superior to the old exterior materialism, the piling up of goods we so often find ourselves engaged in. He speaks of modern myths that need removal from society if people are to change their inner lives. Here are a few of them:

— *Growth*—Forget that bigger means better; it really means more risk.

— *Fertility*—Be ye fruitful but stop multiplying is a better credo.

— *The limited good*—It is not true that one must lose when another gains.

— *Inevitable competition*—Reaching for the brass ring is pointless when there are enough rings for all.

— *The societal will*—The group mind exists in every organization.

— *A separate species*—Man is not separate from the web of life.

— *The separate ego*—We have some separate ego, but we share in the ego of others.

— *The stable elements*—Diamonds, gold, and silver are poor objectives for a person's lifetime.

— *Glory, honor, duty*—These old ideas weaken and change as we get to know other societies better.

— *The law*—We must alter and are altering it quickly.

— *Matter, time, and space*—Science finds little here but energy flows.

Certainly if our times require that we should become nonpolluting and low-consuming, have low oxygen requirement, and be restricted to a limited space, then, like Hindu philosophers, we can most appropriately squat in a cubicle to silently contemplate these inner space issues. But will Americans endure that for long? I doubt it. We're much too healthy and energetic by nature.

Turning back to the affairs of man, it's not surprising that Alvin Toffler's *Future Shock* should have had so much impact on our society. It hit a nerve. People are very much aware of the giant epochal forces and technologies slamming into their lives like meteors. Our politicians try to say all is well, but the public is not very confident about its political leaders these days, to put it mildly. People can see that they are dealing with creaky institutions, outmoded and hopelessly inefficient government agencies, irrelevant charitable associations, and a great many companies trying desperately to do business as usual, ignoring the large-scale problems growing up around them like weeds in a field after the circus has left.

Whether one looks at the aged, the working population, or the young in the 1960s and 1970s, a high percentage of every group wants out from a world system whose voltage has somehow become too great for their fuses. We can see enough of this escapism to ask ourselves: What kinds of goals are we using as we continue to build organizations that worsen our environment for its people? Why must we idealize the kind of organization whose existence depends upon a smaller and smaller group of frantic, driven, high-pressure employees? In the name of what principle do we toss out large segments of both the young and the old on the trash heap of the unemployable? What are we organizing for? In many plants and companies we are pushing harder and harder to eliminate all but a token presence of human beings. Why? Which of our basic, dynamic industries is seeking to expand labor-intensive activities? Who wants more employees every year? Who wants to devise organizations which use people productively to create the future society? As managers review the current options for change, don't many of them unconsciously decide to seek out a quietly humming, completely automated company with no employees but huge profits?

The service industries and our various governments are picking up the slack as business rejects people as reliable organization components. But that may create a world of huge, expensive governments and vulnerable service industries that nobody wants or really needs. The facts are these: In 1900 we had 150 million people, 40 million (27 percent) of whom were employed in business and industry; in 1970 we had 220 million people, 40 million (18 percent) of whom were employed in business and industry. The trend is clear. Our basic economic organizations are hustling to eliminate people from their ranks. What does this leave for a young man to get his teeth into? A travel agency? Are we designing economic organizations so that computers and robots run the production and distribution processes while the people work for the government or a hobby center? Our economic organizations, meaning business and industry, must halt this trend or subsume it in some greater adventure that needs, really needs, people and their human skills to make it work. That is the demand for radical change from the people of the United States in the 1970s. We are becoming a disposable resource for our business organizations, and we don't like it.

Around the world in the underdeveloped societies the demand for radical change from people is quite different. In such societies people want basic jobs for income, food, housing, and self-respect. Most of them live in traditional societies whose leaders and institutions have resisted change even though that resistance has impoverished their people for hundreds of years. But here in the United States we need a new kind of organization that truly needs people and wants an individual commitment from them. Instead, we get a long string of boring institutions.

The overall operation of the United States economy presents a simple thesis: We overwork our resources and technology and underwork human beings. For example, the United States has 6 percent of the world's population and requires 50 percent of the world's energy to survive. Of course, the rest of the world *could* produce a great deal more energy, but is this a viable option for humanity and the thin skin of life it must protect on the surface of this planet?

Our system is what it is: it uses huge amounts of energy and resources. However, it has an unusual byproduct: it tends to use less and less of people's capacities. People in highly industrialized societies really have very little left to do. We can jog around the park, play tennis, keep house, go to meaningless meetings, shuffle papers in an office, or push buttons in a plant, but only where our efficient technology is thus far *unapplied* do we have actual work to do. There simply is not much work left to get your back into. Who really needs you?

To find satisfying work today, many return to primitive but unnecessary tasks. For example, we garden, farm by hand, and build fences, furniture, or houses for our manual satisfaction—just to remember what it was like—but our minds and hearts already know that machines and machine systems can do such tasks quicker and with less fuss. They also spread the benefits of such work to more people. Is it better for one family to have a carefully made home or for 20 families to have mass-produced homes which are more than adequate to their needs? Who is to decide this issue and for whom?

From top to bottom, our organizations reward peculiar kinds of phony busyness while ignoring the fact that most employees and managers are really unused and bored. This is not to say that occasional pressures and emergencies do not arise to challenge people for fairly long periods. Some can remember the overload of commitment and energy expenditure during World War II. Such real challenges of the public's individual energies can happen, but only so long as systems development, technology, automation, and work simplification ignore the challenge of obliterating it.

If a manager's daily experience makes great demands on his time, energy, and thought, it is almost impossible for him to believe in any automated supervisor system which might perform exactly those tasks with all the calmness of a water meter quietly ticking away. Such a manager might well say: "I'll hang on to my job as long as I can" or "We'll unionize to protect our jobs and stop automation" or "I don't believe any other way could be better."

However, a more constructive systems solution is possible; in it human beings and their experience are not discarded on the trash heap. That alternative is to focus clearly on the present, dull reality of our organization life with the idea of changing it radically. We can ask our organizations to make radical improvements in their marketplace functions and wholly new arrangements to meet the needs of the human beings within them. To do so, they will have to reach for goals many times greater than their present tiny objectives. They will, in short, have to prepare to leave the sluggish life of the caterpillar, incubate extraordinary futures, and then realize them through metamorphosis. The modern manager can remember his past and is aware of his present circumstances, but his future still holds mystery and enigma. When we learn to manage radical change, we learn to make our future more familiar by deciding what it will be and then realizing it.

Can a major future goal actually be accomplished for a large organization in view of the increasing complexities of life? If the goal is possible and the complexity of the change process matches the complexity of the situation, the organization's future can be created and realized. After all, the future and the events occurring in it are merely different points in a program for which we already have a great deal of information and over which we even have some control. As we enlarge our understanding of what is going on in ourselves, our organizations, and our society, we enlarge our ability to determine what our futures will be. Perhaps the fact most awful to contemplate about the future is that we are afraid we already know what it will be like and we hope for some unusual event that will make it more interesting to look forward to.

Once the skills of managing radical change become widespread, the capacities of men's minds will create a broad new arena in which to play the futures game. We will devise real surprises for one another when we take a strong hand in creating futures. Life should acquire zest and be full of daily fascinations:

• Business will not stay a mostly repetitive activity, nor will it stifle men's minds. Changes will occur fast enough to make each day at the plant or office an adventure so interesting and varied that men and women cannot resist coming in to find out what is going on.

• Influences from the arts will penetrate the whole culture to enrich its quality and texture in daily artistic experiences.

• Communities will gain sharp identities instead of trying to be alike, and travel will regain its charms. Homogeneity of urbanization will become a crime.

• The planet will regain its natural outdoor beauties in sufficient quantities and distribution for men to enjoy nature as a part of their daily experience. We will renew ourselves in natural outdoor experiences.

• Social adventures to help other cultures, to aid groups who need aid, to venture into outer space or beneath our seas, to create unique life-styles and environments will be set up as large, operating ventures which anyone can join.

To summarize, people want and will support radical change whenever it promises to enrich and enliven the qualities of daily life.

Youth and Radical Change

In his popular and controversial book, *The Greening of America,*[4] Charles A. Reich ably portrays the sharp, intuitive insight of youth as well as its confusion and inexperience. Our young people have sensitized the American public to the cant, hypocrisy, and meaninglessness too often accepted as normal in human behavior. Reich classifies the seven basic elements of our society as:

1. Disorder, corruption, hypocrisy, war
2. Poverty, distorted priorities, and law-making by private power
3. Uncontrolled technology and the destruction of the environment
4. Decline of democracy and liberty: powerlessness
5. The artificiality of work and culture
6. Absence of community
7. Loss of self

Reich feels that the ideals of young people are offended when they see

old people shunted into institutional homes, streets made hideous with neon and commercialism, servile conformity, the competitiveness and sterility of suburban living, the loneliness and anomie of cities, the ruin of nature by bulldozers and pollution, the stupid mindlessness of most high-school education, the coarse materialism of most values, the lovelessness of many marriages, and above all, the plastic, artificial quality of everything; plastic lives in plastic homes.

If we back off from such statements of young writers to consider the facts, what comes through? Well, one obvious fact is that, if they could somehow remove fear of want, large numbers of young people would never go near the organizations of our society. Recruiters from companies of all kinds, from governments, and even from education would find the going rough. Many of the young are on the run from the organizations we have built, work in, and admire. They find them a vicious influence on humanity!

We can use the reactions of young people to better understand what is happening to the whole society. For example:

• Instead of feeling loyalty, pride, and a desire to serve their country, a large segment of young people feel the Pentagon, the White House, and the Congress are their enemies.

• Instead of eager interest in attending high school or college to prepare for a career, enlarge their minds, and deepen their sensibilities, young people too often deny the right of such institutions to exist.

• Instead of anticipating the fun of throwing themselves into jobs or careers in the economy, young people seek ways to extract a living with the least possible personal involvement.

• Because they "see" a world in which our institutions are damaging and injuring people, young people seek the healing and caring professions as "respectable" and avoid the business, entrepreneurial, and managing professions as "disreputable."

In a different vein, John McHale claims the problem is marked not by rejection of the traditions and precepts handed down by elders but by young people "taking them seriously! They believed what was told to them about inalienable rights, the pursuit of truth and justice for all men, and other shibboleths." [5] Knowing that our society's organizations, especially business, can do anything they will, the young say to them, "Make it all come true, Daddy."

A clearer view of the dilemma comes from Konrad Lorenz, the respected biologist, who believes that adults must recognize the valid demands for change and that youth must acknowledge the indispensability of an established culture:

There are indeed many good reasons to revolt against the older generation. It is perfectly true that all establishments on all sides of all curtains are committing unpardonable sins against humanity.

I am not only speaking of actual cruelties, of political suppression of minorities, or the mass murder of innocent Indians by the Brazilians, but also of the deadly sins against the biology and ecology of mankind which are consistently being perpetrated by all the governments: of the exploitation, pollution and the final destruction of the biosphere in and on which we live, of the constantly increasing hustle of commercial competition which deprives man of the time in which to be human, and of similar phenomena of dehumanization.

The youthful do indeed have good reasons to take issue at the goals at which the majority of the older generation is striving and I think that they do indeed recognize the intrinsic worthlessness of utilitarian aims.[6]

"Adam Smith" recently said:

It may be that the era of purposiveness, with its inherent dictum of sacrifice, is winding down, however slowly. That does not mean another era of something else is immediately at hand. The counterculture may not be a proper guide to the future because it is defined by its opposition; it is easier to describe what it is against than what it is for. But it may serve to stimulate some sort of synthesis, to make us broaden the idea of what is "rational," to help crack the consensus. Long before the term counterculture came to be bandied, Keynes had delineated the lopsidedness of the accumulative society. "We have been trained too long to strive," he said, "and not to enjoy." Perhaps in a hundred years, he wrote—a hundred years from 1931, that is— the chief problem of mankind would be to live agreeably and wisely and well.[7]

On the other swing of youth's ideological pendulum, Herman Kahn [8] reminds us of the large counter-counterculture group (67 percent, he says) among young people who are "square and getting squarer." He pinpoints the malaise of youth among the remaining 33 percent, the children of the upper-middle class, and he discounts to some degree their influence on the whole society. Yet it is more likely that the upward-rising, upper-middle class is a fracture zone of our society and that its youth are in fact indicative of things to come.

Samuel A. Culbert and James M. Elden sensibly balance the rejection of our organizations by the young with concern over nonexplosive ways in which our organizations might change. They suggest a rapprochement between youth and the organization as follows:

The irony is that as our society becomes more complex, change is more necessary but more difficult, and violence is more costly. We desperately need to learn new, nonexplosive ways of changing in all sectors of our society —in government and labor as well as business.

Whatever the level, renewal efforts benefit from collaboration. Students are *issue-sensitive* but *organizationally naive*. Conversely, the corporations are *issue-passive* but *organizationally sophisticated*. The challenge of the 1970s is to combine the best of both worlds so that we can begin to manage the change required to actualize new values.[9]

The deep primal scream for change coming from a key segment of our youth is both pitiable and serious. Here again the demands for radical change affect every family with children and every community. Not many could have predicted the carnage we have witnessed in the young people we know in the United States and around the world. They break their spirits as they flail against what they see as the moral wrongs of society's organizations. Among the families of our friends, the malaise hits home. Parents all over the world feel poignant heartbreak over their young people. This is far from normal. It requires us to seek radical change that might once again fill young people with buoyant hearts and anticipation at taking their places in the organizations of society. In short, our youth need radical change in society before they can work out their destinies. *They need radical change to regain hope.*

Modern Business Societies and Radical Change

Sociologists and economists who appraise the United States against other societies would object to our breast-beating and crying out, "We're sick, sick, sick!" By any fair appraisal, United States society is a whopping success that is unique in the world's history. Embodying as we do all peoples and all cultures, we stand out as a kind of United Nations that deserted jawbone and went to work. Also, as Jean Francois-Revel points out in *Without Marx or Jesus,* "the stress and protest in the U.S. scene is part of the tremendous vigor and thrust of a society that is actually moving more rapidly than other countries in directions, such as democracy and diversity, that the world's intellectuals profess to value most highly." [10]

Our advances in societal organization and economic sufficiency have given us two things:

1. Time and resources to devote to unusual goals, that is, going to the stars, emancipating other peoples, eliminating the nuclear threat, and motivating young people.
2. Enough insight into our society to cut out the sick flesh from the otherwise healthy body.

Max Ways [11] presents a strong case for a balanced concern for radical change in our organizations rather than any bomb-throwing hysteria. He feels that people

exaggerate the power of business, its relative importance in the total structure. Business does, indeed, constitute the channel through which many of the new kinds of action flow into society, transforming it. Most of the fundamental social changes of recent decades—urbanization, mass prosperity, mass higher education, mass aspirations toward the good life—are intimately connected with the business system. These changes bring new problems and make old ones painfully visible. It is not surprising or, in itself, unhealthy that society says to business, "Since you can do so much, do better."

It is a sign of social hypochondria when critics, underestimating the intrinsic difficulty of many current problems, blame the morals or the motives or the structure of business for the fact that the problems are not yet solved. At this point, a lot of people start believing that the society is sick because it is "business dominated."

Perhaps it is because the cultural atmosphere of our time is pervaded by books, articles, speeches, plays, novels, and songs proclaiming society's corruption that many of the young and the intellectuals are alienated, that many employees of corporations feel morally unclean and psychologically frustrated.

We should resist such acceptance of guilt without losing awareness of what people in our organizations really think. As Ways points out:

A misplaced and overgeneralized consciousness of guilt can undermine the ability to make particular reforms. A man who says, "I am bad," may be locking himself into guilt. But a man who retains his self-respect while saying "That particular pattern of action is bad and I will correct it" may be on the threshold of moral improvement.

We may not like to think about it, but business really has been the most significant force in United States society. As Otto Bremer [12] claims,

Business is today the most significant force shaping American life and the strongest influence determining the everyday values of the average citizen; the operative values in the management of a corporate enterprise tend to become the operative values in the daily life of society.
. . . I am firmly convinced that the future of our society is going to be determined more by the day-to-day decisions of corporate managers—and the values that dictate these decisions—than by any other single influence. This conclusion is reached after 25 years as a student of business, a pastor to businessmen, and a campus pastor in turbulent Isla Vista watching the Bank of America burn.
I am convinced that if the business community will recognize the challenge that goes with the crucial influence it wields, we will not only insure a better fortune for the American people but also provide a renewed sense of meaning, purpose, and fulfillment for business executives.

Bremer suggests that traditional sources of personal value systems —the church, farm, the extended family, a sense of community, government, and education—have diminished in recent years while the influence of business organizations on values has increased. Again, nobody planned it that way. He suggests we have a new ball game in which all the positive and negative effects of business organizations are magnified many times by a society that knows full well how important business is to their daily lives:

The operative values in the management of a corporate enterprise tend to become the operative values of the average citizen. If this is true, it seems clear that the future will be largely shaped by the business community. The central issue then becomes whether or not businessmen are going to make the kinds of decisions and establish the necessary priorities that will channel their growing influence toward furthering a better world.

If we are to move our society away from "cowboy capitalism to a spaceman economy," as Kenneth Boulding suggests, not only business but government, education, religion, and our communities will have to undergo paroxysms of radical change. Too many organizations of our society depend upon a linear exhaustion of resources, the dumping of waste into the environment, and the automation or burnout of people. They simply have no machinery for recycling resources, reprocessing waste, or making permanent places for people to fulfill themselves in a humane manner. What are business organizations to do? The answer is radical change.

As we create a planetary society wherein more and more decisions must be made by organizations on the basis of their damage or value to people anywhere, to the air, water, or other aspects of the environment, then old allegiances to country and to old moral codes will fade away. We know perfectly well that someone or something will have to step on the toes of about 15 nations or there will no longer be more than a scattering of fish in the seas. Other examples abound. Every business and industrial leader is also well aware that most of the value being created in his enterprise now comes from expertise, technology, and knowledge he did not create and less and less from his invention or from the labor of employees. What will this trend eventually mean as far as who gets what for what? Can the Protestant work ethic dominate our mores when work is meaningless or short? Aren't most of the people irrelevant to the enterprise already?

Perhaps in the course of evaluation of business societies there comes a time when the value system that created initial success must yield to new formulations. John McHale [13] concludes that economic man and all the carrot-and-stick motivations and values that characterized him are behind us and that technology and automation have decreed that global man shall emerge soon. Because of the world business explosion, he can see good reasons for this:

1. Multinational corporations require resources from the entire earth to operate.
2. The level at which we now use the earth's resources creates by-products and products that materially interfere with our own life support systems on Spaceship Earth.
3. Our advanced technology systems are already global in nature— defense, space travel, satellite communications, air and sea transport, and telephone and telegraph, to name a few.
4. Commerce and finance are now frankly global operations.
5. Radio and TV implant a common world culture on top of local cultures.

6. International commissions and regulatory bodies are expanding their control.
7. International, scientific, professional, labor, and trade associations are multiplying their effects.
8. Almost all civilized men are recognizing that few major local problems exist; they're mostly global.

Considering that these vast forces are by their nature stepping up the pace of growth around the globe, what will resolve the environmental impasse they tend to create? In his remarkable work *The Systems View of the World* Ervin Laszlo provides a line of thought which is presented here as a strong argument for radical change in business societies:

The golden age of Greek civilization was guided by the ideal of living the good life. It was succeeded by Christianism in the West, where the good life was shifted to the next: the kingdom of God. It was not until the beginnings of the modern age that the eternal order of things was again subjected to empirical and rational scrutiny and man began to adopt new values. First he was playing "zero-sum games"; he proceeded on the assumption that there are a fixed number of goods, and these have to be distributed as equally as possible. The gain of one man is the loss of another—as expressed by the lonely wit who said that if there is a doll for every guy, some guy somewhere must be going around with two. However, with the rise of modern science and new techniques of transforming energy in the production of goods, zero-sum games were replaced by growth games. The theory of early capitalism, as expressed by Adam Smith, was based on the realization that there can be growth cycles where one thing leads continuously to the next, and by the time the cycle returns to its starting point there has been a gain all around. These cycles—such as saving, investment, production, distribution, consumption, labor, and renewed saving—were recognized to apply only to material goods. The spiritual goods were thought to follow in their wake, when everyone had had enough of whatever he wanted.

Equipped with the technological applications of Newtonian science, modern capitalism led to an unparalleled growth in economic productivity. Its values were materialistically oriented: *the good* is a large production per capita, and *the better* a still larger production. . . .

Western culture reduced the death rate, did not immediately drop the birth rate, increased interpersonal communication, and transformed the face of the earth in its image. At the same time this made for the consumption of natural resources at a compounded rate by a vast population. Whereas in centuries and even decades past, men thought that the sky was the limit, we have come to realize that the earth is. There is just so much of it, and just so much of what is there is usable for human purposes. Not only can we not increase per capita production indefinitely, but we cannot even duplicate its present rate in America and Western Europe for the rest of the world. All the people of the world cannot live as Westerners do today; the earth is not rich enough for that. This is something entirely new for the players of non-zero-sum games. Progress cannot lie in more and bigger, as we have come to believe. Progress must be redefined, and that means a new system of values.[14]

It is extremely unlikely that the world's business societies will arrive at any practical and wholesome new value systems without radical organization change.

United States Business Organizations and Radical Change

The gunslingers in the world of cowboy capitalism—not the whole of capitalism by any means—are both amusing and bizarre to contemplate. As "Adam Smith" says:

Radical change is very hard for most people to contemplate. For the man in the green eye-shade . . . the money manager's attitude is: "Sure, changes, we sell something and we buy something else to fit the changes. You say work is going out of style? We'll buy play. Here are my six Leisure Time stocks, and let me tell you how long I've owned Disney."

Money managers operate on the theory of displacement: the framework will be the same, but inside you move things around. My favorite is a gentleman I ran into after I got back from the Vega plant. I told him that one problem among others in certain localities was dope addiction, and at one plant—though the number sounded very high to me—the rate was reported to be 14%. "Well," he said, "I haven't owned auto stock for years. But 14%! Geez, who makes the needles?"

Now it may be that displacement is all we have to consider. "Ah, things are out, quality of life is in, back to the countryside. There is a waiting list for ten-speed bicycles; who makes the ten-speed bicycles? Ah, the ecologists are gaining strength; where is our list of water-pollution companies?"

That is probably good thinking on the tactical level, but there is also a strategic level, and the strategic level has to consider what the more profound changes are.[15]

More than that, would business really want the world to conclude that it is not fit to occupy its position of leadership and should be relegated to managing used-car lots? This image problem continues to fester and sicken business organizations' relations with society. Harold Marquis [16] points out that "When consumer protests can wring from one of the largest and most successful corporations a series of explanations and apologies for the faults it stands accused of, the critical importance of the corporate image becomes apparent." Marquis signals the passage of older value structures in corporate affairs when he says:

It is no longer enough for a corporation to grow and pay taxes, to pay fair wages to its employees, to make good products and market them honestly. Every business faces new economic and social responsibilities.
. . . To live and grow, to command respect and regard, the corporate image must be more than a product of public relations. It must be an accurate and effective reflection of management's principles and practices, and an accurate picture of what the company is and what it does. This image must be presented in terms stated by the public, not by business alone . . . the corporate image must show that management is progressive, mobile, open to innovation, fair to all, and free of dogma and convention.

Anderson, Sharpe, and Boewadt's [17] sober appraisal suggests that business organizations

are not closed systems [but instead are] essential elements in a complex sociocultural environment. Enterprises mirror society's priorities and goals. The evolution of organization goals, then, cannot be discussed without consideration of the evolution of societal goals. . . . [From the Reformation to the present, the goal of economic productivity has characterized most Western societies, and now] the vitality of an enterprise hinges in its ability to adapt.

Anderson et al. selected six external forces that set the pace and course of this organizational evolution: economic factors, political and governmental forces, ethical and legal influences, scientific and technological variables, physical variables (resources), and sociocultural influences. They believe the more effective marketing systems will adequately account for these variables and will be far more effective with the public than old-style marketers who still see people as "consumers." They say:

The products and procedures of the past are no longer appropriate. These have been invalidated by a shift in consumer priorities and goals reflected in consumer evaluations of the firm's market offerings. The nature of the evolution of consumer expectations can be seen in Maslow's hierarchy of needs. Firms must reorient themselves and their products—the two are becoming increasingly difficult to distinguish—toward satisfying the demands of customers in the era of self-actualization. These demands require that firms develop a social consciousness and, finally, an environmental consciousness. The cost of ignoring these demands is not profit; the cost is survival.

All the exhortation of business from its friends and its critics is not worth two cents, in my opinion, if it has no practical meaning. The point here is that real market advantages can be gained, *and are being gained,* by those who are most sensitive to what is going on and able to organize a new system to meet it. In every case, gaining and holding these advantages depends upon systemic radical change taking place within the business organization.

The Future and Radical Change

A Xerox Corporation study [18] of life in the year 2000 infers that, once automation is complete, competitive advantages will be derived from the quality of an organization's systems technology and from its marketing arm. Production differences will be nominal, and the product now considered so unique will be as unique as the paper clip. If this is a reasonable projection, then the radical change of primitive organization structures should be an important part of any organization's systems technology.

A concern of every top manager is "How can I manage radical change in this huge pyramidal organization without fouling up the works?" Stability is a legitimate concern, but it is not as great a problem as it appears. In nature and in man the hierarchies have everything going for them. Consider an organization that has a hundred equal components, such as a drive-in food franchise operation. When any major external or internal change occurs, like severe gasoline shortages or a change in food habits, the structure is liable to collapse in a heap. However, most major business organizations are hierarchies that have developed strength within divisions operating in different markets. These are hard to topple.

A hierarchy in man or nature, as Ervin Laszlo suggests, can "cut its losses and start rebuilding again." It has the strength to develop into a new form. It will not shatter, like glass, once radical change begins to occur. This is the true source of stability through a change effort. The point is that the hierarchy will come apart in manageable and still functioning segments which can fit into the new and metamorphosed structure. Hierarchies are tougher than managers realize.

In the largest sense, those who search for stability in a time of social transition can best succeed by learning to change faster than others. John McHale claims that we are still a captive of former eras in which change was sporadic and slow and linked cause and effect. As a result we still think of *stability* as a good quality of an organization which is the obverse of change, a bad quality. The problem is one of perspectives and clouded binoculars. Instead, flip to a view of this nature: "We cannot afford to have our radical change processes disturbed by any freezing or holding period that will knock us out of our position in the market."

The point is that, in our past and current view of the merits of organizational stability, we have simply ignored the seething cauldron of change factors building up in the organization and in society, and now they are flooding all around us. True stability today is symbolized by the surfer mastering a giant wave. It cannot come from a rotten little rigid organization whose leaders myopically peer out at an unfriendly world. The stability many managers think exists in their present organizations is very much like the peace and quiet of the old Shafter Ranch in California.

At exactly 5:13 A.M., the 18th of April, 1906, a cow was standing somewhere between the main barn and the milking shed on the old Shafter Ranch in California, minding her own business. Suddenly, the earth shook, the skies trembled, and when it was all over, there was nothing showing of the cow above ground but a bit of her tail sticking up.

For the student of change, the Shafter cow is a sort of symbol of our times. She stood quietly enough, thinking such gentle thoughts as cows are likely to have, while huge forces outside her ken built up all around her and —within a minute—discharged all at once in a great movement that changed the configuration of the earth, and destroyed a city, and swallowed her up. . . . If we do not learn to understand and guide the great forces of change at work on our world today, we may find ourselves like the Shafter cow, swallowed up by vast upheavals in our way of life—quite early some morning.[19]

George Leonard says that "like our ancestors in the late Permian period some 400 million years ago, we have just pulled ourselves out of the waters in which we have lived for millennia." [20] Naturally, we would first turn around and notice that seas exist and can be looked at. You can't see a sea if you're in it; you can see it only when you're out of it. You will know "concern for stability" for what it is only when you're well out of it. This would have been a poor observation in 1950, but it is right on target for the 1970s and beyond.

Change is in the air, and when it blows into our lives as it did in Athens, Rome, London, Florence, Jamestown, Yorktown, Philadelphia, Berkeley, Paris, Appomattox, Kitty Hawk, Hiroshima, Berlin, and many other places where great wrenches of society began, wise leaders trim their sails to the wind. Sometimes, as many predict for *our* time, we can have a pretty good blow. Perhaps it's a good time for all of us to forget about safe harbors.

Robert Heilbroner concludes *The Making of Economic Society* like this:

I believe that American capitalism stands at the threshold of a crucial decade. For almost a generation our society has been identified in the eyes of much of the world as a nation that is rich but indifferent; peace-loving in rhetoric but aggressive in behavior; boastful of its economic strength, blind to the misuse of that strength. Now the years are at hand in which that image —and the realities that are uncomfortably close to the image—can be changed. We will continue to be a rich nation; we must cease to be in so many ways a poor one. We will continue to be a powerful nation; we must learn the limits of our power. We will continue to be an economic colossus, but our economic system must now become the undergirding for a good society.

In view of our heritage, our traditions, our deeply rooted failings, this will not be an easy transformation for America to make. It may even prove to be an impossible one, although I strongly believe that this is not the case. But in any event, the all-important thing is to make the effort. The challenge is to *change America today* into a different and much better America to-morrow. In my view, this will be the most searching test of its character that American society has ever faced.[21]

George C. Lodge puts the issue bluntly:

Is management's function to perpetuate a certain technostructure or to serve the best interests of the community that surrounds and depends on it —shareholders, workers, consumers and so on? Most managers would prob-ably say the latter. If so, I submit they must be prepared for radical struc-tural change in their organizations. They should be looking at the introduc-tion of change as a primary order of work not so much out of a sense of nobility as out of an awareness of the requirements for competitive survival.

The nature of the American system requires that change be varied, many-faceted and multiple. Ours is not a particularly well-ordered society; it is not blessed with any great homogeneity; it lacks consensus; our government is diffuse and lacking in authority; national planning of any sort does not come easily to us. One could say, certainly, that this is our strength: manifold openness within which the many engines of change can move with freedom.

But what if the engines of change do not work hard enough or are throttled so that change is stymied or frustrated by its own chaos? The sys-tem will run down, malaise will spread, work will stop. . . . Let us say that to improve motivation and thus productivity, *radical changes in the nature of the internal structure of the corporation have to be made.*[22] (Italics added.)

From every discipline, from business itself, and in every walk of life, our society demands of all its organizations and of its business organizations in particular, not business as usual or hold the fort, but lead us in radical change to a better tomorrow. The demands for radical change are clear, but what of the supply?

References

The quotation of J. H. Milsum is from "Technosphere, Biosphere and Sociosphere: An Approach to Their Systems and Optimization," *General Systems Yearbook*, Vol. XIII, 1968. Alfred North Whitehead is quoted by W. B. Donham in *Business Adrift* (New York: McGraw-Hill, 1931). George Cabot Lodge's quote is taken from his article "Introducing the Collectivist Corporation," *Harvard Today*, March 1972.

1. Rensis Likert, *The Human Organization: Its Management and Value* (New York: McGraw-Hill, 1967).
2. John McHale, *The Future of the Future* (New York: Braziller, 1969).
3. George B. Leonard, *The Transformation* (New York: Delacorte, 1972), pp. 133–137.
4. Charles A. Reich, *The Greening of America* (New York: Random House, 1970), pp. 4–7, 246.
5. John McHale, *The Future of the Future* (New York: Braziller, 1969).
6. In Donald Schwartz, "Advice to Young and Old Alike," *San Francisco Examiner*, January 18, 1970.
7. "Adam Smith," *Supermoney* (New York: Random House, 1972). Reprinted by permission.
8. "The Squaring of America," an interview by Jonathan Ward, *Intellectual Digest*, September 1972.
9. James M. Elden, "Corporate Survival in an Era of Change," *Harvard Business Review*, December 1970.
10. Jean Francois-Revel, *Without Marx or Jesus* (New York: Doubleday, 1971).
11. Max Ways, "It Isn't a Sick Society," *Fortune*, December 1971. Reprinted by permission.
12. Otto Bremer, "Is Business the Source of New Social Values?" *Harvard Business Review*, November–December 1971. Reprinted by permission.
13. John McHale, *The Future of the Future* (New York: Braziller, 1969), pp. 268–278.
14. Ervin Laszlo, from *The Systems View of the World;* reprinted with the permission of the publisher, George Braziller, Inc. Copyright © 1972 by Ervin Laszlo.

15. "Adam Smith," *Supermoney* (New York: Random House, 1972). Reprinted by permission.

16. Harold Marquis, *The Changing Corporate Image* (AMA, 1970).

17. W. Thomas Anderson, Jr., Louis K. Sharpe, and Robert J. Boewadt, "The Environmental Role for Marketing," pp. 66–72, *MSU Business Topics,* Summer 1972. Quoted by permission of the authors and the publisher, Division of Research, Graduate School of Business Administration, Michigan State University.

18. "Life May Become Too Easy," *The Futurist,* April 1969.

19. Don Fabun, *The Dynamics of Change* (Englewood Cliffs, N.J.: Prentice-Hall, 1967).

20. George Leonard, *The Transformation* (New York: Delacorte, 1972), p. 162.

21. Robert L. Heilbroner, *The Making of Economic Society,* 4th ed. (Englewood Cliffs, N.J.: Prentice-Hall, 1972), p. 259. Used with permission.

22. George C. Lodge, "Introducing the Collectivist Corporation," *Harvard Today,* March 1972.

CHAPTER TWO

The Supply of Radical Change

Human society is not a community of ants or termites, governed by inherited instinct and controlled by the laws of the superordinate whole; it is based upon the achievements of the individual and is doomed if the individual is made a cog in the social machine. This, I believe, is the ultimate precept a theory of organization can give: not a manual for dictators of any denomination more efficiently to subjugate human beings by the scientific application of Iron Laws, but a warning that the Leviathan of organization must not swallow the individual without sealing its own inevitable doom.

LUDWIG VON BERTALANFFY

We must be careful not to subscribe to technological solutions which fall short of serving the human spirit, however well they meet our psychological, economical, or physical needs.

WILLIAM R. EWALD, JR.

The essential task of modern management is to deal with change. Management is the agency through which most changes enter our society, and it is the agency that then must cope with the environment it has set in turbulent motion.

MAX WAYS

M any changes managers say they accomplish do not occur. A poverty program director claims he can cure poverty if Congress gives him money; the record shows little or no change. A college administrator claims his school changes young people's lives; it does this rarely or in the wrong direction. A charity claims it can cure an evil; it does not. A new conglomerate claims synergy and all manner of wonderful managerial skills; but after investors inspect its accounting maneuvers, balance sheet, and operating results, its stock price plummets out of sight. Corporate annual reports over the past ten years have been larded with glowing claims of new worlds being conquered, but most of these claims have proved to be invalid.

We are at the end of a golden, post-World War II era which consolidated great advances for society. Profits increased steadily, but now, toward the close of the millennium, each organization and institution is finding it harder and harder to show the kind of useful growth and profitability it once found easy to deliver. Where will we get such quantities of new technology, cheap resources, and unsatisfied demand again? Can we find it in today's R&D, overseas business, cost cutting, automation, and acquisition? The end-of-an-era strategies for organizations are becoming defensive. Where is the internally generated growth we were counting on? Where can large profits be earned? Do we even want them any more?

Of course, everyone can point with pride to IBM, Xerox, Polaroid, Texas Instruments, and a few others for their growth, public value, and handsome profits records, but what about the other 98 percent of United States enterprises? They do not change much today. The situation is much the same with other institutions of society. For one NASA or Manhattan Project success we seem to be afflicted with thousands of government programs which have never been anything but total failures but which, like ticks on a dog, continue to exist.

The few effective college organizations which deliver educated people to the world must be contrasted with the thousands of baby-sitting associations we have set up as colleges but which produce little more than wind. Only a few years ago our education system was the dynamo and the strengthener of American society; today a great many see it as a blight, as an active degenerative agent in the lives of young people, and as the haven of the largest tax money boondoggle the country has ever known. School administration today makes yesterday's swindles involving river and harbor maintenance funds look like embezzlement from petty cash.

Everything one reads or hears speaks of the great changes going on in our times, so someone must be creating these changes. But are they?

No they aren't. The change on everyone's lips is *inadvertent change.* It is the uncontrolled fallout of growth and technology. It was not planned. Alvin Toffler describes it fully in *Future Shock.* We are just beginning to realize that, as managers, we do not know how to plan change in our organizations. At times of national emergencies, we can get change by dumping vast resources into a venture or by swinging a heavy hatchet, but change is rarely achieved in times of normal operations.

Inadvertent and Planned Change

As we appraise the supply of change, we can now recognize two kinds:
1. *Inadvertent change:* the side effects and spinouts of business structures, technology, population growth, urbanization, government debt, and so on.
2. *Planned change:* the deliberately planned for major changes which many organizations claim but few can deliver.

Inadvertent change is, of course, in oversupply. This indicates we live in a culture which has allowed substantial negative forces to go out of control. We did this to ourselves by developing our primitive organizations to excessive size without equipping them to deal with environmental and social degradation.

Considerable investigation is required to understand planned change. First of all, when it comes to the ability of an organization to plan and create change, we must deal with the "emperor's clothes" effect. The emperor's clothes fable deals with charlatan tailors who convince the emperor and his court that they have clothed him in the rarest, richest cloth. But during a parade through town of the emperor in his new finery, a child cries out, "But he's naked!" And he was.

When people in an organization talk about change and point to differences in internal operations, they tend to agree that great changes are going on; but if we get our terms straight and appraise these phenomena in the proper way, the emperor's clothes will vanish. This chapter explores new ways to look at the change capacities of our organizations.

Only within organizations can we adequately deal with both inadvertent and planned change. Throughout modern history, our primitive organizations have been the source of our troubles. Our organizations lack the machinery required to deliver the radical changes called for today. That machinery is crucial to tomorrow's profits. We have no means, little theory, and poor techniques for creating the changes we want. Thus, the supply of anything but negative, harmful change in society is today far short of our ideal of creating a constructive, beneficial world.

Most managers will admit they cannot see how their organizations might make any radical changes. It is contended here that unless we change the way we seek radical change, we will never attain it. The techniques of the past were sufficient to the past, but they are found wanting today. We must create anew. But where? The answer is plain: right in our own organization, starting Monday morning. That's the place for the most exciting transformations of society to occur. It will be the changes we make inside our own organizations which will eventually enable us to deliver constructive change to society.

To summarize this chapter's thesis on the supply of change in society:

1. We have too much *inadvertent* change.
2. We have too little *planned* change.
3. Planned change comes only from organizations.
4. The organizations we use today must be examined closely because too many of them may lack the capacity to deliver planned change.

To appraise these thoughts in a specific example, each manager can use Test 2 to appraise his own organization. (This test is designed for business, but other organizations can adapt it quickly enough. It is to be used with organizations ten or more years old.) Check each of the 14 questions regarding your organization and indicate your answer with an X in the proper column. As you consider each item, notice the close connection between internal changes and profitability. After answering each of these 14 questions, total all the yes answers. If your organization scores fewer than seven yeses, it is now operating at a low level of change capacity and is far behind its potential development.

Can Organizations Change?

The ability to achieve radical change can be plotted. For most of today's organizations, the resulting curve is skewed heavily toward the negative side. Curve A of Figure 2-1 is my estimate of the present situation in the United States, probably the most flexible large society on the planet because of its multicultural background, openness, system of law, and type of enterprise. This entire book on change systems is designed to equip United States organizations, and indeed organizations in all cultures, to move from negative change rigidity, the effects of which fill our newspapers and plague our lives, to the distribution described in curve

TEST 2

Testing Organizations for Their Change Capacities

Check your answers in the appropriate column.

YES	NO	In the last 10 years, has your organization:
( )	( )	Attained a return on investment of 25% in any one year?
( )	( )	Shifted its total dollar volume more than 50% into new products and services?
( )	( )	Made a major commitment of men, time, and money to developing wholly new outputs?
( )	( )	Steadily attracted more and more entrepreneurs and highly skilled people?
( )	( )	Continually increased its R&D investments?
( )	( )	Developed a practical system to test new ventures?
( )	( )	Become more and more open to new ideas?
( )	( )	Stayed ahead of the technology its operation employs?
( )	( )	Gained a major increase in its share of market?
( )	( )	Originated new markets that now account for over 20% of volume?
( )	( )	Made diversification work well for employees?
( )	( )	Enlarged its capacity to hold onto its best people?
( )	( )	Added a major new technology to its operations?
( )	( )	Created a large and constructive improvement in how people at all levels deal with one another?

B in Figure 2-1. Curve B, the desired future curve, displays the fundamental objective of organizational society.

Managers of organizations are aware that our society's magnificent social, cultural, economic, and individual achievement were gained under the slowly changing but almost rigid organizations described in curve A, and they can project that even more magnificent achievements might open up before us if we transform these same organizations to fall on curve B. Besides the major windfalls of profit this activity could create for corporations and their owners, this leap into the next great phase of human organization should advance many humane objectives, heal our environment, raise our values, and benefit all life. No sound data support or deny the message in Figure 2-1. As we will see later on in this chapter, several preliminary tests of organizations conducted by the author

FIGURE 2-1.   Desired and existing capacity of United States organizations to change radically.

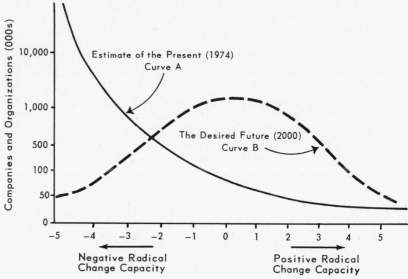

in 1972 tend to support the graphed thesis, but truly authoritative evaluation must await larger-scale testing.

Most well-established organizations or institutions—as we now vaguely understand such human constructs—develop many ways to resist change in all except minor issues that arise. Chapter 3 on the obstacles to change elaborates this point.

Can Your Organization Change?

The direct question "Can your organization change?" digs deeper into the managerial world than those broad societal issues that have occupied our attention thus far. Managers are perfectly capable of arriving at a preliminary answer. Chapter 4 will discuss the techniques for a more detailed and complete approach but at this time consider the basic structure and organization health of your own company or institution.

You now possess sound and credible answers to the question, "Can *your* organization change?" Test 3 is a partial and introductory list of the variables normally appraised when any management tries to answer this question for itself. In constructing this test, the simple organization characteristics that relate to dynamic factors of change were drawn from the three spheres of activity usually present in the structure of complex

TEST 3

Evaluating Change Readiness

A preliminary test to be taken by top managers of organizations.

Read each organization characteristic listed in the left-hand column. Decide which of the two alternatives (center or right-hand column) most closely describes that characteristic in your organization. (For the sake of simplicity at this stage, other gradations and organization variables have been eliminated.) Settle for your best judgment on each item and circle the item you feel is generally true of your organization. Proceed through the entire list before reading the scoring system.

Some Organization Characteristics:	In My Organization This Characteristic Is:	In My Organization This Characteristic Is:
Structure (How is the organization put together?)	Rigid, familiar.	Fluid, alien, unknown.
Communications flow (In which direction do most communications move?)	Down—strong. Up—weak. Interdepartmental— very weak.	Strong in all directions, especially up.
Communications content (What do most messages talk about?)	Work-, job-, reward-oriented, manipulative.	Organization- and social-goal-oriented; treats employees as adults.
Hierarchy (How do ranks and levels operate with one another?)	Insular, entrenched, resistant to outsiders, jealous of territory.	Coming apart by design, wide open, forming new alignments.
Interpersonal behavior (How do people deal with one another?)	Impersonal, frigid, by the book, as if dealing with machines and not human beings.	Involved, sincere, difficult as among equals who consider one another; open, confronting.
New policy adoption rate (How are policies established?)	A steady, small trickle of safe decisions.	Erratic, rapid as in floods.
Span of control	Narrow.	Too large or non-existent.
Work flow	Steady, reassuring.	Erratic, system shows oscillation, "hunting" behavior.

TEST 3 (Continued)

Some Organization Characteristics:	In My Organization This Characteristic Is:	In My Organization This Characteristic Is:
Technology (What is the level of organization technology compared to the state of the art?)	It is considered known; only slight advances allowed.	Floundering; intensive search going on; all basic questions open.
Technical skills	Sufficient to get the work out; insufficient to cause upsets or questions.	In ferment; repeated injections from outsiders; heavy training schedule.
Education activity (How much self-improvement is going on?)	Only when consistent with policy; narrowly job-related.	Wide-open explorations; generous in- and out-of-house commitment.
Intellectual activity (Are experts at home here? Can they be used regularly?)	Experts are suspected. Organization relies on loyal, trained, and unthinking soldiers. Basically anti-intellect.	Experts are in demand by operating executives to strengthen and guide their activities.
Effect on life-styles (What does organization life do to your people's lives?)	Uniformly deadening, an inhuman blight. Boring.	Exciting, absorbing, anxious, dangerous, that is, human.

organizations. According to Talcott Parsons,[1] these are (1) the core technical or production level, (2) the managerial or organizational level, and (3) the institutional or community level.

After Completing Test 3

When you have completed evaluating each of your organization's characteristics, count the number of circled items in the third column, at the right. Ignore all other items circled. A score of fewer than 4 circled items in the far-right-hand column indicates that your organization is extremely rigid; a score of from 4 to 7 items circled indicates a little flexibility; 8 to 11 means you are in an organization which has adapted itself to some outside forces; and over 11 means your organization now has the capacity for a large-scale change program.

A reader with a high score for an organization which is within five years of its birth can discard any feeling of comfort. For a few years new organizations (which busily seek out the rigidities of their future) generally look like mature organizations which have painfully earned some real change capacities. The comfort is illusory. For this reason, in previous administrations of this test we have set aside all scores of organizations less than five years old.

There are other ways you can appraise your organization's change capacity. An obvious one is to have this same appraisal made by your top managers and supervisory personnel; you will see your organization through the eyes of its best and most informed observers. When you obtain the evaluations from your managers and supervisors, you can graphically summarize the scores as shown by Figure 2-2. In this instance, the figure portrays the 1972 evaluations of 144 executives of business and other organizations.

The United States is probably the most changeful society that ever existed, and within this society the business arena contains the highest proportion of change-ready organizations. But my own experience with organizations in business, state, and municipal administration has proved that the capacity for change is low, a disturbing fact that tends to verify the situation of curve A in Figure 2-1 and lends considerable weight to those young and old critics of our society who claim that one "establishment" after another is failing in its mission. A sounder approach might be to remember the incredible achievements of our past, to look at our organization weaknesses with fresh, new eyes, and to anticipate the vast and profitable opportunities for radical change which face us today. In any case, there can no longer be the slightest justification for the common managerial viewpoint that the system is fine, our organizations are perfectly appropriate, and our problems will all be solved "if we farm

FIGURE 2-2.   Change-readiness appraisal.

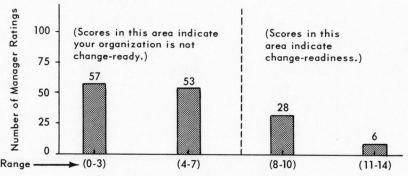

as well as we know how." The chilling effect of low levels of profitability is being felt; the winds of change blow far too hard for these fragile, wishful springtime kites.

Other generalizations about change readiness can be made from supporting information not discussed here.

— Young, new companies or other organizations are initially change-ready, but this quality quickly fades away "as things get organized around here."

— Companies at the fringe of their industry remain more change-ready than those at the core.

— Companies operating in open markets are more change-ready than companies operating in tightly regulated industries, markets, or countries.

— All companies or other organizations facing competition are far more change-ready than are protected, noncompetitive organizations such as governments, government agencies, hospitals, schools, religious organizations, and associations.

— The level of change readiness of most modern organizations is lower than managers assume.

— Some evidence exists that the self-ratings by managers of their organizations may be optimistic. Evaluation by other levels of the organization hierarchy, and by observers external to the organization, would probably produce far more negative ratings.

— Thus far, conglomerates have not been found significantly different from nonconglomerates in change readiness.

Needs for Change

Each manager can further sharpen his focus on his own organization by completing the checklist of Test 4. In this effort the manager uses his best judgment to evaluate a number of conditions that reveal his organization's behavior. Each time his judgment produces a yes in the test, the manager signals an area to explore for the rigidities that limit an organization's ability to function. Any organization that rates five or more yes answers on this checklist should seriously consider radical change as a condition of survival. If, by this time, you are beginning to perceive the need for and the direction which radical change might take in your organization, how do you proceed?

What Is a Change System?

To effect anything like a caterpillar-to-butterfly transformation in a business or other complex organization, we need some sense of an or-

TEST 4

Checklist of Organization Behavior
That Signals Needs for Radical Change

Check your answers in the appropriate column.

YES	NO	In your organization:
( )	( )	Is there a constant need to manipulate employees?
( )	( )	Does downward communication contain a great deal of exhortation, of attempts to develop "positive" attitudes of cooperation?
( )	( )	Do you have substantial numbers of employees and managers who could be described as disaffected, alienated, unsympathetic, resentful?
( )	( )	Have the last three top management changes of personnel proved to have little effect on solving basic issues?
( )	( )	Has the system been increasing its pressure on individuals to conform?
( )	( )	Does your recruiting produce fewer good employees compared to five years ago?
( )	( )	Is the organization's future honestly confusing?
( )	( )	Are you locked into outmoded technology?
( )	( )	Are charlatans beginning to win promotions?
( )	( )	Are competent managers selecting early retirement more frequently?
( )	( )	Is the long-term trend on real profits downward?

derly and reasonable procedure to follow. Management literature now contains few specific, concrete guidelines for creating or controlling high-speed, radical change in organizations. However, it has been the rule that whatever man's mind has attended to, he has been able to improve. If we now concentrate top management attention on how to attain high rates of change, the theory and technique of change systems will prove to be no exception to that rule.

I predict that modifications and improvements in change systems will soon flood the literature and dominate management planning. It is even probable that basic advances will make obsolete all that was developed for this compendium of radical change techniques. Managers who seek major improvement for their organizations and for the society they serve will act in the earliest days of change systems understanding, namely, *now*. Quite probably the greatest gains will be made quickly before new and unheard of sources of inertia and resistance have time to arise among us. Despite the immediacy of the opportunity, most organizations will find that they are not yet ready for radical change as revealed in the tests just completed or in the more definitive evaluations described in Chapter 5.

A change system is a management way to metamorphose an organization out of its present state into the next constructive phase of its potential development. Such radical change is not easily imposed from outside the organization; as in the case of the caterpillar, you spin it out of your guts. Chapters 4 to 7 define change systems in greater detail. (The appendix contains a description of a change system as a general system. Management scientists will want to review the appendix to appraise the theoretical underpinnings of the concepts presented throughout the book.)

The Supply of Change in Society

In the largest sense, human society has changed radically many times over the millions of years it can be presumed to have existed. The prime cause of these changes has been the development of the mind of man. In most historical periods, man has been reluctant and usually unable to change his institutions; he has been far more successful in changing matter, tools, and even other species, as in the case of dogs, horses, vegetables, grains, fruit trees, and flowers. Over the last few thousand years, however, he has developed an enormously more complex set of systems which now dominate this planet and has opened up his options to other parts of the solar system and to other star systems.

The records of most societies reveal many basic social and economic advances in recent years. Here in the United States the greatest explosion of human energy ever recorded produced the results listed below:[2]

	1910	1960
U.S. percent of world's land	7	7
U.S. percent of world's population	5	6
U.S. percent of world's wealth	15	50

Notice that in 50 years the United States jumped from 15 to 50 percent of the world's wealth, a remarkable achievement which has never been equaled. In 1960 the United States had 35 to 40 percent of the world's annual income, an annual gross national product of over one trillion dollars, and a net worth of about three trillion dollars. Each measurement continues to increase. Also encouraging is the obvious fact that the United States has not secured growth by taking new territory—thus eliminating claims about Yankee imperialism—and in 1972 its citizens had dropped its birth rate, for the first time, *below* what is needed to replace its existing population. Admittedly, wealth is not everything in life when one considers what it is to be human, but in the classic expression, "It sure beats hell out of whatever is in second place."

Besides exploding the quantity of wealth within the United States, our remarkable system distributed that wealth in a topsy-turvy fashion. In most societies the rich are few and the poor are many. In this society, however, the pyramid is inverted. Using the $7,000 to $10,000 annual income as a balance point, arbitrary as this is, more American families are above the line than are below. The Conference Board projections for 1990 suggest that families with incomes exceeding $15,000 (in 1971 dollars) will number well over 40 million, and these people account for close to 60 percent of all families. The rich may be getting richer, but the mass of the United States public as well has made extraordinary gains in personal income. Figure 2-3 illustrates the 1970 figures and the 1980 and 1990 projections.

Those 50 years between 1910 and 1960 did not write a record of management or organization ineptness; quite the opposite. Managers from all over the world now study and imitate the United States systems, procedures, and manager styles that created this record. Americans, however, are quickly sated with self-congratulation. A hallmark of their nature is the question they ask themselves after every success: "But what do we do for an encore?"

Our experimental, scientific society is perfectly willing to try any

FIGURE 2-3. The changing pyramid of income distribution (1971 dollars).

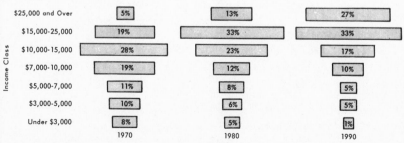

SOURCE: Department of Commerce. The Conference Board, prepared for the White House Conference on the Industrial World Ahead: A Look at Business in 1990.

encore that comes along. Along those lines, the theme of this chapter can be stated in four sentences:

1. We are handicapped in creating new futures by our too rigid organizations.
2. It is time to pick apart our organizations to see what they are made of.
3. Only new designs for organizations will deliver radical change.
4. Only radical change will deliver the environment, the profits, and the quality of life we want.

How Do We Attempt Change Now?

As Chapter 1 indicated, many responsible observers criticize our organizations and institutions for being too slow in delivering radical change. On the other hand, we have adopted a great many devices and even wrong-headed ideas in our attempts to supply radical change in large organizations. The measures least likely to succeed, listed at the top of Table 2-1, consist of historic and less sophisticated attempts of managers to redesign individuals and thereby create change in their organizations. In some circumstances, any of the 15 concepts listed could be the one "best" answer, but for modern United States organizations the strategies most likely to succeed are given at the bottom of the list and deal more directly with the system itself. We are learning that to get change we must change the system, and not its leaders or its participants.

Any set of leaders in history will claim at times that if it tries a little harder, it can change its own group mind and thus can change the minds of the people it rules or represents. But that is not all there is to the process of making great changes in the world. As Eric Hoffer says succinctly:

Only here, in America, were the common folk of the Old World given a chance to show what they could do on their own, without a master to push and order them about. History . . . lifted by the nape of the neck lowly peasants, shopkeepers, laborers, paupers, jailbirds, and drunks from the midst of Europe, dumped them on a vast virgin continent and said: "Go to it; it is yours." . . . They went to it with ax, pick, shovel, plow, and rifle; on foot, on horse, in wagons, and on flatboats. They went to it praying, howling, singing, brawling, drinking, and fighting. . . . Small wonder that we in this country have a deeply ingrained faith in human regeneration. We believe that, give a chance, even the degraded and the apparently worthless are capable of constructive work and great deeds.[3]

TABLE 2-1. Concepts used by managers to attempt change in large organizations.

PRIMITIVE ERA
1. Make a plan and command people to obey it or else.

MANIPULATIVE ERA
2. Manipulate the attitudes of people in the organization.
3. Manipulate the behavior of people in the organization.
4. Change the location of people in the organization.
5. Manipulate the information available to people in the organization.
6. Manipulate the status of and rewards and incentives for people in the organization.
7. Manipulate the work group composition to squeeze "troublemakers" out of the organization.

ERA OF SYSTEMATIC APPROACHES
8. Change the work environment of people in the organization.
9. Eliminate as many people as possible from the organization.
10. Change the technology of the work itself.
11. Change the education of people in and out of the organization.
12. Change the culture of the organization.
13. Change the exterior environment in which the organization fits.
14. Change the participation of people in decision making and problem solving.

CHANGE SYSTEM ERA
15. Change the system of people, technology, throughput, goals, intellect, and values and its relationship to the whole environment.

Table 2-1 clearly shows that managers who earlier tried to change large organizations stumbled with and gradually downgraded those methods which were based on attitude change, behavior change, or the manipulation of reward systems. Instead, they have moved steadily and intelligently toward total systems concepts. To enlarge on these strategies used by managers to supply change, first consider the general type of management style and organization which created those remarkable 50 years described earlier in the chapter. An excellent way to do this was laid out graphically by Dr. John F. Mee. Figure 2-4 shows the model that did the job.

In 1910 so-called scientific management emerged; management came to be viewed as a system of authority over the activities of workers. Industrial engineers began establishing standard operating practices and improving, through time-and-motion study, the efficiency of operations. Within a relatively short time our open society and what Servan-

FIGURE 2-4.   1910-to-1960 model for management as a system of
authority.

Scientific Management — Autocratic Management
Activities-Oriented Management
Management as a System of Authority
Power-Over-People Position

The
Managers

Centralized Decision Making
Emphasis on "Reacting" to Situations
Through
Organization and Control
Destiny Determined Future

1. Manager designed the organization structure.
2. Manager delegated authority and responsibility.
3. Manager set the tasks for workers.
4. Manager determined "one best way" for work.
5. Manager hired and trained workers.
6. Manager used financial incentives only for work.
7. Manager provided close supervision over work.
8. Manager established tight executive controls.

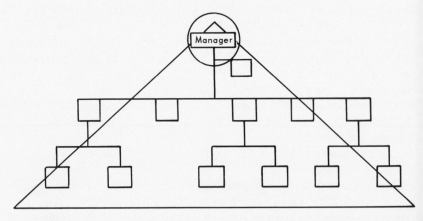

SOURCE: John F. Mee, "Changing Concepts of Management," *S.A.M. Advanced Management Journal*, October 1972.

Schreiber calls our "secret of social justice" had radically improved the effectiveness of this relatively rigid model through the

General Motors organizational philosophy of the 1920s, the human relations movement in the 1930s, the engineering science and management training program for World War II in the 1940s, and the popularity of the management process in the 1950s. Now we see this generalized concept of management, for all its improvements, as "Theory X" (described by Douglas McGregor) or as "9-1" in the Managerial Grid (described by Blake and Mouton).[4]

The 1910–1960 model generally produced a pyramidal structure which culminated in the man at the top, as shown in the figure, and which represented a centralized, activities-oriented management. Dr. Mee suggests that today a number of major managerial trends are brewing a new model:

Futures forecasting and its fulfillment
Results-oriented management
Management by objectives
Management as a resource rather than as a system of authority
Network-based management systems
Systems analysis
Organization development
Participative management
Self-actualization

These trends have resulted in the new general model for organizations shown in Figure 2-5 where the pyramid is inverted and represents a decentralized, results-oriented management.

These informative concepts lead to questions about organizations: What are they? What kinds exist? What are the differences? How do we know which form to adopt? How do we uncover new forms of organizations that will outperform the ones we know so well? Can we uncover large new veins of profitability by changing our organizations? From these questions emerges a logical inquiry: If an explosive *demand* for radical change exists, then through what medium can the change be supplied most efficiently? And there is only one possible answer: through our organizations and institutions.

What Is an Organization?

A quick answer to the question "What is an organization?" should suffice: It is a systematic arrangement of people, materials, technologies,

FIGURE 2-5.   Post-1960 model for management as a resource.

Participative Management — Supportive Management
Results Oriented Management
Management as a Resource
Power Through People Participation

Management

Decentralized Decision Making
Emphasis on "Proacting" to Desired Results
Through
Objective Setting and Causative Thinking
Organization Can Shape Its Future

1. Management resources determine operational and strategic objectives.
2. Authority and responsibility are taken from the objectives.
3. Personnel work for objectives, not activity tasks.
4. Personnel participate in determining methods of work.
5. People are employed and developed for achievement.
6. Financial incentives augmented by personal incentives.
7. Supervision develops self-commitment for results.
8. Control is evaluated by results, not activities.

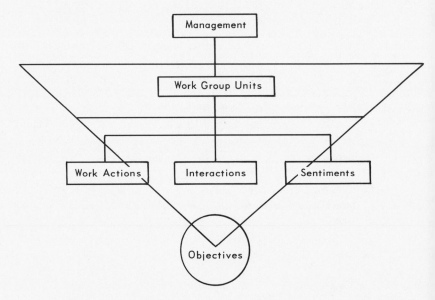

SOURCE: John F. Mee, "Changing Concepts of Management," *S.A.M. Advanced Management Journal*, October 1972.

processes, policies, and objectives that reveals an overall identity or "wholeness." Nevertheless, a considerable body of literature * attempts to describe organizations—what they are and how they differ, how they operate, their functions and role in society, and their effects upon people and the environment.

Increasingly effective work in these areas provides enough grist for the organization analyst to classify organizations and their behavior.

In looking at organizations *for the purpose of achieving radical change,* it is sufficient that a simple classification system be used to aid the manager to describe *his* organization. We can also describe an organization as a set of limits and restrictions on individual rights and behavior that enables people to pool and multiply the value of their efforts and thereby accomplish goals they probably could not accomplish by themselves:

The eight-hour day
The five-day week (or four or three)
Disposable income
High living standards
Use of specialized talent
Peaceful value exchanges
Application of sophisticated technologies
Civilization
Government

In short, each organization says to us: Here's the deal. You do thus and so and we will give you so and thus in exchange. Within such an exchange, the organization must find some means—exploitation, technology, labor-saving arrangements, monopoly, economies of scale, more production, demand creation, supply controls—to develop a retained surplus of value from each exchange (internally with employees and externally with the market) or it will not survive. A single organization may be so poorly conceived that the only way it can show a profit after all input/output transactions is to poison the environment by dumping waste chemicals, products, or gases into it. The more efficient and humane organizations clean up their waste, support themselves, and distribute sizable benefits in *all* directions—to society, owners, employees, communities, consumers, and the quality of life.

The entire spectrum of organizations can be classified from those which are highly negative in their effects upon society to those which

* Indebtedness is acknowledged here to the writings of March, Simon, Stafford Beer, Lawrence, Lorsch, Bennis, Weber, Steiner, Litterer, Merton, Caplow, Rice, Burns, and Woodward, among others.

TABLE 2-2. Judgmental rankings of selected human organizations in modern society.

SCALE OF OVERALL VALUE IN SOCIETY		ORGANIZATIONS
Of maximum positive benefit	+3	Advanced business organizations Most free enterprises Open education systems
Moderately beneficial	+2	Scientific research groups Medical care systems Compulsory education systems
Slightly beneficial	+1	Welfare organizations Business and trade associations
Neutral point	0	Religions Cities Governments
Slightly detrimental	−1	Unions Business monopolies and cartels Militaries
Moderately detrimental	−2	Crime and dope syndicates The Mafia Anarchist-terrorist groups
Of maximum detriment	−3	Fascist movements

have proved highly positive, as shown in Table 2-2. These judgmental rankings by the author are sufficient to start many a debate, but that is not their purpose. Table 2-2 is presented as another way for managers to back away and look at their organizations through new eyes and with new value judgments. The next section of this chapter accelerates that process.

The Vehicles of Change: Organizations

To better understand how we might deliver radical change in human society, we need to dig deeper and deeper into how we think about our organizations. In recent years organizations have also been described as bureaucracies, sociotechnical systems, information-processing systems, social systems, and decision-making systems. Valuable as some of these lenses are for looking closely at the organizations we live in and work for, something more of the reality people experience remains undescribed.

Some time ago, Kenneth Boulding developed an interesting hierarchy of systems concepts ranging from the simple framework of the atom to the far-flung transcendental unknowables beyond the galaxies and beyond our comprehension. This seemed like a powerful organizing idea to me, yet it was too global—or rather, too galactic—for my purposes. I have narrowed the focus considerably, with acknowledgment to Dr. Boulding,[5] and constructed a list of systems of which human beings are components. Seven systems are described in this grouping. They range from the system most often used in human history—the leader/follower cluster—to the system just ahead of us in the evolution of organizations —the organic organization, human type.

The table printed on the endpapers at the front and the back of this book presents the seven organization concepts. Each manager can decide which one most nearly matches his own organization. As a first step to change, you can examine the more complex forms of organization to conjecture if any have potential for your organization's future. The gap between your organization today and the class of organization to which you aspire represents the problem space which your change system must close. If, for example, you decide your organization is a mosaic and you feel it should be an organic plant type (OPT), the specific differences between mosaic and OPT operations are the things you are going to create as you reach for overall transformation. Managers of the largest organizations will soon realize that their organizations have some components of one class and some of another. This need not invalidate a decision about the core organization. What class is it? How many of your peers agree?

If we are to deliver radical change in a world that normally sees little of it, new approaches such as this one must precede the development of new goals and new status-to-goal gap reduction programs. A gap reduction program merely moves an organization from where it is now (present status) to where it wants to be (goal). It will prove useful to consider each class of organization in detail to understand its structure.

  The Leader/Follower Cluster

Few things are as natural to boys and girls as to follow a leader they respect. The pattern is begun in childhood with the earliest games and amusements, and it continues in Boy Scouts, Girl Scouts, Campfire Girls, YMCA, and YWCA. We start life within a family structure that around the world most often appoints the father as leader and the rest as followers. (Many fathers find this natural and are completely unaware that they classify their wives and children as second-class citizens for life.) The irrational enthusiasms of youth flounder from one youth culture leader to another while seeking someone to admire, someone to imitate, someone to identify with. Our education systems use the leader/ follower image more than any other. It is built into the raised teacher's podium, the lecture hall, and the classroom. Later, in the world of work, we quickly find the value of working *under* a good supervisor or a good boss. As a matter of fact, however, we hope to avoid working *for* poor leaders.

A graphic symbol for the leader/follower cluster could be the leader exhorting his followers to obey him; that would exemplify the all-too-human nature of a relationship that is as old as man. We are considering the substantial pros and the important cons of a dominance/submission relationship between people. Such basic characteristics must have appeared from the first day a near-human sought a mate or men got together to organize their hunting. Therefore, I date this concept of organization from the earliest potassium-argon dating system record of near-human bones, namely, 5.5 million B.C. Since then, through tens of thousands of generations, you might say this pattern has become fairly firmly engrained in all cultures. Here are some examples of leader/follower organizations that will help to define the class:

The leader/tribe model of nomad cultures	Most performing arts companies Some doctor/hospital relationships
Napoleon's army	The corporal and his squad
Hitler's Germany	A union leader like Cesar Chavez
Mao's China	and his followers
Chiang's Taiwan	Morgan and his pirate crew
R&D groups that cluster around a key scientist	The guru/novitiate relationship in arcane religions

In distinguishing this group, remember the strong and sometimes almost psychotic human relationship between the leader and his follower. Each feeds the other what he needs. That must be present. A citizen can submit to a policeman's orders and yet have no leader/ follower relationship with him over time.

As to the structure feature of the leader/follower organization, one individual occupies the central role and all the others are on the periphery. Management control is maintained by one centralized authority who dominates the entire organization, which is literally "the shadow of one man." The local interaction in such an organization is restricted almost entirely to the downward transmission of orders from master to slave.

The individual follower practices his skills for the benefit of the group, but he gains few personal rights. He is in a master/slave relationship. The authority of the commander is absolute or nearly absolute at least within the organization framework and occasionally on life and death issues as well. There is usually no recourse among followers against this arbitrary power. The follower might opt to leave the cluster or to set up one of his own, but if he does so, he usually runs grave risks of ostracism, discrediting, or destruction. To leave is to betray the cluster, and that is why to leave a union of this type is to lose your job at once. Vindictive retribution is swift, as in a street gang.

Several evaluations of the cluster seem reasonable. The leader/follower organization's ability to accomplish work, achieve objectives, and carry on long and arduous tasks has been strong throughout history. We can assume that it has been equally effective, for practical reasons, ever since men first banded together in their own interest. One man could not have stampeded a herd of woolly mammoths over a cliff to get the winter's supply of meat, nor could one man defend an extended family, protect a hunting territory, or develop a culture. The prehuman life forms undoubtedly began such activities by clustering around a strong man and following his orders. It was, and is, effective; it was, and is, personal. Today a member of a street gang knows who he is, where he stands, and what his group identity means to him. He prefers this to the anonymity of his unformed self.

Speaking of youth, as a revealing aside, the extraordinary needs of young people for a relationship as direct as this may be thwarted by modern societal arrangements which prematurely plunge them into organization forms just too complex for their capacities. We know that, from fertilization of the egg, the child's development replicates many stages of evolutionary history. Considering the limited civilizing skills of most parents, we could well conclude that the child arrives at the Neolithic period somewhere in his teens. It is intriguing that, in the 1960s and 1970s in the United States, teenagers have been nomadic and tribal (Woodstock), have wandered in typical Australian aborigine "walkabout" style, jumped about to primitive tribal music forms (rock and roll, hard rock), sought out leaders and messiahs (Manson family, Jesus freak communes), practiced amoral sex, shrunk from the world of their parents, filled their heads with sentimental philosophies and religions, decorated their bodies rather than furnished their minds, acted out roles and played dress-up in clothes of bygone eras, and deserted the cities for the woods—all quite reminiscent of the behavior of a Neolithic tribe when faced with civilization for the first time.

Perhaps we should heed these signals more attentively. Instead of locking young men and women into insufferably boring schoolrooms and antiseptic life-styles during these years, we should give them alternative leader/follower cluster situations which would help them work through the Neolithic phase profitably. The thin trickle of youth into the Peace Corps, Voluntary Action, and Vista suggests the way to do this to everyone's benefit when the mismanagement that has afflicted these agencies is eliminated. Large-scale, socially positive tribal movements for about 25 million American young people at home and around the world should turn out quite well. Impersonality should be avoided, however, and the full power of the leader/follower form of organization should be invoked in all its Neolithic fun, dress, sentiment, and glory in the sharply identified group.

Aside from this example, power in a leader/follower cluster is centered in one individual. For this reason the leader's strengths are implemented, but so are his weaknesses. Too often this means a spotty record as far as willingness to adopt new technology for the group is concerned. Each advance in technology or in organization structure must first be appraised as to its effect on the leader's absolute power. The leader is not likely to dissipate his power to the group's advantage. Normally, this also means that an organization built on this pattern has little ability to alter its own structure because that comes down to "changing the leader's mind" on the fundamentals he represents. Historically, with kings, dictators, et al., necessary changes could come only by deposing or killing the leader in favor of another autocrat. Unfortunately, such revolutions cure only temporary emergencies; rarely do revolutions dissipate the power to dominate others. Most substitute one ruler for another with no lasting public benefit.

Because each of the organization forms given in the endpapers should be considered as a possibility for the explosion of multinational organizations—economic, governmental, and educational—now being formed around the world, I feel it is advisable to discuss such potential for each class. In my judgment, the leader/follower cluster has little to offer multinational organizers except as a temporary organization structure for youth missionary movements or in the case of development organizations working in very primitive areas of the world.

 *The Mosaic Organization*

As the name implies, the mosaic form involves the putting together of separate, distinct pieces, glued only at the edges, to form some pattern. Most mosaic organizations form random patterns because of the autonomy of the pieces. They are held together by the merest traces of adhesive. This organization form is a social interdependence concept. It involves connectedness only for a few particular purposes; in all other respects the parts are independent, disconnected, and autonomous. As so little yielding of independence to hierarchical structures occurs, the chief vehicle for decision making in a mosaic is jawbone; hence one of its main characteristics is incoherence, or all talking at once.

As to the structure, the mosaic is a loosely connected assembly of subsystems. Authority in such an organization can be secured only through negotiation between the groups or segments and almost never from individuals. The mosaic is composed of independent subsystems each with its own authority base. As might be expected, each subsystem has its own data fund with little social interaction able to penetrate the partitions of the subgroups.

Examples of mosaic organizations include

The Holy Roman Empire	Voluntary associations
The United Nations	IGY (The International Geophys-
NATO, SEATO	ical Year)
U.S. Articles of Confederation	The American Indian nations
European Common Market	Medical groups and law partner-
Urban communities	ships
Public and private universities	The League of Arab Nations

As the examples indicate, the key problem with mosaic organization is the tenuousness of the relationship between groups and individuals. A clockwork is far more dynamically interconnected. In a mosaic it is as though we have said to one another, "In this one way and no other will our people deal with your people; we relinquish nothing to you, and we accept nothing from you." For example, Robert Hutchins is reputed to have said that the University of Chicago was held together only by its heating system, and Clark Kerr, former president of the University of California at Berkeley, suggested that the sole relationship in his organization seemed to be conflict over parking lots for automobiles.

Mosaics can be useful. There are times when no other relationships are possible or desired, but over time their strictures and inefficiencies chafe the individuals. In this form the component group rights dominate; each group is able to veto all the rest to thwart most attempts to take action. The United Nations is a glaring example. While it has value in providing an arena for jawbone, its ability to accomplish work is limited to a few committees which operate as clockworks. The main assembly— a mosaic—is impotent indeed. The mosaic form was first visible in about 9000 B.C. when tribal leaders got together in "nations" to confer and tell stories. The pattern has not changed much. In the vacuum left by our inability to yield rights to superior forms of organizations, we are creating mosaics even today.

The mosaic structure is rarely able to produce much of value or to accomplish more than a small part of its stated purpose. An exception to this rule is found in scientific and professional pursuits: the International Geophysical Year, law partnerships, and medical groups are reasonably effective relationships, although the characteristics of mosaics still are visible in them.

A mosaic has little ability to adopt new technology or systems advances. Like a clockwork, it tends to reflect the state of the art at the time of its formation. Little machinery exists for changing goals. For the same reason, it can rarely alter its own organization structure. Each participant jealously fights against any sensible relinquishment of the veto or any other separatist power to an effective central administration. In effect, all central authority is ruled out in this arrangement. For example, we will have to wait for an attack from another galaxy or star system before we can bring ourselves to organize a space patrol and defense system. The UN could scarcely consider the task today.

Finally, mosaics already have multinational existence and represent the first step to multinational organization forms with effectiveness and substance. They are still largely political in nature and possess too many managerial loose ends for a multinational corporation to consider adopting, yet they are being formed all over the planet.

 The Clockwork

The third class of organizations is best represented graphically by the works of a windup clock. All parameters of its activity are preset in its design. Its operation requires only a simple motive power, the unwinding of a spring. Such an organization is mechanical in its working, predictable as to output, and rigidly interconnected internally. Its operation is almost completely impervious to the world around it, and its structure is inhuman and mechanical.

Once the basic pattern is set, usually around the needs of a piece of machinery, a process, or a service, all that remains is for the general forces in the organization to spin out predictable results. In such an organization the original design controls almost all efficiency. Little that managers attempt within a clockwork makes any real difference to operations in the long run. A great many managers who have recently been trying to change clockwork organizations will discover here why they found the change to be impossible.

In a clockwork structure, work processes are rigid and mechanical without room for variation in the works, which is marked by inflexible interdependencies. As to the authority process in such organizations, that has already been completely programmed into the original design. Authority is centralized, and an extremely limited dispersion of power and privilege is "designed in" only in the tiny amounts necessary to facilitate the work processes of the "machine." In a clockwork organization, social interaction is meager because the data base was fixed at the time of origination and uses only the most rigid channels.

The following examples of clockwork organizations will probably raise many hackles, but I suggest that the reader consider how little performance is gained from the relatively large resources which such institutions require.

Individual departments and agencies of the United States government

Economies of countries run by dictators

Public utilities

Telephone companies

The union movement

The public school system (K through 12)

Religions and charities

Public corporations like the New Jersey Turnpike Authority

Foundations

It is interesting to note that, without the power to tax, without monopoly or some other means to regularly and arbitrarily extract resources, such clockworks would soon exhaust their springs (that is, succumb to entropy) due to their fundamentally uneconomic and rigidly conceived operations. Such organizations are free from the whip of competition and unable to create surplus value or internal independence despite huge allocations of resources from a generous society. Naturally, the people in these organizations attempt to make this glaring weakness appear to be a virtue.

In understanding clockwork organization output, it is essential to prevent the organizations from comparing themselves with their peers or with their own past records. This reveals little. A public school's efficiency in getting output from its resources should be compared with diesel mechanic schools, pilot training programs, or Sesame Street, not with other public schools. A public agency like the U.S. Agriculture Department should be compared with International Harvester Company, Food Machinery and Chemical Company, or the hybrid seed developers as to the value of its effect on farming per dollar invested.

How do individuals fare in clockwork organizations? The rigid interconnectedness of clearly defined and impersonal parts allows some personal right to emerge in such organizations. The segmentation of functions creates cadres of specialists in each area. A general coordinating program binds all parts and, as in clocks or public schools, this tends to repeat itself year after year. Very little environmental or market demand creates any change in clockwork organizations, although political or ideological movements do stir them up slightly from time to time. Change is a pious hope expressed by students, citizens, users, commuters, union members, and the general public. It is not actionable because no action contrary to the clockwork design is really possible.

Scrapping clockwork organizations is usually immensely expensive, and so we are stuck with them. In later chapters, however, ways to change them will be discussed. It will be apparent that in each case a basic societal decision must be made. That comes only after an extraordinary paroxysm of effort. We may be getting close to this stage in education and in the union movement also.

Another interesting exercise with a clockwork organization is to try to discern the locus of power. Being conceived as a piece of machinery—and not anything human—such organizations have everyone inside saying "Not me" when the question "Who's got the power?" comes up. True power within these organizations resides with the public which created them. It is expressed in laws, Internal Revenue regulations, donors, and believers. The clockwork itself can do little but try to operate with slightly greater efficiencies. These brave efforts usually cancel each other out. Most clockworks get less and less efficient, that is, "wear out," as the years roll by; again, our schools and unions are partial examples of worn-out clockworks.

As to their record in society, clockwork organizations were set up in early civilizations, probably around 1000 B.C. In the United States we converted through the lead-cow thinking of advanced companies to a process society in about 1950, and that broad movement limits the market for clockwork organizations. Clockworks will be around for a long time to come because they are often useful at early stages of an industrial society, but the better and more responsible ones still visible in the United States will soon transform themselves to more effective and more complex systems.

Because clockwork organizations embody some organized conceptual thinking about how to accomplish a given function, they have been of value to society, especially in accomplishing its routine tasks. I would judge their capacity to produce value as moderate to low in comparison with the six other organization forms. Their ability to adapt to new advances and new technology is almost zero by definition, except that by dying out and being redesigned—in the phoenix process—they can be reborn with new clockworks that embody the current instead of a former state of the art. However, this rarely happens—today we are building new schools, new unions, and new government agencies that imitate the old patterns much too often.

Thus it is clear that the clockwork model system cannot alter its organization structure by its own efforts. Only outside forces can do the job. Public schools provide many examples of this truism.

 Pyramidal Organizations

Pyramids of authority are so familiar to us that in almost every human activity—even in other kinds of organizations—we build or imagine the pyramid naturally as a way to make sense out of organization. In virtually every field of effort, critics assume that some Machiavellian group "at the top of the pyramid" is responsible for whatever they see as evil. It is always disconcerting to achievers to get to the top of some pyramid and find nobody there but themselves or someone far less effective than they had imagined; it is much like Dorothy's dismay to find a dear, bumbling old gentleman posing as the fierce, mysterious Wizard of Oz.

The pyramid is a geometric figure, and it symbolizes the structure of the classic hierarchy we know so well. In pyramidal control authority is arranged hierarchically. Within the system, specialized subsystems are also arranged hierarchically. A good example is the military organization with its levels of squad, platoon, company, battalion, division, and army.

Operational interaction within a pyramid conforms to the hierarchical structure of the organization and emphasizes superior/subordinate relationships. A cardinal sin in a pyramidal organization is to fail to go through channels in trying to get an important message to the top. Control of what is transmitted upward is a key means of self-protection in a pyramid. It is also an example of the stratification and compartmentalization allowed for, as well as the delegation of authority under rigid rules. The pyramid is a far more efficient structure than the leader/ follower cluster. Examples of pyramidal structures are:

Militaries	Most small businesses
Organized churches	Police forces and fire
Courts of law	departments
Political parties	Military academies
Governments in general	Ships' crews

An investigator of the major sports in the United States would tend to classify football as a pyramid in which the strategy of the game is under the control of the quarterback or coach; baseball, in contrast, is more of a nine-man mosaic in which the playing of each position perfectly usually results in victory. Football requires the continuous giving and receiving of orders; baseball has far less and subtler signal calling which affects only a few players at a time. An organizational classification of U.S. sports and games might help to illustrate the various classes. Notice in Table 2-3 that most of the individual games use no organization other than that inherent in the individual human performer. The team sports tend to fall in the mosaic and clockwork classes. Perhaps only football can be classified as a pyramid organization which processes a steady stream of information in several directions, alters the direction of effort regularly and by choice, and deals with changing situations by shifts of strategy that affect all participants. Football generally varies the group's responses to a degree equaled in no other sport.

No sport really exemplifies the simple leader/follower cluster organization class, yet we can remember rare individuals whose personality overwhelmed a team and set up the classic love/psychosis leader/follower relationship. Games for the future could well be based on the complex relationships that exist within organizations of the conglomerate, organic plant, and organic human types. We are not there yet. Finally, most of the sports and amusements listed in Table 2-3 have no organization at all. They are widely popular. This line of analysis might be used to buttress the thesis presented earlier that we are too accustomed to primitive types of organizations.

The pyramidal concept has many useful attributes:
— It allows for levels of status that are large at the bottom and small at the top, and that implies a weeding out to find the "fittest" to rule.
— It permits specialization in that any kind of job can be assigned a level.
— It combines pyramids that clearly rank the people within them.
— Its large base and shape imply stability.
— It informs the member exactly where he is in the ranking order and reinforces the value of all the places, especially at lower levels.

Pyramidal organizations have been around since about 2600 B.C. Many exist today; in fact, most organizations are pyramids. Now they possess only a medium-size capacity to produce wealth and value, but they produced most of the world's wealth in the preceding few hundred years. They are losing their dominance because rising expectations of personal autonomy among their members is creating a continuous series of internal disruptions and dislocations. People no longer find great virtue in taking or receiving orders and then acting without allowing the message to pass through their minds or be appraised by their value systems. Now they regard such behavior as improper or actively evil; once

TABLE 2-3. Estimated distribution of U.S. sports and games among the seven organization classes.

Playing Entity	Sport or Amusement	Organization Class	
Individuals	Golf, tennis (singles), skiing, individual track and field, chess, checkers, gin rummy, poker, cribbage, bowling	None	
Individual/team	None except for rare people like Connie Mack, Knute Rockne, Casey Stengel, and Vince Lombardi, who unnaturally dominated a team	I	Leader/Follower cluster
Teams	Baseball, cricket, soccer, hockey, basketball, bridge, tennis (doubles)	II	Mosaic
Teams	Rowing, bobsled, swimming teams, track teams, all racing	III	Clockwork
Teams	Football	IV	Pyramid
None	None	V	Conglomerate
None	None	VI	Organic plant type
None	None	VII	Organic human type

they considered it as loyal and trustworthy as the people involved in the Watergate affair did.

Pyramids have a low but visible capacity to adopt new technology and organization system advances. Their subsystems in particular can gain rewards by improving their operations as long as the improvements do not too greatly or too quickly threaten hierarchical authority. They also possess a fair ability to alter their own structure; we have seen truncated pyramids developed and, as the next class of organization demonstrates, clusters of pyramids are among us now. Finally, as to their use in multinational expansion, pyramidal organizations are in existence and will remain one of the available, if modestly attractive, options for future multinational corporation growth.

 The Conglomerate Organization

Perhaps it would be well to discuss one of the confusions buried in the widely used term "conglomerate" as applied to organizations. To conglomerate anything means to bring together, to cluster, to work into a ball various disparate materials. The example in geology is conglomerate rock, in which different kinds of hard materials are stuck together with a binder such as sandstone. In conglomerate corporations, however, it is more likely that, whatever their lines of business, the organizations being clustered together are virtually identical. They are all pyramids as a rule, so the definition of a conglomerate used here is a cluster of pyramids.

The conglomerate organization tends to create value by coalescing the potentially least efficient and highest-cost segments of a group of working pyramids—usually high-salaried managers but occasionally staff groups such as accounting, advertising, and purchasing—to gain performance, particularly in earnings per share. As we have seen in recent years, some conglomerate structures are formed solely to manipulate capital stock values for the benefit of a small group—a not too admirable goal. To the public, which is often left holding the bag, such management ethics provides good reason for distrust of the whole business system.

When a conglomerate structure works well and the inputs and outputs of the pyramids relate well to one another, a strong (synergistic?) multiple of horizontal activity can occur and substantially improve the entire system. Normally, however, the pyramidal hierarchies are united only at their summits and are subject to control by the core hierarchy. Authority over the entire structure is marked by a core management group which prevails—often crudely—over the authority structures of the pyramids and thus gradually erodes their spirit and drive. Needless to say, in those conglomerates which were thrown together solely on the basis of inflated stock prices and lack any organizing rationale whatever, almost no horizontal interaction occurs and internal confusion eventually creates a negative spiral.

In the more effective conglomerates, however, the pyramids do possess products, services, and skills useful to their brothers. The resulting horizontal interaction—the prime justification for this form of organization—can be wholesome and beneficial. However, some historical examples of the main waves of conglomerates illustrate the problems inherent in this form of organization.

In 1900, trusts in the United States (began trust busting)

In 1929, holding companies in the United States (led to the SEC), European cartels

In the 1960s, ITT, LTV, Litton Industries, Sperry Rand, Monogram, Glen Alden, Allied General, City Investing, Marcor, Boise-Cascade, Gulf + Western, the Pentagon

Conglomerate organizations have probably been around since about A.D. 1000. We show little sign of growing out of the habit of periodically turning to them, and it is worrisome that so many times they have been destructive. Conglomerates have not yet distinguished themselves for creating value because of the merits inherent in their form; value is instead inherent in their components, which might well, in some cases at least, have done better outside than in. Because conglomerate core managements (referred to by some as shark pens) on many occasions have torn up the managements of their component pyramids, they have opened up opportunities to install advanced systems and higher technologies by fiat. Also, by the same willingness to snap off heads, they have shown a capacity to alter their own internal structure, that is, to change their organization, but at what human costs!

Many multinational corporations are conglomerates partly because the core managements saw obstacles to growth within their borders and reached out to build or buy operations in other markets. This remains a manipulative approach, and yet—as a first step to create world businesses—it was effective in creating momentum and enlarging management perspectives. If the conglomerate form is to survive internationally, its key internal change will have to be in the form of radically different goals and values.

 Organic Organizations of the Plant Type

It is provocative to learn that of all the systems man can distinguish around him, the most advanced and complex are of a biological nature. Nature is far ahead of our comprehension in its ability to construct systems. Nature gets huge output from minimum input and can develop flexibilities in her systems that we cannot yet fathom. In Kenneth Boulding's words, the plant-type system has a "division of labor among cells to form a cell society with differentiated and mutually dependent parts —roots, leaves, seeds." This model for human organizations to consider suggests an organic unfolding of structure from minute, core inherent characteristics and determinants. This is demonstrated when an oak tree results from an acorn. Quite a systems feat.

As to structure, the plant-type organization is a loose network but a unified whole. Internal and external identity is of a single cloth, which is much different from the lower forms of organization we have discussed thus far. Authority in the plant-type organization has traditional hierarchical structures strongly affected by concepts of corporate citizenship for the participants and by the effects of organic growth upon the system. As a result, individual freedoms are enlarged to some degree and individuals tend to flower in this lively, growing environment that considers some of their needs.

As might be expected, the organic plant-type organization depends upon relative freedom of communication flows in many directions, especially in from the environment which nurtures it. This necessary and built-in sensitivity to the environment accounts for the considerably greater ability of all organic forms to deal with their own and others' environmental degradation. Channels of communication are interwoven into an integrated communications network, much as the simple sensing system of a biological organism connects differentiated components and coordinates them fully as a single organism. This happens when a plant turns to the sun for its benefit.

Valuable and advanced as this simple organic organization is, the reader is reminded that, although it is alive like a plant, in its essence it is mindless. This point of description is not negative when we compare this organization to simpler forms. It will be elaborated later on in this chapter. Examples of organic plant-type organizations are:

General Electric	U.S. Steel
General Motors	Unilever
Eastman Kodak	Philips
Du Pont	Nestlé
Sony	Alcoa
International Harvester	Oil companies

These clearly defined and relatively well-integrated organizations are representative of that large group of companies in the United States and around the world which have contributed the largest single wholesome influence on modern times. Plant-type organizations have existed in society since about A.D. 1800, and they should be reasonably viable until about 2050. This short a time span is allocated because these organizations—in contrast to governments, schools, churches, and unions—are extremely sensitive to the world around them, and it is predicted here that they will advance rapidly to the next higher level of human organization—the organic organization of the human type.

Plant-type organizations have a capacity to produce value that is high compared to that of the other forms so far discussed. Their ability to adapt and grow into new techniques, new technologies, and new systems advances has marked their history. This ability to adapt and grow may now be on a plateau, however, due to their top-heavy growth in recent years. In the same way, these organizations have been able to evolve new forms of their organization structure over short generations, but again much of this has slowed due to the problem of digesting unusual recent growth in size. Many changes that have occurred recently are restricted to small segments of the structure; few are general throughout.

In the multinational corporate future, organizations of this form are already powerful and expanding, especially where they have allowed their natural sensitivity to other cultures and other environments to guide their growth into new markets and ventures. As in nature, however, the plant form when thought of as a model is but a way station on the way to man.

 Organic Organizations of the Human Type

In consideration of the success of organic-type organizations, it is not too surprising that a simple operation like putting a head on the organization shoulders should be thought of. If we want vibrant, alive, goal-seeking, and life-giving organizations to inhabit, we cannot much longer use arithmetic or mechanical models for organization conception. As a model for human organizations, even a tree has shortcomings.

Observers who caution against ascribing human qualities to things have neglected to provide a superior conceptual model. In all of man's mechanical, arithmetic, and geometric mental baggage of organization design, nothing compares to the exciting prospect of using man himself as the model for the organizations of his future. Out of all the systems we know, only man has demonstrated perfectability, changeability, mobility, mind expansion, introspection, deduction, feeling, analysis, action, coherence, and goal seeking on the highest level for his own as well as for all other life forms. Man is the open-ended model of living, working systems we can most easily work with. He also has the highest radical change potential of any organizational model thus far developed. His brain and his mental processes are again the most expandable we know; compared to mechanical or arithmetic systems, they are unlimited.

In addition, an organization built with the idea of man as its model would possess a many-sensed awareness of the realities of existence and of life which more rigid forms could never achieve. In such an organization we could blend human minds with an organization consciousness and work together to achieve goals hitherto thought impossible. Within such a symbiotic relationship, NASA took us to the moon. Tomorrow, such organizations will take us to the stars as well.

No better model for an organization exists. Man conceived as a system is the blueprint for the dominant organizations of the future.

All other organizations we have used in our history—with the exception of the leader/follower cluster—are patterns of mechanical or geometric constructs. The word "pattern" is used because the parts, connectors, and components of our organizations have been assembled without thought of their needing a black box or central intelligence. We give leadership power to people who have heads and use them; but they use their brains within a system that itself has no designed-in brain. Our primitive organizations are now arrangements of men, resources, machines, and techniques to produce a figure (arms, legs, innards, nervous system, and trunk) guided by other intelligences, namely, men. Do we handicap ourselves by this omission? The men in the organization think and act, but the organization itself is merely a mindless and valueless array of parts, processes, records, and meters. To remedy that, if we choose to, we must advance beyond our primitive models of clusters, mosaics, clockworks, pyramids, and trees to the truly human model and then give it a mind of its own. The change system defined in Chapters 4 to 7 will take the first steps toward accomplishing that task.

Breakthroughs in organization conception never come full-blown. The idea that we have been getting along rather well with mechanical or headless organizations is both disturbing and incomplete. A company president's response might well be: "What the hell do you mean? My organization has a head and I'm it!" In this instance it is suggested that the mind of the leader, regardless of its effectiveness, is no more than a substitute, a surrogate, a borrowed intelligence being used by a headless organization. Let's try this notion another way.

Most organizations simply fulfill a program. Like a computer, they grind out whatever their instructions require them to. Inside these organizations men are scrambling to untangle problems, remove blockages, and counter the effects of exterior forces and interior disturbances, but basically their drive is to run the system the way it is as hard as they can. The whole activity—not the people in it—is mindless. It's valuable. It can distribute values throughout the society, but it does this much as an automated Telstar satellite does. It follows the program built into it while resisting all else.

I repeat, this has been a useful but mindless organization environment within which live human beings are spending most of their lives. Can we do better? Why not? Imagine what advances are possible for organizations that possess their own intelligence, their own awareness, their own conscience. If we add this capacity of organization consciousness, I suggest the following will occur:

— Organizations will take far better care of their members and will receive far greater contributions from the people now dozing in our primitive structures.

— The organization will become a full participant in the development of applied intellect and in the elevation of a society's values and goals.

— Every incentive will exist to automate repeatable activities now being performed by humans and to send human beings off on the exciting organization missions that only humans could handle.

— Intellectual activity in organizations will expand by thousands of percent. Computers, remote terminals, advanced software, and display devices will finally come into their own as the organization concentrates on improving the quality of its thinking network as well as its action network.

— Knowledge people, leaders, and doers will have a more natural communion of interest as they seek organization goals.

— A large educating, training, computing, sensing, message-sending, and recording brain will emerge as the organization's group mind tied by its nervous system to every part of the organization and aware of its environment. Much more complex and difficult goals and missions will be possible. Like what? Like sending a man to the moon as NASA did in contrast to manufacturing windup dolls for the Christmas trade. Like attacking all the great problems of mankind and making this planet congenial for its inhabitants, half of whom live in want. Like creating wholesome and beautiful environments for man's future and realizing the full potential of his development as a human being instead of being trapped in his most primitive animal aspects.

— Finally, instead of apologizing for the winding down of the free enterprise system, organizations with heads on their shoulders can affirm by their behavior the power for good in high profits, the benefits to mankind of large-scale operations, and the capacities of the human race to eliminate the remaining vestiges of our primitive eras.

With these possibilities in mind, let us consider the organic human-type organization. First, it is clear that it embodies a biological concept of growth *using man himself as a model*. The structure of this model features a tight network governed by an artificial intelligence. Its authority mechanisms too are governed by an artificial intelligence which assists in developing conditions for the free expression of individuality by humans in its structure. The broad general distribution of authority throughout the system exceeds the delegation of any other form of human system.

Within the organization, social interaction is marked by the complete freedom of relationships in all directions. The channels of communication are fully coordinated in an intricate, wide-open network. Finding examples of organic organizations of the human type is difficult because quite probably no organization which is built on this model yet exists. Until we can see how we can live and protect our humanity in organizations of this form, no doubt we'll be a bit nervous about the task. Although no organization has crossed this threshold of development for mankind, probably several are very close. These may be:

IBM	Battelle Institute
Xerox	3M
NASA	Volvo
Texas Instruments	Comsat
Polaroid	CSIRO (Australia)

These organizations reached their present advanced form by a variety of means, chief of which is their ability to concentrate intellectual activity on useful, value-creating operations. In one way or another all are immensely profitable. When and if they break through to the full transformation suggested here, they should be leading the way for all other human organizations for the next thousand years.

The human type of organization has the highest future potential to produce value efficiently from the resources it utilizes. It will prove to be more flexible than any other type of organization in adopting new technologies and systems. It will prove especially effective in developing large and unusually profitable operations which will be environment-improving instead of environment-degrading in their primary, secondary, and tertiary effects. Its ability to alter its own structure will be the highest. Before too long, it should pass through radical change processes more and more rapidly until it acquires the ultimate organization skill: the ability to remain in a state of permanent metamorphosis. In this condition, the organization will change continuously, implement new data it finds or creates, and adopt new technologies and systems concepts as they appear useful to enlarge and enhance its beneficial effects upon its people, the public, and the environment.

Life in such an organization will be extraordinarily stimulating and exciting. Every day the facts of life will in some way be literally different. In an environment so stimulating and encouraging to their drives and needs, the main problem of human beings will be to get away often enough to a quiet place to rest up from the intense and pleasurable excitement of work. That will be a situation quite opposite from the one created in our organizations today.

Organizations and Environment

Once these seven forms of human organization are understood, we can
see why many of the worst problems of advanced societies have arisen.
As we expanded our mechanical and rigid organizations all over the
world, we placed human beings in an essentially inhuman and cold
environment. A pyramid is no place to live, nor is a clockwork. Whatever their other benefits, mechanistic and mathematical environments
destroy what is human about humans and leave behind robots and zombies. To make certain that you understand how far-reaching this process
has become, let me quote the late Ludwig von Bertalanffy, father of
general systems:

> The concept of man as robot was both an expression of and a powerful
> motive force in industrialized mass society. It was the basis for behavioral
> engineering in commercial, economic, political and other advertising and
> propaganda; the expanding economy of the "affluent society" could not sub-
> sist without such manipulation. Only by manipulating humans ever more
> into Skinnerian rats, robots, buying automata, homeostatically adjusted con-
> formers and opportunists (or, speaking bluntly, into morons and zombies)
> can this great society follow its progress toward ever increasing gross national
> product.[6]

Earlier in his history, man was so deeply involved with nature that
he brought its inner light with him as he moved from an agricultural
to an industrial society. As time went on and generations succeeded
each other, that inner light went out for men and women working steadily in our bloodless, lifeless mechanical bureaucracies. It is the specific
nature and structure of our primitive organization forms (and their
rules and regulations) which destroy man's humanity, his needed renewal from natural surroundings, and his social will.

A most important reason to move to organic forms of organization
is our slowly degrading environment. In the long run, we have seen
that it just is not possible for mechanistic and mechanical organizations
to deal with nature, either with man's nature or with the nature of the
web of life we are part of. In the calculations of most organizations,
nature and man do not compute. However, the organic organization's
natural sensitivity to the exterior environment helps it to develop capacities to grow and to protect other life forms at the same time.
Our one best hope for environmental protection is not to bay at the
moon or to carp at politicians for more laws, but to move our organizations promptly into organic forms that can deal directly with the

problems they created. When we do this in all the organizations of society, but especially in business and industry, then we will have the head, the heart, and the hands to work us out of our current environmental impasse.

The problems with organization structure in modern or postindustrial societies, as just described, are not the problems uppermost in people's minds in less-developed areas. Each environment and each culture must be accurately appraised and understood before any organization form can be recommended to it. In the Libyan desert, for example, French, British, and American companies are pumping up huge quantities of water to sprinkle the desert sand 24 hours a day. Ten cuttings of alfalfa can be made each year! Crops explode from these desert food machines. The Arab employees wander in and out of the work crews, still deeply immersed in their religion and their desert milieu, even though the latter is vanishing before their eyes. Language and comprehension problems abound. It is doubtful whether anything but a leader/follower cluster form of organization could get out the work, yet this is foreign to many of the Europeans and Americans. Two cultures, plus the needs of modern machinery, of a bountiful agribusiness, and the surrounding desert sands, are in conflict. The example illustrates why organization forms should logically relate to the people, the technology, and the environment.

Probably Japan's preceding hundred years of industrial development is the best example of how a society can carry mores, loyalties, habits, and expectations from a well-formed and traditional culture into an industrial revolution and make it work. At the same time, the rigid forms of organizations Japan used automatically replicated the social and environmental problems of other industrial societies because they were not designed to deal with them. Such an adaptation by a whole people has not eliminated the challenges of creating new organization forms that actualize their employees, preserving the rare quality of life inherent in Japanese tradition, and protecting the rapidly degrading environment of the Japanese islands.

In Table 2-4, as a general guide, the seven organization forms have been arrayed on the basis of where they are most likely to fit into society's various stages of development. Nothing in the table should be interpreted to mean that high urbanization is better than other stages; in fact, if people in those parts of the world relatively underdeveloped today will just use their heads, they may be able to gain the benefits of highly sophisticated technologies without incurring the curses of urbanization and overpopulation.

TABLE 2-4. Fitting organization forms to environments.

	ORGANIZATION FORMS RATED MOST SUITABLE						
	I	II	III	IV	V	VI	VII
CULTURE AND SETTING	L/F CL	M	CLO	P	CO	OPT	OHT
Highly developed, urban and suburban						X	X
Medium development, some urban				X	X	X	
Low development, rural	X	X	X	X	X		
Primitive, mostly rural	X	X	X	X			
Primitive, tribal herds or light farming	X	X	X				
Primitive, wandering	X	X					

L/F Cl = Leader/Follower cluster; M = mosaic; Clo = clockwork; P = pyramid; Co = conglomerate; OPT = organic plant type; OHT = organic human type.

In moving ahead the concepts of change systems, new perspective can be gained by contrasting the distribution of these seven organization types worldwide with their distribution in the United States. Confirming data for this evaluation are simply not yet known and the ratings are based on the author's judgment, but the issues raised are worth considering. When such measures are generally taken, we'll at last have the facts. Again, by suggesting what ought to be the development of organizations in society, Table 2-4 illustrates the too primitive nature of the organizations we actually possess. In our industrial societies most organizations fall into classes III, IV, and V.

Several concepts usually expressed in words are given estimates in Table 2-5 which might stimulate some organization to go out and get

TABLE 2-5. Dispersion of organization classes.

CLASS	NAME	WORLDWIDE FREQUENCY, %	U.S.A. FREQUENCY, %
I	Leader/Follower cluster	40	10
II	Mosaic	30	15
III	Clockwork	13	20
IV	Pyramid	10	30
V	Conglomerate	4.5	15
VI	Organic plant type	2	9
VII	Organic human type	0.5	1

the facts. As it is, the table portrays the worldwide dispersion of organizational classes. Again, the percentages given are my estimates; no hard data exist.

A Case History

As another way to help today's manager develop and use these new concepts about his own organization, a meeting of a leading multinational corporation's executive committee (imaginary as befits a view of the future) is here presented:

CORPORATE PLANNER   You don't need anything but a clockwork for our new plant in that country. The production processes are well known, and our chief reason for being there is the location behind their borders and an oversupply of labor. We are protected behind their tariff walls. All we need to do is to crank the mechanism up and help them to get reasonable performance out of it.

PRESIDENT   All right. Set up the design for it and go ahead.

PERSONNEL V.P.   What about our problem in the Boston area? That's a high-technology plant we operate there, and we're having trouble hanging on to our technicians. They are going over to competitors and to other high-technology plants in the area.

ORGANIZATION CONSULTANT   Would an organic organization, plant type give you something new to talk about in recruiting and in holding people in that area?

PERSONNEL V.P.   It might. We've tried everything else.

PRESIDENT   Very well then. If no one objects here, take a year to put it in. Keep track of whether it was worth it too.

CHAIRMAN   Gentlemen, now that your main business is finished, I would like us to consider some of the long-term implications of what we are doing. In about six of our divisions, over the past few years, we have installed clockworks, pyramids, and organic organizations with remarkable results. However, word of this has traveled around the organization with some unique consequences. Our people have learned a new vocabulary of organization structure, and it is not at all unexpected that with this new learning they should ask, "What about corporate headquarters?"

PRESIDENT   Well, what about it? We're doing fine and the balance sheet proves it.

CHAIRMAN   Let's not invalidate that in any way. What I am talking about is a phenomenon visible throughout human society. When you raise a man's condition—say by giving him a job—you raise his expectations. Now he wants to learn his job and earn a raise. Later he'll want to earn a promotion. Similarly, as we have improved and concentrated people's attention on the fit of organization structures to each individual operation of this company, we too have raised people's expectations of us.

PRESIDENT   I'm afraid I see what you mean.

CHAIRMAN   Yes, there is some reason for dismay if I read you correctly, but there is a good deal more reason for excitement and relish in the situation. I have been leading up to the idea that we can no longer duck the question: "When do we set up corporate headquarters as an organic organization, human type?" What do you think?

PRESIDENT   You're suggesting our own people are in the pool. They say the water is fine and what are we waiting for. Is that it?

CHAIRMAN   You've caught it exactly.

PRESIDENT   Well, what does everyone else think about this?

CORPORATE PLANNER   We're long overdue. Let's go for it.

PERSONNEL V.P.   It is a logical move. It will excite our young people and give our recruiting and promotion tracks a good deal more vitality.

MARKETING V.P.   Nothing could help us more to get on with our job.

FINANCIAL V.P.   The financial community will love it, I'm sure. Besides I can see some great opportunities for us internally. However, how do we calculate the risks?

ORGANIZATION CONSULTANT   Before talking about risks, let me say from experience that by placing the most difficult job, the most challenging tasks, and the most complex and human structure at the core of your organization, you will energize the entire group of companies. This should fire up performance, pride in excellence, self-development, and ambition to move up to a core group really worth joining. You'll give bite and permanence to the whole organization structure. Now as to risks. We know some of this area is uncharted, but the journey across it can be confident of a passage. You'll make it. To put dollar figures, time, and other resource costs together will take me about two months.

PRESIDENT   Go ahead on that task, and we'll put this item forward until then.

In *The Future of the Future* John McHale [7] points out that mankind's immediate future will most likely be created by nontechnological means. Technology has created most of our past and present conditions. As a result McHale feels that men know how to create the hardware they need but are vague about the software. They have some doubt that the social and behavioral sciences are equal to the task.

If we put a head on our organization's shoulders and give it organic life (in simulation), we will have created a practical way to use our action vehicles—our organizations—to play a dominant role in developing the software we need so badly. As McHale says, "The models . . . of our institutions . . . restrict much of our futures thinking within obsolete historical conditions. . . . We need to experiment more consciously with innovative social organizations."

We have examined organizations as the chief vehicles and suppliers of radical change and have found most of them wanting. To some degree, ambition to advance to higher levels of organization may have been stimulated in the reader, but any manager knows that monumental obstacles stand in the path of every major effort he makes to create a change. Thus, it is prudent to consider, aside from the inadequacies in organization structure, what day-to-day obstacles prevent radical change in most organizations.

References

Ludwig von Bertalanffy is quoted from *General Systems Theory* (New York: Braziller, 1968). William R. Ewald, Jr.'s remarks are from *Environment and Change* (Bloomington, Ind.: Indiana University Press, 1968). The quotation of Max Ways is from "Tomorrow's Management: A More Adventurous Life in a Free-Form Corporation," *Fortune*, July 1966.

1. Talcott Parsons, *Structure and Process in Modern Societies* (New York: Free Press, 1960). For a more recent review of this area, see Fremont Kast and James Rosenzweig, *Organization and Management* (New York: McGraw-Hill, 1970).
2. Statistics and graphics reprinted with permission from John F. Mee, "Changing Concepts of Management," *SAM Advanced Management Journal,* October 1972.
3. Eric Hoffer, *The Ordeal of Change* (New York: Harper & Row, 1952), p. 149. Used with permission.
4. J. J. Servan-Schreiber, *The American Challenge* (New York: Atheneum, 1968).

5. Kenneth Boulding, "General Systems Theory—The Skeleton of Science," *Management Science*, Vol 2 (1956), pp. 197–208.
6. Ludwig von Bertalanffy, *General Systems Theory* (New York: Braziller, 1968).
7. John McHale, *The Future of the Future* (New York: Braziller, 1969), p. 11.

CHAPTER THREE

The Obstacles to Radical Change

The great barrier to major entrepreneurial innovations within the modern corporate framework is the organizational hierarchy itself, which operates to protect the status quo and fend off attempts at innovative change.

ROBERT KIRK MUELLER

Our institutions—and this includes business organizations as well as other kinds—are the "chromosomes" of our society. . . . They preserve in them the successful "gene" mutations of previous social, cultural and technological innovations. To protect themselves against further change, institutions harden their resistance by formalizing rituals, customs and traditions. In a rapidly changing technology, the social organism thus preserved becomes unable to cope with its new environment and either must give way to the innovators or fail to survive.

DON FABUN

To avoid wasting your time, here I state flatly that, although most managers are aware of and use techniques to install programs that create low or medium rates of change, it is still true that most managements now possess *no* techniques that have any chance at all to deliver radical, high-speed change in their own organizations. If you are a manager who has already learned this hard-to-take truth, you can skip to Chapters 4 and 5, where you will meet entirely new guides and climbing techniques for the thus far inaccessible mountain of radical change.

Existing techniques cannot change your organization in any but a slow and evolutionary fashion. If you are not yet convinced of this, you will find ample evidence here. Because the record and the evidence in this chapter are so unilaterally negative and discouraging, this book specifically reminds you that *radical change is possible* and that any reasonably intelligent and able manager *can* attain it in his organization.

External Interdependence

We have all heard of the "web of life" in the forest or at the seashore, wherein many life forms interact and occupy "niches" in their environment. Such niches and interactions are best when they are stable and friendly to life. Extremely harsh or wildly fluctuating environments tend to limit the numbers of individuals, the numbers of life forms, and the amount of interaction. For example, not much life or interaction goes on at the North Pole, but things are jumping in a tropical jungle.

The same principle applies to organizations, of which men are components. We are life forms too. Our organizations are a life form into which we—as gods—have breathed life. We should remember that what the gods have given they can also take away. In free societies we have a wide multiplicity of organizations, perhaps the widest range possible. They are affected by all the other systems with which they interact. In hospitable environments, a single system can become so tightly interlocked with other organizations that what happens to one affects all. Because organizations in most environments must deal with other systems and must use man as a system component, it is not hard to see why they naturally prefer order, stability, predictability, and reliability; in short, organizations generally prefer low or medium rates of change as a way of life.

A manufacturing plant in a small community, Company A, strongly affects the lives of the people who gain employment from it and want that benefit to continue. The plant affects local natural resources and suppliers by enlarging their economic interdependence; it influences the price of real estate, the flow of economic development, the costs of schools, and, most importantly, the air and water that everyone shares. These interdependencies created by the natural operation of Company A become very strong regardless of individual or managerial preferences. All interacting systems prefer predictability from their fellows; therefore, any radical change up or down in the fate of Company A stimulates adjusting or demanding forces throughout the community in which the company operates.

In larger urban areas, manufacturers can avoid, but only to some degree, the lockstep pace of interdependence clearly visible in a small one-company town. Any system has a network of external systems affecting it. Most of the external systems tend to keep it operating today as it operated yesterday—for *their* convenience.

Books about organizational change usually come to life with graphic detail when they describe the *obstacles* to change but fade away in abstractions when they describe techniques to get around the obstacles. Like giants facing Lilliputians, the great long lists of obstacles flowing from author after author stare down at short lists of change techniques. Not much on change management was in print before 1950. Perhaps we can conclude that it was proper in those early years for writers on change to focus on the obdurate realities of organization resistance to change. Recently, however, many new change techniques have swelled the Lilliputian ranks. With the ideas developed in this book, it is hoped they can at last shoot up to a height greater than that of their obstacle giants.

We should abandon this win-lose image of change techniques versus obstacles. The optimism now being felt about attaining radical change stems from a superior understanding of the change process. We now know that it avoids useless win-lose confrontations on minor issues and moves ahead smoothly toward larger goals. The concepts in change literature have gotten more complex, and they present more useful arrays of techniques. Now, in an inclusive framework, the entire field of inquiry advances a step to the idea of change systems, a concept proposed in these pages.

A change system is a general system. This means that it is a system for your organization which is superior to your present management system. How is it superior? In these ways:

— Instead of management assumptions that tend to use men as robot components or controls for machinery, the change system will push toward management systems that use men as human components of the system. This means the new system's operations depend on the values, quality of performance, ethics, and morals of its human components instead of on how well a man can simulate an automatic control.

— Your present system is likely to possess a buried assumption that men and women are objects to do things with—to persuade, lead, manipulate, threaten, and dominate so as to adjust and control their efforts. The new system will regard people as the active and dynamic determinants of its success.

— Your present system is not likely to affirm that man has a mind, that he can create symbols to live by, that his perspective extends beyond his organization existence, that he knows he will die, and that he can create an infinite variety of futures and live in them. The new system will deliberately open the door to these traits of man.

— Your present organization has been conceived as a closed system needing no basic redesign. The new system will be an admittedly open system capable of developing organically into new forms, transforming itself, and lifting itself on the lever of its new-found openness.

— Many present organizations are neutral or amoral on many basic ethical issues in a way that insulates them from the challenges of their time. The new system will abandon neutrality for a specific set of organization values, ethics, and morals.

The final difference is crucial. The new system will have integrated [1] this idea of organization conscience with capacity to attain higher levels of performance, widespread benefits, much higher profits from the use of its resources, and a better way of life for the people inside the organization. The real life aspects of this new human condition are in some respects beyond our present imaginings. A specific goal of the advanced, organic organizations will be to make life inside them one of man's most exciting adventures instead of the insufferable boredom that afflicts most of us today.

Although many change practitioners still rely on the simpler levers to change, the overall progression of thinking from simple to complex is made explicit in Table 2-5. In 1957, Ginzberg and Reilly [2] pointed out that many company attempts at change failed because:

Top management refused to alter its own behavior.
Change was seen as a matter of giving the right orders.
Top managers were unable to delegate the power of decision.
Managerial training was weak and spotty.
The founder of the business was still alive, and to make needed changes would be viewed as an affront to his life's work.
Organization inertia was too great.
Resources were unavailable or the will to use them was inadequate.

Economic conditions were unfavorable.
Previous managerial attempts had failed.
Men do not relinquish status and authority easily in any hierarchy.

In many companies and institutions those same conditions exist today. J. M. Juran deals with resistance to change in his book *Managerial Breakthrough*.[3] His still sensible counsel for the manager seeking to overcome what he saw as massive obstacles to change is paraphrased and briefed in the following 29 points:

1. Separate and understand both the social and technical aspects of change.
2. Learn the scale of values in the culture you intend to change.
3. Remember that what is different is not necessarily wrong.
4. Violent resistance can stem from unwise uses of power.
5. Change is a potential threat to any culture.
6. Get social values working in the right direction.
7. Resistance to change can be signaled by lip service; general belligerence; thefts and vandalism; immature, childish behavior, and insistence on former practices; substitute outlets—sports, gambling, alcohol, or community activities; or flight from reality.
8. Never attack a culture head on.
9. Remember that advance of any kind requires a lot of unlearning.
10. Teach the new.
11. Remember that you are the product of one of many environments.
12. Translate esoteric counsel into the language of the culture you are working with.
13. Do not overdesign your system.
14. Do not fall in love with your recommendations as the sole cure.
15. Get everyone to contribute to the change process.
16. Provide time for people to change attitudes or habits.
17. Start small and introduce changes gradually.*
18. Allow no surprises.
19. Watch for the right time to initiate action.
20. Use outside experts to second-guess change.
21. Keep it simple.
22. Work with the recognized leaderships.
23. Treat people with dignity.

---

* The author believes that today Dr. Juran would feel that the state of the art makes "large-scale, high-speed change" a legitimate option and that the "gradualism" recommended in item 17 is relegated to eras in which an organization is consolidating the gains made from radical change.

24. Put yourself in the other fellow's place.
25. Use persuasion.
26. Change the environment.
27. Allow for the saving of face.
28. Create a social climate which favors the new change.
29. Avoid win-lose situations.

Goodwin Watson, in Warren Bennis' excellent reader *The Planning of Change*,[4] describes resistance to change as an acceptance/rejection cycle in which:

1. At first resistance is massive and undifferentiated; "everyone knows better."
2. Proponents of change are called crackpots.
3. The strengths and weaknesses of pro and anti forces are appraised.
4. Status and power elements are examined. Who has gotten to whom?
5. Direct conflict and a showdown occur.
6. Somebody wins; somebody loses.

Watson describes the many intertwined factors of this rigid resistance to change as a group of system factors and a group of individual behaviors. He describes resistance among individuals as due to the following characteristics:

1. *Homeostasis,* the sum of the built-in regulatory mechanisms in all our attitudes that maintain stability and the status quo. Those who seek change for personal stimulation are a small minority.
2. *Habit,* the pleasure of repeating learned responses. We keep our noses in grooves that satisfy, much in the way a phonograph repeats one record endlessly.
3. *Primacy,* the first image that is hard to alter. Our first impressions dominate our attitudes.
4. *Selective perception,* the power of old constructs to screen out new information.
5. *Dependence,* the common life-long habit of orienting to father figures.
6. *Superego,* the effect of unwarranted expectations of self imprinted on the young child by his parents and his culture.
7. *Insecurity and regression,* the age-old urge to return to the infantile paradise lost.

Complementing the obstacles to change visible in *individuals,* Watson lists the following resistances in *social systems* (that is, organizations viewed as social systems):

— *Conformity to norms.* Standard operating practices, dress, forms of address, adherence to schedules, statements of loyalty, forms of am-

bition, approved community participation, approved family arrangements—all these are signs of conformity by organization members to
institutional norms. The group polices the individual and squashes deviant behavior as well as deviant thoughts. This group tendency to
weed out deviance, that is, change, is as alive in the boardroom as it is
in a street gang. Its essence is denial of individuality and the group's
urge to make obedient zombies out of men.

— *Systemic and cultural coherence.* In this kind of resistance the parts
take on characteristics of the whole; therefore, if you change a part,
you attack the whole. Thus, attempts to start radical change in one
small part of an organization will soon invoke repercussions, counter-
actions, and obstacles throughout the whole outfit.

— *Vested interests.* The economic and prestige interests of groups and
individuals entrenched in the present system are obvious obstacles to
change.

— *The sacrosanct.* Every culture and every organization cling to some
shibboleth about what can and cannot be done, which is beyond the
reach of reason. Most shibboleths are assumptions about people or
organization life visible only to the trained anthropologist or sociologist.
They silently prevent change. A good example is NIH: most organizations automatically reject any idea if it is labeled not invented here.

— *Rejection of outsiders.* If the person carrying a new idea is a for-
eigner, he's "no good" or at least irrelevant to "the way things are
around here." Newness is usually killed unless it is generated from an
accepted leader "inside" an organization.

Watson goes on to illustrate quite clearly that an innovation will
encounter obstacles unless it is minor in scope, affects few individuals,
does not threaten organization culture, and does not threaten traditional,
erroneous shibboleths. Radical change, which by definition penetrates
all these screens and attacks the homeostatic tendencies of our primitive organizations, thus has little or no chance.

Watson also states a positive argument in favor of no change in
organizations: "The forces which contribute to stability in personality
or in social systems which can be perceived as resisting change . . .
permit the duration of character, intelligent action, institutions, civilization, and culture." Thus he suggests that most of the hallmark institutions of civilized life have natural stakes in the prevention of change.
These are formidable obstacles.

Another observer of organizations, Herbert A. Shephard,[5] makes
it clear that most organizations were designed to accomplish a few
specific tasks reliably and to resist all innovation-possessing unknowns.

In such an organization—an automated production process, for example —efforts to innovate can be classified as "error, irresponsibility, and insubordination; and appropriate corrective action is taken to bring the would-be innovators 'back into line.' " Shephard points out that rigid hierarchical organizations obey orders precisely and that learning or change can take place only at the top, short of the revolt from below which is almost inevitable in modern times.

Further, a rigid innovation-resisting hierarchy must, by definition, screen out as "disturbances" all innovations occurring to employees who are familiar with the work itself but are low in the pecking order. This force is so rigid, says Shephard, that most organizations develop an "underworld" of better and easier ways to get the work out (which employees carefully conceal from their primitive managers lest their production goals be raised). The process is certainly self-defeating for all; but when the sharks are set loose, no one can blame people for getting out of the pool.

"Beating the system" to install innovations in combative, hostile organizations requires an individual or group with paragon qualities, says Shephard. The change manager should possess:

Creative but pragmatic imagination
Psychological security
Autonomous nature
Ability to trust others and to earn trust
Great energy and determination
A sense of timing
Skill in organizing
Willingness and skill to be Machiavellian

Maybe it would be easier to make an organic, radical change in an organization than to find enough nonpareil Galahads to fight the ever-renewing dragons of innovation resistance. My own list of obstacles to radical change embodies much of what others have included and also factors in the change system concept. I am deeply indebted to the definitive research of Bennis, Watson, and many others.

The System's Obstacles to Radical Change

Homeostasis

The maintenance of a balance between all internal and external forces is called homeostasis, and we underestimate the need for and the power of it. After all, the biggest task of man is to find a homeostatic relationship between his numbers and the life-maintaining resources of Spaceship Earth, or all will perish. We vary our body temperature at risk of death; we vary social arrangements at risk of antagonizing our peers; we vary our ideas at risk of being classed mavericks. In many ways variation from the balance point in any system means a larger and much more likely loss; ergo, our world possesses great homeostatic forces which resist change.

Vested Interests

Any system benefits some individuals but penalizes others. Those who are benefited become firmly entrenched and have no intention of altering the situation for the sake of some remote organizational goal. One cannot take the nipple out of a baby's mouth before he's through and convince him that hunger is good for him. You can expect screams and violent opposition from the entrenched beneficiaries of your present system.

Economic Problems

The constraints of cash flow, capital, and ownership comprise economic problems. Radical change requires money and uses it to finance ventures in unknown seas. However, most suppliers of capital want predictable earnings and dividends from visible, known, and familiar sources. The two kinds of venture are in basic conflict. Only the growing intelligence of management, the investing public, and the money market offer any hope here. Some day, capital will be withdrawn from familiar, and often low-profit, ventures and invested in organizations with the skill, courage, and adventuresomeness to attempt the journey to radical change. In a time of transition the latter investment policy will turn out to be the most conservative one.

Tradition

Tradition is a dead weight on change attempts. Every organization develops some traditions or adopts them out of the culture or community. These traditions can add color and reinforcement to wholesome interpersonal relationships, but they can also stultify innovation when the two conflict, as they usually do.

Cultural Rigidities

Inviolate organization assumptions include certain ways to speak, manners to use in submitting proposals, and forms to use in obtaining funds. All these cultural patterns can vitiate change efforts. Explanations of "how we do things around here" usually make it clear that "there's only one way." That way almost always seeks to recreate the past and avoid unknown futures.

Value Conflicts

The hallmark of our times is the value conflict. We espouse honesty, but we lie in our advertising; we honor integrity, but we conceal product or service weaknesses; we ask for open communication, but we violate confidences; we extol the future to gain investor capital, but we conceal mitigating costs or incapacities; we talk about change, but we protect rigid policies. All these and other "normal" events in organizations tear at the individual's values and encourage the kind of alienation which is incompatible with confidence in the possibility or the merit of radical change.

The Uses of Power

Power is the chief weapon of the ignorant. Any radical change process which does not deal directly with power and the crucial need for its distribution and limitation will prove irrelevant. It is shocking to contemplate yet literally true that the Declaration of Independence and the Constitution of the United States—and any other Magna Carta of human rights—are left outside the factory gates and the office reception area. Nobody really planned it that way; it just happened. A core reality of all the primitive organizations now in use in our companies and institutions is that individuals are *not* equal. They do *not* have the protection of the Bill of Rights in daily affairs on the job, and they have few recourses from arbitrary management or union actions that at times match in fairness the rulings of a Tartar chieftain. The equality and democracy of a political election, once a year, is gone from the daily time-clock-punching line which is restricted to one class of employee.

Win-Lose Psychology

The cultural assumption most difficult to overcome is that someone must win and someone must lose. Because we have not yet developed

satisfying ways to compete with ourselves or with the challenge of ac-
quiring a skill, we still compete with one another and thereby create a
sense of victory and domination in the winner and defeat and submission in the loser. Our society concentrates on football, baseball, golf,
tennis, and other fiercely competitive games. How much longer can we
afford to regard these games as the source of our culture's values? Even
in radical change proposals to benefit all, some will make a game of
defeating the proponents. In any future society, arrangements in which
everybody wins will be the best ones, win-lose situations will be the
lesser, and the worst arrangements will be those in which everybody
loses. Unfortunately, in most organizations today the latter two styles
of confrontation prevail. Their automatic side effect is to block change.

Adopting Safe Goals

Organization cowardice is typified by the adoption of safe goals. It is
appropriate to remind ourselves that we walk this way but once. Twenty
years is all most people will give to the organizations in which they
work. Usually organizations discourage the individual's idealism and
his constructive ideas for change, which leaves him with little more than
the motivation to hang on to his job. If all employees want is a sinecure
and retirement pay, why should they support any organization goal
other than a 5 to 10 percent increase per year, roughly comparable to
inflation? Corporate files on marketing programs and long-range plans
are loaded with such nongoals. They effectively block all thoughts of
change; more than that, they invite corporate raiders, stockholders, the
public, and government agencies to attack management.

The Downward Spiral of Negative Change

Change can go up or down. Nothing guarantees that change is always
improvement; in fact, the annual death rate of business organizations,
associations, schools, churches, and government agencies around the
world makes it clear that organizations regularly spiral down and out.
The average age of organizations is less than the human life span. Most
failures are caused by refusals to face the challenges of our times. The
only change *that* management policy creates is that it blows everyone
out of the water. An upward spiral is reinforced by the positive, optimistic expectations of people in the organization; a downward spiral
speeds and reinforces dissolution by negativism and expectations of

doom. In the present sense downward spirals can also represent radical change. By now, however, it should be clear that our target is radical *constructive* change.

Long-Range Planning

So-called long-range planning can actually be building in sameness by planning. In recent years, planning for the future of government and business organizations has accelerated. Far too often long-range planning convinces managers that new options or new directions are remote. Too many plans challenge nothing of importance in present systems because planning directors do not have the options for creating radical change. Many organizations hesitate to upset carefully built plans for orderly growth based on assumptions of the past even though massive evidence encourages radical change. Managements that can set aside the idea of using planning to prevent new options can now allow planning departments to be in at the beginning of radical change efforts.

Resistances to Change in Group Behavior

The urge to obliterate self. Most people prefer that their individuality be lost in the group or in the safe back alleys of organization structures because they have been taught that visibility of self increases personal risk. Aside from that factor, if all one wants is a paycheck, why attract attention by being a human being?

The effects of systemic coherence. Because an organization has interrelated subsystems which contribute to or take from other subsystems, the predictability and reliability of output of each work group become virtues. Each subsystem wants every system that affects it to be consistent and regular; that is, *nobody wants change.*

The sacrosanct. Every work group quickly translates the accidents of its formation, situation, supervision, assignment, and informal leadership into taboos or customs. These are often used to "train" new managers, put down recalcitrant employees, block new ideas, or debunk top management programs.

Rejection of outsiders. No group ever existed that did not require outsiders to qualify, that did not define "in" and "out," and that did not defend its status quo from new ideas, especially outsider new ideas. This group characteristic is useful when it screens out erroneous or harmful new ideas but destructive when it refuses constructive ideas.

Resistance to Change in Individuals

Stability satisfies. We enjoy stability and routine in our jobs. Although some few individuals welcome the stimulation of new ideas, new routines, and new challenges, most people find it a burden. This is particularly true among alienated employees and managers, who comprise by far the largest group in most organizations. Habits and grooves get one through the workday. Because they are often classified as second-class citizens, employees have little interest in major organization issues and prefer to go through the regular motions each day without any mental or physical disturbance. A janitor or a president will resist any force that threatens his groove.

First images dominate. The first clear-cut image each person gets of "what things are like around here" dominates his thinking for the duration of his employment. Most individuals refuse to relinquish these constructs under any but the most violently contradictory circumstances.

Selective perception. Related to the primacy of first images is the way people select from communications those parts that reinforce their constructs but will not see or hear contrary evidence no matter how well it is presented. It is no news that, from top managers to assembly line workers, old prejudices yield most reluctantly to new information or superior argument.

Dependence and conformity. Starting in the cradle, children are taught to remain dependent on others and to conform to others' dictates. Many adults make a virtue of such obedient submission—as do managers or generals who want loyal minions—and secure their whole personal identity from the submission process. When they are confronted with a supervisor who behaves as though employees were his equal, they refuse to permit his notion of equality to affect their behavior. In time they will make him reassert a traditional role of dominance to feed their need to submit.

Superego. We've been carefully taught at home, by our peers, in school, and through the media that life-styles and achievements impossible for most of us are what we should seek. So we seek them. Thus most organization members are forcing themselves to want what others (advertisers, political leaders, managers) say they should want. These irrational expectations of self lead to character impairment. They are frequently found within organizations whose official goals sound as though they would be more appropriate for androids or robots than for live, diverse human beings. The process of encouraging unreal expectations in people kills the humane, personal talents and skills needed for radical change.

Self-distrust, the acceptance of guilt. Our society is replete with pur-
veyors of guilt; they discern in every human action a reason to feel
guilty of some social crime or other. For example, the social messages
of the counterculture and the socialist-liberal wings of both political par-
ties in the United States concentrate on making the public feel guilty
of its sins. In this way we have ennobled its acceptance until guilt has
become a virtue, although our common sense should give us a healthier
view of ourselves. Guilt blocks constructive change because it encourages sick, sentimental responses to problems.

Insecurity, regression to childhood. Many organizations are im-
pacted with infantile, regressive behavior on the part of large groups of
employees who have long since lost respect for management. The managers themselves have created this condition. Change for these groups
is uphill all the way. They lack organization mental health.

Orneriness, intransigence. In the course of their development, pyramidal organizations and large bureaucracies create islands of influence
around specific functions. People in these secluded areas often imagine
they are a law unto themselves. Sometimes, because they know of some
corporate officer malfeasance or management peccadillo, they *are* a law
unto themselves. Such autonomous rebels, secure in the belief that they
are immune, ignore organization programs. Government agencies are
famous for this phenomenon, but any large organization displays it in
one way or another. Such encapsulated groups gut radical change
efforts.

Systemic Constraints Set Up by Agreements

1. Established policies of payout to stockholders can reduce available resources to levels so low that investment in change or growth
   is nearly impossible.
2. Massive investment in a single technology may require so many
   years to pay out that change too is automatically ruled out.
3. Labor contracts can preclude change.
4. Government consent decrees or other lawsuit settlements can
   prevent consideration of the most useful change options.
5. International market agreements can require no change.
6. Agreements with subcontractors or suppliers can lock an organization into a situation.
7. Agreements and commitments with bankers or financiers may
   prevent change options from being considered.
8. Pledges to authorities in various regulatory agencies can require
   organization behavior which, over time, is destructive.

A Checklist of Change Obstacles

Test 5 assists the top management team that wants to define how and why its organization resists change efforts. This checklist does open up most of the areas of legitimate concern, but only the quality of investigation and analysis contributed by the organization itself can determine whether new information of strategic value is produced in this process.

Are Large Changes Possible?

Many managers and management analysts have been bewildered by the enormous obstacles their organizations have thrown in the way of "obviously useful and beneficial changes." Lawrence K. Williams [6] of Cornell University sees resistance to change as a problem of attitudes which are often not logical, whereas the new systems proposed for introduction usually are logical. Williams catalogs some of these attitudes as prejudice, fear of loss of status, fear of inability to learn, loss of self-respect, loss of reliance on experience, violation of identity, and mistakes of myopia among "logical" reorganizers who seem to be unaware of the depth and importance of the informal organization's policies and techniques for getting the work out.

Too often, Williams states, planners and administrators use a "bulldozer approach" with the idea that power will prevail, the motto being "If logic won't do it, try force." While this approach may jam the new program into the organization, it will almost certainly insure that the secondary and tertiary waves of adaptation necessary to make any large-scale program pay off will have to be accomplished over a lot of dead bodies. In such processes, internal goodwill is dissipated. In considering more intelligent ways to introduce change, Williams suggests:

— People will be more likely to adopt a change if they can help to design it.

— New systems that embody understandable and acceptable objectives will earn cooperation when the people affected can fully discern the potential benefits.

— Management too often assumes change is beneficial. A given change may be beneficial to international operations or to stock prices, but it also may be directly detrimental to employees' livelihoods, status, sense of personal worth, and work experience.

— Planners and managers should remember that technical feasibility is only one minor aspect of change acceptability; yet most changes proposed by management—many of which are not very successful—

TEST 5

Checklist to Appraise
Resistance to Organization Change

1. Describe the vested interests protecting your organization's status quo.
2. What basic problems of cash flow, capital, ownership, and profit margin prevent change?
3. What organization traditions must be removed to allow change?
4. What values (honesty, integrity, service, etc.) does your organization deliberately espouse but violate in practice?
5. How much equality and inequality exist among all your organization's employees?
6. On what issues (right to decide futures, right to speak, right to equal pay, etc.) can you distinguish inequalities?
7. Exactly what kinds of competition between people does your organization require?
8. How safe or meaningless are your organization's goals?
9. Over the last ten years has your organization been on a plateau, in a downward spiral, or in an upward spiral? Why?
10. Do your long-range plans account for and plan for any radical change possibilities? What is the reason?
11. Define who can use outside experts to contribute to organization policy decisions. Exactly what do you use outside people for? Why?
12. What image of the organization is presented to new employees in fact? What image do they hold six months later?
13. Does the organization propagate irrational and self-destroying expectations in its salesmen, managers, supervisors, middle managers?
14. What groups does the organization feel it "can do nothing with"? Exactly why is this true?
15. What accounts for your organization's existence? Does it have a monopoly, own a resource in short supply, have a license or some other non-free-enterprise saving factor?
16. Describe the sources of active opposition to radical change efforts likely to arise in your organization.
17. How much phony professionalism afflicts your organization? Describe it clearly.
18. What major investments, sunk costs, prevent any thought of change?
19. What are the official constraints on what your organization can do? Describe regulations, consent decrees, laws, debt, overspecialization, too many SOP's that seriously limit your future planning.
20. What other major constraints affect you, such as labor contracts, lawsuit settlements, supplier commitments, or pledges to government agencies?
21. Can you discern a major impending dilemma which might force your organization to consider radical change? What is it?
22. What situations or conditions among top executives continually block change system planning?
23. What factors in your hiring and personnel policies seem to be producing look-alike employees and the weeding out of those who might be inclined to deviate from SOP's because they have better ideas?

are planned, proposed, and authorized solely on the basis of technical feasibility.

As a manager reads these analyses of problems in introducing change to complex organizations, he might recall specific events in his organization and wonder, "How come? We experienced a major change without all these troubles." What probably happened was that the press of inadvertent change from outside the organization over a long period of time gradually created a situation in which some manager said, "Why don't we do this?" and all was already prepared to do exactly that with a minimum of fuss. *This is change by evolution.* It is a matter of adapting to changes created elsewhere in society. It is not change by *design.* Little or no credit is due management for its implementation, although such managerial behavior is far more beneficial than using force to introduce change or refusing to change despite all signals to the contrary.

All too often we note that the organizations which survive longer than the human's average span of 70 years have managed to do so not by superior performance or stronger design but by *force* (government agencies), by *monopoly* (telephone companies, utilities), by *control of a resource* (steel, banks, aluminum, lumber, cement, oil, gas, copper), by *licenses* that limit competitors (airlines, railroads, truckers, taxicab companies), or by *defense business or national emergency* (North American, Lockheed, Boeing, General Dynamics, McDonald-Douglas, Thompson-Ramo-Woolridge). Such survival is ordained when a society appoints a specific elite; it is *not* an example of the survival of the fittest in the free marketplace.

Willis Harman [7] points out that our ability to affect the future is limited. He sees the continuity of cultural changes, unexpected events, deep social forces, and the inertia of institutions as factors that make it unlikely that we can design our future, that is, overcome the obstacles to planned change. The choice we have, says Harman, is not whether a great transformation is taking place in society but whether we choose to understand it and to move with it instead of against it.

The "economic institutions of the society seem to be at odds with the society's highest values," says Dr. Harman. As long as this condition increases in intensity, as it has in recent years, further "alienation, economic decline, and social disruption" seem likely. I would add that not only economic institutions but *all* institutions are in varying degrees unsynchronized with today's emerging value systems. In short, although many have not yet caught up with the idea, large groups of the United States population see their churches, schools, governments, and business enterprises as damaging and repressive to the life forces of human beings and to the quality of life everywhere. This is a serious societal impasse. Something must give.

The invention of new ways to manage and to relate to organizations which include human beings as components occupies the rest of this book. The first step to radical change is a radical improvement in how we decide upon organization goals. Any change goal worth its salt requires us to raise our sights much higher than we ever thought possible in our organizations.

References

The Robert Kirk Mueller quotation is from *The Innovation Ethic* (AMA, 1971); Don Fabun's quote is from *The Dynamics of Change* (Englewood Cliffs, N.J.: Prentice-Hall, 1967).

1. William Gray, "Bertalanffian Principles as a Basis for Humanistic Psychiatry," in Erwin Laszlo (Ed.), *The Relevance of General Systems Theory* (New York: Braziller, 1972).
2. Eli Ginzberg and Ewing W. Reilly, *Effecting Change in Large Organizations* (New York: Columbia University Press, 1957).
3. J. M. Juran, *Managerial Breakthrough* (New York: McGraw-Hill, 1964), pp. 141–157.
4. Goodwin Watson, in Warren Bennis, Kenneth D. Benne, and Robert Chin (Eds.), *The Planning of Change*, 2d ed. (New York: Holt, Rinehart and Winston, 1969).
5. Herbert A. Shephard, "Innovation-Resisting and Innovation-Producing Organizations," *Journal of Business*, October 1967. Used with permission.
6. Lawrence K. Williams, "The Human Side of a Systems Change," *Systems & Procedures Journal*, July–August 1964, pp. 40–43.
7. Willis H. Harman, "Key Choices of the Next Two Decades," in *A Look at Business in 1990: A Summary of the White House Conference on the Industrial World Ahead*, February 7–9, 1972 (Washington, D.C.: GPO, 1972).

PART TWO

Changing
Organizations

CHAPTER FOUR

Change Goal Formulation

It takes just as much creativity and energy to solve wrong as well as right problems, to ameliorate phantom as well as real concerns. The task of technology then begins with interpretation. . . . Defining problems in the component-oriented analytical fashion of the past will only lead . . . back to the same kinds of questions. . . . Totality-oriented synthetic [definition], however, will expand technology's horizon to new qualitative heights.

RALPH G. H. SIU

We are living in a time of growing suspicion about the purposes and effectiveness of the major institutions of the United States—business, government, the universities, and the churches, among others. We are also living in a time when great things must be done quickly.

GEORGE CABOT LODGE

Human institutions and societies function best when they are spontaneous expressions of the freely chosen activities of their interrelated members.

ERVIN LASZLO

C hange goal formulation will shortly become one of management's most exciting practices. Like all uninspected areas of human behavior such as motherhood, goal formulation at first looks like an exercise in the obvious.* Managers say, of course, that their goal is to earn more profits. If they manage a government agency, they say their goal is to implement policy set by political leaders or the legislature; if they are in a college, they say their goal is to educate. These broad-brush oversimplifications, valid though they may be in the largest sense, are, in effect, discussion closers. They are designed to end further questioning or discussion of an organization's true goals. Most imply, "We're going to keep running the system as it is."

Let us agree in advance that the pious goals usually advanced by managers to their organizations are well-meaning but illusory. If profit is accepted by management as an organization's credo but is consistently ignored by the organization's members as a day-to-day goal *they* can live with, then to continue to insist upon its adoption is jingoistic obstinacy. Maybe the problem is that such a general goal is either not understood by employees in terms of the work or else they consider it improper.

A company management which decides all issues and sets its goals exclusively on the basis of short-term profitability is out of place in the free enterprise system. Such policy is no more ethical than that of an untrained child, left alone in a candy store, grabbing everything in sight to stuff his mouth and pockets.

Simple greed is the most destructive policy humans can share in a free economic system—whether in the stock market, at the races, in Las Vegas, at home, or in organizations. The market produces profits as a function of the legitimate exchange of values, and that exchange is seriously impaired by those who approach it with greed. The psychic damage of greed, its erosion of character and self-respect, and its unconscionable social cost have too long a history to be detailed here. As a goal, greed is not an adult organizational objective, nor is it effective over time for an individual to adopt. We ought to be grown up enough to be embarrassed and upset when any top manager says, "We're here to make a profit." Of course this is partly true; but as a summation of part of the life of a number of human beings, it is a narrow and destructive caricature of human nature. Let's leave such naïve statements to children and devise more fundamental goals for ourselves and our organizations.

* Management planners have developed terminology which ranks the word "objective" highest in the organization and ranks the word "goals" as suitable for subsidiary targets. On that basis, the phrase "change goal" describes a temporary, time-scheduled target that fits within overall objectives.

The American entrepreneur has always had a healthy interest in making a profit, but he would rarely endure the stress, the personal agony, and the long effort needed to build his enterprise just because he wanted to fondle money or use it to gain power over others. No matter what he has said, his behavior has consistently revealed larger, more wholesome objectives, a high sense of adventure, and a clear-cut desire to be of service to his fellow man. The current crop of sophomoric doomsayers like to think of entrepreneurs as vicious exploiters of people, but the American record displays more healing, helping, sharing, giving, and hope-instilling behavior coming from entrepreneurs than from any other employment category. After all, in any reasonably well-developed enterprise, profits are no more than a tool for continued growth and development and not an end in themselves, except for the weakest among us.

We have larger objectives than money in running our huge businesses and other organizations, and we will be better off if we frankly admit them. If current leadership is inarticulate on this subject, an inspection of the American record of emancipating people in every category of life should be enough for the thoughtful person. It is possible to hide such a simplistic goal as "more profits" behind a marvelously complex armory of strategic and applied long-range plans. In this process, vast complexities of interior and exterior conditions and constraints are explicitly set forth in a painfully detailed plan. The illusion is created that management in its wisdom has provided for a vast array of contingencies in its long-range plans, which are always the most modern, the latest, and the most "in" procedures. Too often, however, these portfolios of plans fail the test of time. How do your 1950 or 1960 long-range plans look today? The whole complex array of now dusty charts, objectives, and performance measures probably shakes down to a goal of more profits by running the present system a little faster.

What realistic goals are found in organizations today? Here are some possibilities that might strike a chord among thoughtful managers, although they rarely are seen on a framed "company credo" that graces the wall of the reception area:

For the business enterprise:

Our goal is really
　　To keep everything quiet and nice.
　　To suppress external and internal challenges.
　　To acquire a fortune by organizing the efforts and investments of others.
　　To dominate others in order to demonstrate our superiority.

To erect a structure higher or larger than anyone else ever has.
To maintain the position in society of a "class" of people.

For the government agency:

Our goal is really
To keep a low profile.
To impress our superiors.
To minimize the risk of investigation.
To create jobs.
To assist political or ideological movements.
To manipulate the public.
To retire.

For the college administration:

Our goal is really
To provide a haven for incompetents.
To extend the privileges of retirement within a pretended employment status.
To support uneconomic activities.
To protect teacher privileges.
To baby-sit juveniles.
To keep job seekers off the market as long as possible.
To disseminate propaganda.
To satisfy the egos of professors by providing situations in which they can dominate the minds of others.
To insulate society from the drastic bungling of youth.
To manufacture docile employees.

The intent here is not to be unkind, for there is no one among us who cannot be made a bit uncomfortable by searching questions. Rather, the intent is to open up the process of goal formulation to at least a few breaths of fresh air.

Most official decision making on goals at top manager levels is polite hogwash; yet no more important decision can occur in any organization. Management consultants and theoreticians writing in this area have tried their best to be polite and inoffensive in pointing out to managers that glaring inadequacies and hypocrisies exist in corporation and other organization goals. Because such politeness has had the effect of condoning a general condition of goal superficiality, this chapter on goal formulation begins flatly with the claim that: *Among modern organizations, the most broadly acknowledged goal is survival. We have not yet defined many goals for human organizations which are much more complex and value-oriented.*

In 1958 NASA had great aims for the United States space program.

Its intentions were sound, patriotic, and general—it would achieve complete capabilities in space. Billions were spent; many activities were initiated and carried on with dedication; but results were difficult to evaluate or account for. After the fact of Sputnik finally sunk deep enough into our consciousness to hurt, President John F. Kennedy declared and committed NASA to a specific goal: "Put an American on the moon and return him safely before this decade is over." Now the diffuse, activities-oriented NASA had a goal that met the criteria for results management: [1]

The objective was specific and could be understood by everyone.
The objective was quantifiable in both time and space.
Progress could be measured daily.
The goal was both realistic and extremely difficult.

NASA began with the end result—the goal—clearly defined. Then, by backtracking through time, hardware, human resources, software, technology, and resource requirements, it could and did realistically accomplish what is still hard for the world to believe. We went to the moon! This illustrates a crucial step in the radical change process in large organizations of any kind. There is now no need for the almost unlimited resources NASA utilized because we know more about change, but we still must begin by finding the *end result* as soon as possible. In short, the feasibility study, change-readiness program, and early parts of the change system are designed to uncover the end result, the true goal, the next great phase of reality which is inherent in your present organization's structure. Therefore, all awareness, consciousness, data sensors, information, and analysis going on early in this process must focus on finding out what the end result really is. Let me give you some more examples:

1. Packaging Company A might think its goal is the faster, cheaper production of buyer-motivating product packages. That being so, it is in hot competition for each percentage point of market share with competitors who have identical goals. Yet, because of societal pressure against waste and pollution, particularly in packaging, Company A has almost worked itself into position to become a recycling utility which can cut out 80 percent of a community's inflow and outflow of these "disposable" resources. Its end result goal is now to design and operate recycle systems for new and old communities, an entirely new enterprise.

2. A college may at last face the facts of too little capital, excessive personnel costs, low staff output, limited teaching efficiency, and student disinterest to discover that it should become a lifetime learning

institution that provides education services at a price to people of all ages. That is its *end result*.

3. An airline wakes up to the weakness of selling seat sizes, hotel and car reservations, meals, drinks, and pretty stewardesses and decides to seek out the true end result everyone wants: a short, certain, and easy way to get from here to there, regardless of weather or other conditions. No one has yet been able to put it all together for the traveler.

4. A large bank wakes up to the fact that people don't like banks very much and see little value in checking accounts, safe deposits, and loans at high interest rates. It sets out to become what people need but cannot find anywhere in the world of finance: the sober, impartial, but informed counsellor on personal financial matters. The *end result* will transform the institution completely.

5. A leading advertising agency decides that the U.S. public will not much longer abide its high-paid lying on behalf of marketers. It decides to finance and develop, community by community, product and service information systems available at a price to consumers who will pay for the truth. The rest it will continue to fool, but with a clearer conscience.

All this is not just a matter of seeking out or dreaming up goals really worth seeking. The end result must spin out organically from the people, the technology, and other specific realities within each organization. An organization goal worthy of a change system effort can be arrived at by this general formula:

$$\text{Change system goal} = \frac{\text{management ambition} + \text{generic possibilities}}{\text{all constraints}}$$

where

> *management ambition* is the quality and extent of management's desire to achieve.
>
> *generic possibilities* are your organization's history, its present status, and its actual potential.
>
> *all constraints* are the risks and limits imposed by resources and internal/external environments.

Expressed in words, what you may hope to accomplish, plus the goals which are inherent in your *nature,* will be amended by the internal and external constraints we face in all organizations. The final product could be a *worthy* change system goal, but it rarely is. The quality of worthiness in that sentence is expressed by being:

> Great enough in potential value to be worth the effort in human energy
>
> Financeable and profitable

Difficult but not impossible
Beneficial in many directions

Every manager is aware of several goals his organization might seek. It is quite important to take each one seriously, to develop a deeper understanding of its potentiality, and to arrive at a system one can use to appraise its value. Test 6 provides such an appraisal method. Its use should be considered the beginning of intensive goal appraisal. Managers can score goal appraisals as follows:

1. Select three of your organization's major goals.
2. Appraise each goal on Test 6. (To enlarge your information, have other managers do the same thing and plot the scores.)
3. Total the score for each goal based on the values noted numerically. (The weights used in scoring were developed on the basis of probable relationship to low, medium, and high rates of change.) Discard all goals scoring less than 20 (out of a possible 50). They are suitable for normal management programming but too minor to use as the object of a change system.
4. To obtain stronger goals, follow the goal-setting techniques discussed later in this chapter.

Another simple approach to the setting of organization goals is to focus management attention on this question: *What could we become to fulfill our missions better?* This overall concern has several logical components:

1. In what stage of organization development are we now?
2. What are our resources?
3. What are our organization's chief risks, dangers, and obstacles?
4. What do experts and innovators in our line of effort think we could become in the future?

Regarding the list, it might be useful to consider question 1: In what stage of organization development are we now? Organizations evolve much as plants and animals evolve from birth to death and over generations as well. Chapter 2 defined several different species of organizations —clockwork, mosaic, organic, and so on (see endpapers). Assuming that you are now aware of your organization species, we can go on to consider in which stage of its life cycle it is. The following are some relatively loose categories for you to consider. They are adapted from the excellent work of Larry Greiner,[2] who has carefully considered the effect of life cycle on goal selection. Table 4-1 describes the overall picture as I have adapted it. Notice that the roles of managers tend to change, depending upon the stage of the organization's life cycle. You

TEST 6

Top Management Goal Appraisal

The first step to change: How to set a change goal. What one must evaluate in a change goal to decide if it is worth seeking by change system methodologies.

Use this form to evaluate each major goal you are considering. Each goal automatically implies a number of process considerations if it is to be implemented. Goal and process aspects are therefore intermingled in the form shown below.

Write in specific organization goal here: —————————————————

——

——

Now choose the one statement that most closely answers each question:

What are the time span aspects of this goal?
( )   0   Short term (less than three years)
( )   2   Medium range (three to five years)
( )   5   Long term (over five years)

What is the change content of this goal?
( )   0   It improves present system without altering structure.
( )   2   It adapts present system to new conditions.
( )   5   It completely transforms current operations and structure.

What level of concern for people does it display?
( )   0   It blocks change by an overconcern for people.
( )   1   It amputates weak operations and subsystems, regardless of people problems, to gain overall organization health.
( )   4   It provides opportunities for those willing to grow but gets rid of the rest with some consideration for their problems.
( )   5   It organizes to achieve its goals by encouraging the self-actualizing of employees and managers.

What is the strength of its imagery, its evocative power?
( )   0   It is dull, narrow, selfish, weak, or out of touch.
( )   1   A dutiful, obvious, typical goal.
( )   2   A strong, exciting concept that should stimulate some groups.
( )   4   Will enlist most employees' long-term dedication and enthusiasm.
( )   5   This goal will help form the structure of future society, and it should gain wide approval from people internally and externally.

What is the human energy commitment (other than machine-replaceable energy)?
( )   0   It reduces the human energy needed in our organization.
( )   1   It uses no more than low-level effort.
( )   2   It requires a modest increase of effort in one or two departments or levels but does not involve the rest.

TEST 6 (Continued)

( ) 4 It wholly commits two or three departments; others must stir themselves to adapt.

( ) 5 It demands a large-scale effort from all departments at all levels.

What are innovation requirements?

( ) 1 It depends on ideas from elsewhere or on existing technology.

( ) 2 It requires some innovations from standard sources.

( ) 4 It cannot succeed without planned and unplanned innovations at many levels and in many areas of the operation.

( ) 5 It organizes for deliberate innovation, stimulation, and application on a large scale internally and externally.

What is the scope of the goal selected?

( ) 0 It is fundamentally a one-department, one-division, one-subsidiary, or one-level effort.

( ) 1 It involves one main organization function and its immediate interfaces.

( ) 3 It establishes interdepartmental machinery to expand its benefits generally.

( ) 5 It establishes a complete extra-system (temporary system or project system) to conduct the change processes.

( ) 5 It involves the entire ecosystem in which the organization operates.

How democratic is the planning that created this goal?

( ) 0 The goal was completely designed by a few managers.

( ) 1 Goal was manager/staff group determined.

( ) 2 Goal-setting process was mainly carried out by management with allowances for some participation at all levels.

( ) 4 The process was started and the main goals/issues were decided by management, but it was wide open for participation at all levels.

( ) 5 The goal-setting process depended upon systematic contributions from all levels and the entire organization network gave its consensus.

How well is it attuned to social forces?

( ) 0 This goal ignores current social trends, value shifts, advances in sensitivity, and other exterior secondary effects.

( ) 5 This goal reflects the value structures of exterior and interior publics directly and indirectly involved and provides benefits for them.

( ) 5 This goal predicts the future dominance of particular value systems and designs for that eventuality.

What is the scope of the intellectual activity this goal requires?

( ) 1 It uses current capacities, procedures, and resources.

( ) 2 It adds expert counsel and creates some new information processing and new data.

( ) 4 It requires a systems model regularly fed and measured by data from operations.

( ) 5 It establishes a full-fledged artificial intelligence to direct and illuminate the processes of change.

TABLE 4-1. The organization cycle.

MANAGER STYLES FOUND IN EACH CYCLE	STAGE
Innovators and technologists	1. *Initiate.* Create a salable product or service and find a market for it.
Basic business managers	2. *Develop.* Surround and support the basic function with a homeostatic system.
Market developers and business acquisition teams	3. *Diversify.* Exploit strengths, expand operation, acquire, integrate, delegate, divisionalize.
Systems managers for cost effectiveness, central controls, management by exception, management by objectives, management information services, computer usage	4. *Standardize.* Focus internally on improving all systems and procedures to squeeze out marginal efficiencies.
Industrial statesmen involved in government missions, public and community relations, charities, the arts, social issues, internal education, job enlargement, politics	5. *Socialize.* Become socially responsible, control environmental input, build a nice headquarters, improve life for employees, self-develop. (Give up on major profits growth.)

get one set of clues by examining manager styles and another from organization behavior.

Any single organization's system can be located somewhere in the five stages of Table 4-1. Unless there are compelling reasons to revert to a former stage, it will be normal for each organization to move ahead from one stage to another much as biological life forms do. One does not become a grandfather or a sage on his third birthday, nor is it seemly to adopt teenage behavior at age 50. Not too much is known about how long organizations remain in each stage of their five-stage cycles, but a good guess would be between 10 and 15 years. Most organizations expire after about 70 years unless they are unusual or have developed taxing powers to keep them alive long after their productive years.

It should by now be clear that goal formulation will be deeply affected by two prior considerations: (1) What kind of organization are you dealing with? (2) Where is it in its life cycle? Here some examples might be of value.

Example A

The ABC Drug and Chemical Company is a simple pyramidal organization serving general medical needs. After 50 years it has reached stage 4 (standardize) and it is now considering internal and external pressures to move to stage 5 (socialize). Certainly our management literature as well as counterculture charges and government pressures encourage this. In effect this decision would mean lower profits to stockholders, fewer raises for employees, and fewer investments in R&D or innovative ventures. After much agony, management decides that these goals are too shallow, too easy, too other-directed, and too likely to be reached by other societal means in the near future; therefore, it opts for a basic change system to accomplish the following mutually necessary goals:

1. Transform the organization from a pyramid to an organic plant type.
2. Develop R&D and marketing for a new range of drugs that directly affects and helps to improve human performance under stress, in adverse environments, and in special tasks and conditions of life.

Example B

The city of Urbano is a loose, completely urbanized mosaic that nobody controls. The city administration is a clockwork that performs a few basic urban functions such as security, street maintenance, school finance, and some regulation. After 100 years, the city administration is still in stage 1 of its development and has just begun to consider more efficient ways to manage, control, spend, plan, and fund its activities.

The city council and the mayor are aware that the community is surrounded on all sides by a great city called Megalopolis and that no reason for Urbano's continued existence can really be discovered. Urbano's local identity and small-town life have long since been swallowed up by the big city; its downtown has lost out to the suburban shopping centers; its citizens work elsewhere in the area; its local media have given up in favor of the big city media; and almost no integrating factor is now holding it together. Local pressure groups are asking for more parks, less pollution and noise, more community services, lower taxes, and more welfare. Now the city council decides to seek out a general community consensus for the following goals:

1. The city's administration will immediately systematize to stage 4 to cut city costs by 50 percent for today's services. Taxes will stay the same or rise slightly with inflationary forces.
2. No new services will be adopted, nor will old ones be expanded for five years.
3. The tax savings will be devoted to buying up peripheral land and internal blocks of land for parks, open areas, wildlife preserves,

campgrounds, and recreation areas. Other government sources will be exploited for the necessary funds.

4. Public corporations will be set up to build, fund, manage, and expand the utilization of the resources of goal 3 with the aim of improving the quality of life in Urbano. Use of the environment by taxpayers will be by permit based on carrying capacity. Non-taxpayers will be allowed to buy permits depending on the availability of environmental spaces.

5. The city administration will continue Urbano as an entity rather than abandon it to the eager Megalopolis agencies. The effort will be to develop a local identity suitable to the plural modern world.

Example C

A modestly endowed college finds itself unable to survive under the current costs of education and plant upkeep. It realizes that it is a mosaic organization and that it has arrived at stage 2 (develop). Faculty and students are interested in a radical change to a school without walls that revokes its diplomas and sells all past, present, and future students on a program of lifetime education using all modern telecommunications and education-by-mail techniques. The board of trustees, however, wants a demonstration of the efficacy of such measures before taking the plunge and decides to move to a combination of stages 3 (diversify) and 4 (standardize) to experiment with the market for the new concepts among past, present, and future students. It suggests the following goals:

1. The college administration will standardize operations, reduce staff, and cut costs by one-third.

2. Experimental projects will be set up through the internal savings plus foundation or government funding.

3. A project center for change will be established to control projects, disseminate findings, and prepare for future development.

4. The college organization will change from a mosaic to a conglomerate of education enterprises. Some will prosper; others will fail.

Example D

A large stock and bond brokerage firm has realized that it is a mosaic and that its basic service function to the various classes of investors is in question as to value and fee. Management appraises its development thus far as stage 4 (standardize) and is contemplating pressures to move to stage 5 (socialize) and greatly increase its levels of service while reducing its fee structure to more modest and "legitimate" levels. The organization's financial analysts are deeply interested in the emerging multinational corporations and the possibilities for financing their future expansion by many innovative means involving stock ownership, especially through pension and mutual funds.

Management decides that its people and structure are best suited for the pioneering and development of an area that needs financing for new enterprises. As a result it decides to:

1. Retain its structure (stage 4) and diversify into a number of underdeveloped areas around the world.
2. Focus local and international capital on smaller ventures.
3. Cooperate with governments in providing some management aids to enterprisers.
4. Seek new ways to make capital generation conform to the aspirations of emerging economies.
5. Develop profitable and useful services for multinational corporations.

Examples A to D suggest that each management might make very different decisions based on circumstances, kind of organization, stage of development, resources, available leadership, ambitions, and societal pressures. This is as it should be; we should expand our awareness of alternative futures that relate directly to our present status. Obviously in stages 4 and 5 it will not be easy to interrupt the normal life cycle and recreate the vigors of youth, yet this is the challenge of radical change.

A linear view of the goal-setting process is laid out in Figure 4-1. Once the change-feasibility study and the change-readiness program are complete, a number of goals (shown as 1 to 7) will have emerged from inside and outside the organization. These are then screened and prepared for more intensive analysis by the organization's change system team. The team will further reduce the number of goals based on its deliberations and, after developing plans for them, will submit perhaps three to internal and external experts in the organization's field of operations. The expert counsel is then digested and top management is asked for a preliminary commitment to one or two final goals.

Next the entire organization (or appropriate samples of its people and its leaderships) should have a full and repetitive opportunity to consider the following:

Which goal is worth seeking?
Are there any better goals?

What should be considered in the goal selection process?
What benefits can you see?
What risks or negatives are there?
Would you support or oppose this goal? Exactly why?

This can be done in information meetings, bulletins, discussion groups, or by anonymous survey. It should be conducted throughout the organization with the thoughts that:

1. Management and outside experts have done as well as they can as experts in developing the next goals for our future in this organization.
2. But you as an employee have knowledge, experience, and opinions which may alter, eliminate, or change their goals.
3. For this reason, and because management does not want to attempt a goal which employees will not support, we are seeking your reaction to what has been done so far so that we can improve the entire effort.

FIGURE 4-1.   A linear goal formulation track.

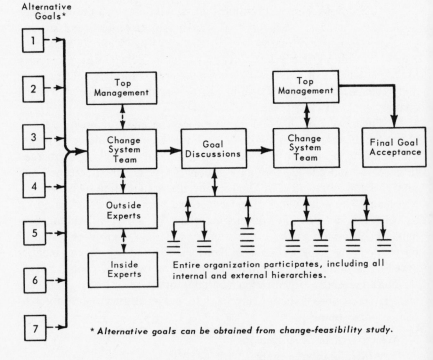

When the discussion, amendment, and possibly a redo of the entire process or a rescue of some previously discarded goal result in a reasonable consensus throughout the organization, the change system team can in good conscience report to top management that, for example, the agreement of experts and organization members is 75 percent on goal 1, 43 percent on goal 2, and 15 percent on goal 3. At the same time, the change system team will be prepared to submit reasonable cost estimates for goal 1 implementation. Then top management can establish change system schedules and commitments with reasonable certainty of their long-range pertinence, value, acceptability, and accessibility.

Whose Reality Do We Change?

Exposure to other cultures and awareness of the cultural and biological limitations of our senses and mental constructs should, by now, have convinced us all that, within reason, the world we experience contains a large dollop of personal preference. There is little doubt that galaxies, stars, and planets exist outside our skins and beyond the range of our vision, but a great many aspects of relationships between humans seem to have more life inside the skin than outside. Such a mental construct is the idea of organization.

If this is generally true, why shouldn't we select a future goal for human/group/society organization and then deliver it? Why can't we choose the future we prefer for our organizations and then realize it? In fact we now can, within limits. Many have already grasped this lesson and are well on the way to delivering not very admirable goals for segments of the United States. Some examples of this are the determination of much of our media in the United States to realize a self-hating society and the drive of some of our upper-middle-class young people toward a life of total despair coupled with the solace of religion, sensory burnout, or drug addiction.

In practical terms, there is little excuse for an organization's management to endure creeping obsolescence, takeover, legal and regulatory shackles, attack by pressure groups, or organization ennui. Every manager can take hold of his organization's future, form a powerful goal, devise a systematic approach, and make it work. After gaining a superior understanding of organization structure and change processes, he can plan and program constructive and unusual goals. Chapter 5 will explain the how-to-do-it aspects of this process in more detail. Some examples of areas of human enterprise needing superior goals and futures delivery are:

— NASA, which has prepared itself and its people for an ambitious program of star travel, sits around waiting for someone to decide whether it should exist at all.

— Our railroads, which surrendered their rights as managers to their union bosses and to government regulatory committees, now give less service to the public and, in many instances, less profit to their stockholders.

— Our age of environmental concern is marked by political puffery, yet our state governments commit huge blocks of unspoiled forest and agricultural land to development into asphalted suburbs by their deliberately destructive policy of land assessment and taxation.

— Our energy utilities waste huge amounts of money—which they charge to the public—while they fumble their main assignment: to provide the public with power.

— The nation's steel, aluminum, electronics, and ship-building industries accept labor, marketing, and taxation arrangements that allow their competitors around the world a success beyond their fondest dreams.

— Our oil industry displays an embarrassed smile as it quietly faces expropriation of its assets by bandits who call themselves government officials in some countries. This is a business-as-usual policy carried to the gallows.

Contrary to popular management axioms that the future is cloudy, or that technological breakthroughs are impossible to predict, or that economic cycles are beyond anyone's control, or that we can't do anything about the government, a viewpoint is advanced here that *you can create any number of futures you might prefer*. This is not to say that constraints do not exist on our futures as they have existed on our pasts and presents, but they are far less restrictive than we believe. In all but the most rigorously regimented societies, managers have far more latitude to create constructive goals for their organizations than they now imagine. The issue really is this: Will our leaders move toward radical change, or will they sink to homeostatic nongoals in their organizations while they await retirement?

Goals conflict. It is normal for goals to conflict with one another. Each goal reflects its own pattern of values and implies certain benefits in which organization participants have vested interests. Organizations embarking upon any intensive investigation of their past, present, and future—as in a change-feasibility study described in Chapter 5—will uncover a surplus of goals. "The key to planned organizational change as a concept and as a working social device is found in well-conceived and realistic organization goals." [3] A carefully conducted feasibility study will assist in setting such goals.

Part of the problem of finding a suitable change goal is that each organization is already a "multilevel, multigoal system . . . and concerted action for the achievement of one goal is, indeed, a rare phenomenon." Conflict between stated and unstated goals is more normal. A strong change goal can be considered within an organization as:

The future we seek
The justification for our existence
The standards on which we will judge our performance
The final source of judgment on whether we are a success

One Last Word on Goals

When a change goal is powerful enough to electrify an organization, inspire its people for years, and sustain the pressure of the costs of radical change, it will be marked by the characteristic of harmonic form. A harmonic chord has different notes, each separate and distinct yet vibrating to a common frequency. If all notes are the same or are merely the same note octaves apart, the music is dull and uninteresting to the ear. Through the wise choice of different notes we create a superior musical harmony. Such harmony will be found in superior goals for radical change wherein many of the most constructive realities of an organization's existence can be fitted together innovatively to create the next phase of its future.

A new future completely different from the past will draw strength from many resources and strengths now present in your organization structure. Every organization has within it the seeds of its future, the solutions to its problems, and the source of its demise. Deciding where your organization is today in its ability to reach for its highest future potential is the subject of the next chapter.

References

The quote of Ralph G. H. Siu is from *Environment and Change* (Bloomington, Ind.: Indiana University Press, 1968). George Cabot Lodge's remarks come from "Introducing the Collectivist Corporation," *Harvard Today,*

March 1972. And Ervin Laszlo's are from *The Systems View of the World* (New York: Braziller, 1972).

1. Many of these concepts were stated in James Webb, *Space Age Management* (New York: McGraw-Hill, 1969).
2. Larry Greiner, "Evolution and Revolution as Organizations Grow," *Harvard Business Review*, July–August 1972.
3. Garth N. Jones, *Planned Organization Change* (London: Routledge, 1969), p. 199.

CHAPTER FIVE

Change-Feasibility Studies and Change-Readiness Programs

If we are to think of building the future environment in comprehensive *human* terms, we need a way for the different sciences, professions and interested laymen to converge— to organize their thinking and communicate with each other.

WILLIAM R. EWALD, JR.

I, for one, am convinced that a man can play over his head, indefinitely, if he has the good fortune to be immersed in a vigorous and adaptive enterprise—one which has a challenging social mission and a dedication to technological and organizational innovation to achieve it.

J. A. MORTON

Without doubt the most radical organizational changes made on a practical, day-to-day basis in the United States have taken place at Procter & Gamble, one of America's largest companies and well known for its hard-boiled aggressive management practices.

DAVID JENKINS

B efore initiating a change process, managers will find it essential to conduct a thorough change-feasibility appraisal—a coordinated complex of studies leading to a single go/no-go decision on whether to attempt radical change in a given organization. This effort prepares the top management team to decide if a radical change system can be constructed and to recognize when the odds against success are much too great. The latter alternative should occur fairly frequently, as the description of the natural obstacles to change in Chapter 3 has suggested.

Yielding to temptation to go ahead with a radical change process without the results of a thorough feasibility investigation is an unwarranted gamble. Some organizations under heavy economic pressure or in unusual circumstances may simply barge ahead with a radical change system and skip the feasibility appraisal, but this decision is risky.

Organizations Are Different

Each organization *is* different, as the people within it will confirm. The effects of particular leaders, the accidents of history, the environment and culture in which it lives, the nature of personnel, and technological differences make each organization unique. All organizations have similarities, yet each will require a different change system. A manager might borrow another man's car, but he would be ill-advised to borrow another manager's change system.

If we are to change a particular organization to realize the next great phase of its potential, we must plumb its depths to understand how and why it works. That need for understanding is much greater than what managers need to run the organization as it is now. Many examples can illustrate this point:

- To fly an airplane a pilot does not need the knowledge of the aeronautical engineer who designs a new model.
- The mayor of a city does not need the skills of a new town planner.
- The home gardener can get fine results without the gifts of a Luther Burbank.

It should be clear that if we are to attain radical change, levels of knowledge and understanding much greater than those needed to run the system must be added. It is legitimate to question whether a particular organization can develop the capacity to operate on those new levels if only for a brief time. Thus the feasibility study is basically necessary to the process of radical change for these reasons:

1. To find out if the organization is strong enough

2. To gain some idea of what form the organization could reach for

3. To assess the odds for and against success

Feasibility Information Characteristics

Two kinds of information should be considered during a feasibility study:

1. *Qualitative data* from nonstatistical sources; it flows out of top management experience, change discussion, depth interview, and expert analysis. Expert analysis will be drawn from inside and outside professionals practicing their disciplines. The change process deliberately expands the application of intellect to organization problems by employing the industry technology consultant, communications expert, economist, anthropologist, sociologist, long-range planner, management scientist, behavioral scientist, organization development consultant, futures forecaster, management information system consultant, and change systems adviser.

2. *Quantitative data* from statistically based sources such as employee and management surveys, measurements of events, financial records, the counting of events in operating records and sales records, measures of other organization behavior, and market research data.

Feasibility Study Design

An outline for a change system feasibility study of a large metals manufacturer is presented in Table 5-1. It should be stressed that this is not a pattern for imitation, even by metals manufacturers. Each company, organization, institution, or government agency seeking radical change must formulate for itself the depth and extent of information it needs to make a go/no-go decision. Also, the outline of Table 5-1 does not describe the many feedback loops through which the study information will go before a good decision is reached. These formulations will vary considerably among types of institutions, cultures, and governments, but the general guidelines presented throughout this work, *when combined with common sense,* should prove adequate to the task of designing change-feasibility studies on a do-it-yourself basis.

Some Study Management Suggestions

To avoid creating either obstacles or overcommitment to change during change-feasibility studies and change-readiness programs, the following areas merit scrutiny:

1. Maintain or increase managerial credibility.

TABLE 5-1. A change system feasibility study outline for a large metals manufacturer.

WHAT CHANGE SYSTEM FACTOR IS BEING MEASURED?	IN WHAT AREA?	HOW ARE THE DATA CREATED?
1. Organization's readiness for change (internal)	Top management	All top managers get interviews in a systematic survey
	Middle management	Middle management interviews in a total sample survey
	Supervisors	Supervisors are interviewed in a probability sample survey
	Employees	Employees interviewed in a probability sample survey
	Work groups	Group sessions by group theory practitioner or transactional analyst
	Special groups	Group sessions by production process analyst or technology specialist in management information system, R&D, long-range planning, engineering, marketing, or finance
2. Organization's readiness for change (external)	Industry or service area	Consultant or industry expert interviews and delphic systems
	Customer/client evaluation	Sample survey of customers and clients
	General public	Opinion survey
	Government and/or other pertinent external evaluations	Industry association data, public records analysis
3. Organization's present status and its past history	Organization headquarters	By analysis of internal records and management reports
4. Present level of communications effectiveness	Internal communications	By content analysis and from opinion survey data
	General level of communications in the industry	By analysis of findings from a literature search in the organization's technology, markets, financial competition, and peer group

TABLE 5-1 (Continued).

WHAT CHANGE SYSTEM FACTOR IS BEING MEASURED?	IN WHAT AREA?	HOW ARE THE DATA CREATED?
5. Organization's economic situation	Internal economics	Management plus outside economists and other management analysts
	Market economics	Economic consultant to industry
	Ecosystem economics	Ecology consultant
6. What cultural factors affect change capacity?	Internal cultures	Anthropologist or sociologist consultant
	Interfacing cultures	Anthropologist or sociologist consultant
7. What are the organization's key issues and what are its blocks to change?	Internal	By change team study of all internal opinion surveys and of expert appraisal of the organization
8. How strong are the organization's sources of change?	Internal organization	By the ratings of managers using Test 7
9. At what level of our technology do we operate now?	Operations and R&D	Outside technology analyst appraises technical gaps and strengths now employed in operations versus sophistication available elsewhere
	Self-appraisal of current operations	Operations personnel, quality control, and R&D people rate internal technology gaps and strengths
10. What specific major changes have emerged thus far?	Change system components	Change team appraises the design factors for a change system and ranks them as to feasibility by using all the above data
11. Change system considerations	System design	Change system consultant, OD consultant, and change team begin to build a systematic approach to large-scale changes
12. What major preliminary goals are we developing?	Goal refinement of the change system target	Change team *

* Note: Inside and outside consultants are important inputs early in the process, but management's internal change team gradually takes over all responsibilities, decisions, and activities in the change system feasibility analysis.

TABLE 5-1 (Continued).

WHAT CHANGE SYSTEM FACTOR IS BEING MEASURED?	IN WHAT AREA?	HOW ARE THE DATA CREATED?
13. What are the futures forecasting factors we must consider?	Preliminary data net design	Change counsel, MIS head, or futures forecasting expert
14. Feasibility decision?	Summary of all analyses	Change team members
15. Can we design a change system?	First cut	Change team members plus change counsel
16. What project controls and budgets do we need?	Design projections	Change team members
17. What will be our feasibility report to top management?	Go/no-go recommendation and preliminary change-readiness or change system program design	Change team members

2. Maintain a wide-open investigation to create a better future for all.
3. Put top management men on the pan first.
4. Notify all hierarchical leaderships of the facts in private before public announcement is made.
5. Stress the odds both pro and con on eventual success.
6. Classify the effort as evidence of one of many management concerns for the people and the organization. If it fails, other routes will be tried.
7. Ask for full, fair, and honest participation.
8. Avoid all threat.
9. Make it clear that the smartest, sharpest, most-respected, and wisest management people are pushing for this investigation. Identify it with your best leadership group.
10. Maintain the uncertainty of the outcome.

Initial Measurements

In the sample feasibility study outline just presented, reference was made to a form to use in measuring an organization's present status as far as the ten sources of change are concerned. (See Chapter 6 for a detailed discussion of the ten sources of change.) Test 7 presents a simplified first appraisal of this area. In each organization, if confidence in impartiality can be given to lower-level managers (perhaps aided by anonymous rating sheets), ask each manager to rate each item on the basis of what he knows of the *entire* organization by placing an X in the appropriate column of Test 7.

TEST 7

Appraising the Ten Sources of Change for Feasibility Studies

A rating sheet for use by department heads and staff group leaders.

Factor to be rated in our organization	This is how our overall organization works				
	It does very poorly	It's poor	It's fair	It's good	It's excellent
Innovating of new services, products, procedures	( )	( )	( )	( )	( )
On improving the way we get the work out	( )	( )	( )	( )	( )
In improving relations between employees, managers, departments, levels	( )	( )	( )	( )	( )
In forecasting its future growth	( )	( )	( )	( )	( )
In understanding the background and beliefs of the people we deal with	( )	( )	( )	( )	( )
In policies that encourage the education and training of all employees and managers	( )	( )	( )	( )	( )
In projecting a vision of the organization in the future that excites and motivates everyone	( )	( )	( )	( )	( )

TEST 7 (Continued)

Factor to be rated in our organization	This is how our overall organization works				
	It does very poorly	It's poor	It's fair	It's good	It's excellent
In being careful to consider and deal with all of those who really control what happens around here	( )	( )	( )	( )	( )
In being willing to bring in outside experts regularly to keep us advanced in every area	( )	( )	( )	( )	( )
In setting up special task forces drawn from many departments to solve major problems that affect everyone	( )	( )	( )	( )	( )

To score the results in a simple and general way, use these principles for the first time this area is examined:

1. For each item subtract all good ratings from all poor ratings, counting all as equal, to get a net plus or minus score. Ignore the fair ratings.

2. If over six scores are negative, you can begin to get concerned that radical change may not now be possible, but look further at all the information being created by the feasibility study before deciding.

3. The distance from present ratings to having over six items rated good or excellent (assuming reasonable manager awareness and honesty in ratings) is the problem space within which your change-readiness program will operate. By beginning with simple appraisals of this kind, a manager can begin to conceptualize the subject matter and the methods with which he can later set up practical programs for the radical change process.

Several of the analyses listed in the sample feasibility study shown earlier are familiar to managers and need no further description, although their purposes and content will naturally be much more intensive and change-oriented than is usual. They are:

Organization attitude and opinion surveys using personal and self-
administered interview procedures

Customer/client/industry opinion surveys

Organization status and history analysis

Communications content analysis

Economists' analyses

Many managers are familiar with these tools, but it should be cautioned
that the quality of what they produce varies widely between a thorough
(usually professional) performance and inexpensive or inexperienced
simulations often described as "just as good." Really good information
is almost always expensive and difficult to obtain. The depth and extent of information adequate for manager decisions in "running the
system as it is now" simply will not qualify for the change process.
Superior information produced by thoughtful, honest self-analysis and
the good detective work of inside and outside impartial analysts is vital
to success. Other elements of this feasibility study require some description:

What cultural factors affect our change capacity?

What are this organization's key issues and what are its blocks?

How strong are this organization's sources of change?

Each of these will be described in turn in the paragraphs following.

What Cultural Factors Affect Our Change Capacity?

The two cultural appraisals of Table 5-1 will define a great many unspoken and assumed behaviors, mores, and assumptions affecting activities throughout the organization and impinging on it from the outside.
Managers are unaccustomed to a cultural review of their own organization, although such appraisals are used frequently in studying
other institutions. It is again necessary to caution managers who are
contracting for a sociologist's or anthropologist's aid in this effort that
the quality of such analysis varies widely. Some professionals, in studying other cultures, are unable to set aside the assumptions which guide
their own. When this happens, data can be hopelessly distorted.

Seek out professionals whose experience, published works, and
personal integration suggest maturity of mind and the ability to relate
honestly and openly with very different people. They will provide you
with original and useful insights to your own organization's cultures.
They are not easy to find. Brief them thoroughly on what you are attempting; let everyone in your organization know they are arriving and
why; and cut them loose. Specific techniques for cultural appraisals
are given in Chapter 6.

What Are Our Key Issues and Blocks to Change?

One ongoing activity of an organization's change team is to isolate key issues of concern and blocks to operations which are already prominent throughout the organization. Every organization has hundreds of issues and blocks. They cannot and should not be dealt with all at once or serially. It is crucial, however, to isolate and attack those which are uppermost in general employee/manager awareness early in the change process to demonstrate alertness to peoples' concerns. Their resolution has a great effect early in the game on peoples' attitudes toward the entire process of change.

Issue/block attention by the change team will insure that some of the team's earliest activities will affect people in the areas of their highest concerns rather than attempt to interest them in issues which are perhaps more important but are remote to their current concerns. To impart immediacy and pertinence to a change process and to remove it from the category of "another vague management effort," start with where your people's thinking is *now*. The first 12 steps outlined in the feasibility study of Table 5-1, as an example, will provide a wealth of data from which the change team can evolve a priority list of the issues and blocks most important to change in the organization.

From another standpoint, we concentrate on issues and blocks because the change process is most likely to begin in the sensitive areas— the fringes, the sectors where conditions accepted as constant and true at headquarters begin to blur. Whatever our overall goals, if we begin change activities at those points where movement is already visible and the attention of organization members is highest, then we get the effort off to a good start.

How Strong Are This Organization's Sources of Change?

People in organizations naturally love numbers. They want to know the score. How are we doing compared to last month? Managers often wish employees would consider larger issues and are frustrated when they concentrate on the manipulation of scoring mechanisms; however, we all know that in the game of golf, as in life, it's "How many strokes did you take?" and not "How compact was your swing?" We seek results we can score. Of course, in organizations that have alienated their people there is little interest in the score or in any other aspect of performance except what is needed to get by and get out.

Change systems, as well as change system feasibility studies, regard the counting of important process events as crucial to eventual success.

These methods of counting will be new to most managements. The change team will count events which reveal whether the organization's potential for change is high or low. Examples of two change process measures and the graphs they produce are given in Figures 5-1 and 5-2. By using these measures publicly, everyone in an organization can be shown movement toward or away from change readiness. Visibility is vital to the effectiveness of any measure.

In Figure 5-1 two classes of events are being measured each month: (1) Organization events in which information is requested and granted. (2) Organization events in which requested information is denied or delayed. There is no need to evaluate what kind of information is involved. Obviously, some requests are wholly improper and should be denied. That is irrelevant to this measure. What we are seeking is some way to enumerate, say, 100 communication events regardless of content to decide if they are information-granting or information-repress-

FIGURE 5-1.   Change-readiness scale of information availability.

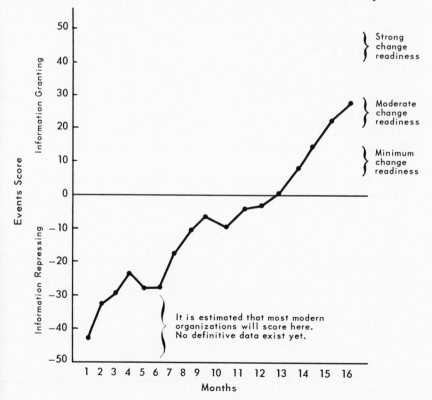

ing. Then out of that 100 events that took place, say, in April, we'll have something like this:

62   information-repressing events
34   information-granting events
8   not classifiable

All we do then is subtract 34 from 62 and forget the unclassifiable events to get a repressing score for April of −28. This is so scored in Figure 5-1.

Clearly, getting information for such measures will be difficult. Another possible data source for this scale is the manager/supervisor survey, which can define enough of the problem to reveal the organization's health or sickness. Make it a point to include in organization surveys conducted in the feasibility study such directions as "Describe any important event in which you requested information you needed and got it" and "Also define and describe any important event in which you requested needed information and could not get it." These critical incidents can then be analyzed by the change team for their applicability to this measure of information openness, scored as to their repressing or granting of information, and then enumerated to construct the scale.

The purpose of devising a scale such as that of Figure 5-1 is to measure a basic aspect of change readiness—in fact, of organization health. Like the fruit tree or rose plant innovator, we cannot create a new variety without grafting onto healthy root stock. These change source measures tell managers, with painful clarity, whether they can deal with change in their particular organization. That is entirely separate from whether they can manage their system as it is. Radical change

FIGURE 5-2.   Organization performance in supplying information for those areas most important in employees' opinion.

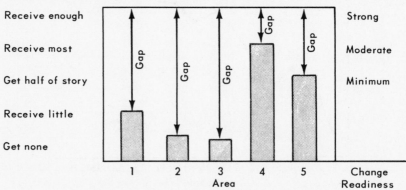

can rarely be approached by weak or hopelessly frozen organizations; we need healthy, growing root stock to succeed. Information openness illustrates one aspect of such health.

Figure 5-2 illustrates the particular content areas of communications which have large gaps and those which have been reasonably satisfied by current communications practice. To construct such a measure, change team members review the content areas which were used in the communications content analysis as well as the one proposed for the employee opinion survey. Keeping the needs of change in mind, they then decide on the most important and basic information areas to measure change readiness, which are represented by numbers 1 to 5 in Figure 5-2. Some information categories which might be measured for gaps are employee knowledge of organization objectives, management interest in new ideas, and management interest in employee job security.

Scales similar to those illustrated in Figures 5-1 and 5-2 are also described in more detail in Chapter 7 in areas such as the following:

1. The rate of innovations proposed in the organization versus the rate of innovations killed. In this case, the data-gathering methods account for the fact that most ideas are not usable, as well as for the problem of finding out not only how many ideas are killed before they get to the innovation-appraising state but why they are killed. Needless to say, these scales will be set up one way for R&D, engineering, or other innovating groups and another for plant and office operations.

2. Company image clusters. As seen internally and externally in corporate image measurement systems, each organization possesses a vague and largely positive reputation. Most image measurement systems used in surveys reveal only the weakest, thinnest kinds of company reputation factors. With our current new knowledge of organizations and with the help of communications experts, a company's internal image can be measured fairly clearly and changes for the better can be charted and defined.

3. In the range of supervisor/employee relations, positive versus negative items can be scored and plotted to form a useful scale.

4. The stream of work process improvements, a category not in the class of innovations, merits a measurement system. Here workers at all levels can provide data, in employee surveys, on what happens to what they regard as sensible suggestions for improving how the work is done.

5. Organizations vary widely in the amount of managerial confidence they possess as reflected in the ratio of outside experts utilized to outside experts proposed. This scale might reveal that proposals for outside counsel are regularly killed to discourage further suggestions,

although this is the kind of cultural assumption the anthropologist's analysis should pick up.

6. Another important scale is formed by counting monthly the hours of on-the-job and off-the-job education and training provided by the organization compared to the monthly record established by IBM. IBM was selected because it has done so well in using education to create a change dynamic in its structure. In some divisions of IBM, employees and managers are committed to job-long education. A rough estimate of the IBM standard expressed in education hours per month is 10 for employees in general and 15 for supervisors and managers. This information is sufficient to construct a scale for every organization. Regard 5 hours per month as a minimum change-readiness level, 10 as a moderate change-readiness level, and 15 as a strong change-readiness level so far as employees are concerned. For managers use 10, 15, and 20. Score your organization's actual use of education compared to the standard.

7. Still another useful scale is obtained by simple enumeration of the committees or task forces which regularly have more than two departments or divisions represented and those which have only one. This measures interdepartmental relations versus rigid territoriality.

Several other scales can reveal organization behaviors and attitudes affecting the ability to change. Change team members and their consultants can easily devise them. Their objectives are:

To widen awareness of organization characteristics
To portray change strengths and weaknesses more accurately
To obtain an overall sense of organization openness that correlates loosely to the openness or closed-mindedness behavior observable in humans

On this latter point, it is useful to think of an overall *agapation score* to characterize organizations. In the change source measures just described, we are trying to find out if the positive events in the organization exceed the negative ones. That is the base for this score. Use each measure selected to create a combined total score to portray whether positive, constructive events that occur every day are greater or smaller in number than negative, destructive events. The product of both measures is a score—a plus or minus number—which is daily getting better or worse in every organizational process.

How to Obtain the Agapation Score

1. Obtain 3- to 6-month records of scores for the 10 to 12 scales your organization is using in its change-readiness evaluation.

2. Average the scores in each scale to gain a single rating.
3. Subtract the number of negative scores from the number of positive or zero scores.
4. The answer is your organization's agapation score. For example:

Positive scale results	6
Negative scale results	4
Agapation score	+ 2

The term "agapation" was developed by the author to suggest the concepts now evolving from the interesting word "agape." In usage here, high agapation means to be sufficiently alive and stimulated by the organization environment to be open and ready to receive new information, enlarge awareness, and learn new skills. Low agapation— its opposite—is mental rigidity and the rejection of any change. In the case of an organization, we can use the term to ascertain the general receptiveness to change which has thus far been built into the organization's structure and behavior. Because we are at the beginning of the era of deliberate manager-involved organizational change, we have few records that would provide perspective on what is pro or con in agapation scoring. On a judgment basis (to be amended as scores accumulate) we propose the following guide.

GUIDE TO CHANGE-READINESS DECISIONS

Agapation Score	*Organization Status*
Plus 6 or more	Adequate change readiness.
Plus 3 to plus 5	A minor change-readiness program is needed.
Plus 2 to minus 2	A major change-readiness program is required.
Minus 3 to minus 5	Large-scale organization development effort and other loosening is recommended. Radical change effort should be postponed for a year or two.
Minus 6 and less	Almost complete organizational rigidity. Maximum risk of extinction. No radical change system or organization development program recommended until the more obvious survival and organization health needs have been satisfied by existing management.

Change-Readiness Programs

If most organizations were generally ready for it, there would be a lot more radical change around now than we can perceive. In short, although the hurdles are really not too high in the change-readiness race, few organizations have yet reached the state of training necessary to leap all of them. Almost inevitably, each organization will get through its change-feasibility study with the realization that in four or five areas it must immediately cure situations which are negative in their influence on change. This should mean massive or modest change-readiness programs. The feasibility studies, and in particular the components of the agapation score, should provide:

1. A list of the areas needing correction
2. The priority rating of each area
3. The probable time and budget for each task
4. The composition of inside task forces and outside consultants required for success
5. The date on which reasonable change readiness should be achieved
6. The measurement system that will substantiate the date of (5) to top management

These initial processes of change might take six to eight months for a change-feasibility study and nine to twelve months for a change-readiness program to remedy weaknesses. In short, within a year and a half most reasonably well-run organizations could prepare themselves to begin a radical change system. The feasibility study and the remedial efforts it uncovers as necessary would not need to be long drawn-out affairs in organizations which are now able to move smartly to meet emergencies.

In slower, more muscle-bound organizations these schedules will stretch out. Organizations with too negative an internal situation will, of course, give up rather than endure the five- to ten-year program of basic internal strengthening necessary before radical change can be attempted. As stated earlier, healthy root stock is needed before the better alternatives of an organization's future can be sought out.

Managers can quickly calculate that feasibility studies and change-readiness programs of the scope and depth described here will involve serious time and money expenditures. It is the intent of this book to provide as much counsel as possible to encourage do-it-yourself activities. Nevertheless, substantial inside and outside costs are apparent. A clear perspective on these costs must be maintained. Many costs can be absorbed in ongoing budgets—in particular, some time charges of top managers, change team managers, and key personnel working on particular projects. Most internal costs, however, must be budgeted to demonstrate commitment and reflect sound cost control.

Table 5-2 provides some rough approximations of change-feasibility budgets based on organization size. As more managers attempt radical change in their organizations, these estimates will be improved; however, it should be apparent that the approach to a radical change process is a major management decision from the standpoint of budget alone. It could also be the organization's wisest investment for its future success.

In summary, the change-feasibility study is a vital part of the change process. It has important internal and external costs, yet it is not nearly as expensive as inaction on the issues of change. Many capital improvement costs are regularly incurred by managements. Such expenditures may be traditionally correct, but the benefits in profits and growth that they produce may at times fall on a diminishing curve. The organization structure is also a capital asset which requires *renewal, strengthening,* or, in the case of the need for radical change, *replacement.* At these times, investment in the process of radical change can return extraordinary and constructive dividends. Once management decides to move ahead to gain large-scale charges, the question of change system design comes to the fore. This is the subject of the next chapter.

TABLE 5-2. Estimates of feasibility and change-readiness budgets.

Num- ber of Em- ploy- ees	Internal Budget *	Probable External Services Costs for			
		Feasi- bility Study	Change-Readiness Program		Total Costs
			Minor	Major	
100	$ 25,000	$ 40,000	$ 20,000	$ 50,000	$ 85,000–$ 115,000
500	50,000	75,000	35,000	80,000	160,000– 205,000
1,000	75,000	85,000	50,000	130,000	210,000– 290,000
5,000	100,000	150,000	90,000	270,000	340,000– 520,000
10,000	200,000	250,000	150,000	500,000	600,000– 950,000
50,000	300,000	500,000	250,000	1,500,000	1,050,000– 2,300,000

* Estimates are in 1974 U.S. dollars and include all internal costs, meeting times, costs of services, travel, and other components. In most organizations operating at "normal" levels, from 30 to 60 percent of the internal costs shown here need not be incurred due to low workloads.

References

The remarks of William R. Ewald, Jr. are from his *Creating the Human Environment* (Urbana, Ill.: University of Illinois Press, 1970); those of J. A. Morton are from *Organizing for Innovation* (New York: McGraw-Hill, 1971). David Jenkins' quotation is from "Democracy in the Factory," *The Atlantic*, April 1973.

CHAPTER SIX

Designing
Change Systems

Our society has reached a point where its progress and even
its survival increasingly depend upon our ability to
organize the complex and to do the unusual.

JAMES E. WEBB

Where there is the necessary skill to move mountains
there is no need for the faith that moves mountains.

ERIC HOFFER

To decide wisely, problems must be looked at from an
eminence. . . . We do not get progress in naval
disarmament when admirals confer. We do not get legal
progress from meetings of bar associations.
Congresses of teachers seem rarely to provide the means for
educational advance.

HAROLD J. LASKI

What is decisive now is not the IQ of the individual, but the
IQ of groups associated with computers—the IQ of
corporations, or "social systems" as Bertrand Gross calls
them, including in the term associated non-human
resources and technology.

PIERRE BERTAUX

The designing of systems that can deliver radical change to large organizations depends partly upon the quality and theoretical accuracy of organization theory. Today this field is exploding with new ideas and concepts, but it still has many gaps. Purists insist upon the highest professional fidelity to the limitations and restrictions of our current understanding of organizations. This caution is well taken but we spend our lives in organizations which we or our forebears have put together. We know we can take them apart, rearrange their patterns, and put them back together; in fact, we are doing that in life regularly. If we do not yet understand organization systems perfectly, of course we should reach for all new knowledge and training that enlarges that understanding; but the imperatives of our age—as Chapter 1 made clear—do not permit delay in seeking radical change until a perfect theory is evolved.

Perfection is not claimed for the change systems concept. What is specifically advanced in its behalf is that all the major sources of organization change have been arrayed here in a sensible pattern which the organization manager can use "starting Monday morning." Beyond that, the usefulness of this kitbox of tools depends on the artisan's skill and on the wisdom of the counselors he selects to help design his organization's future. No doubt superior kitboxes will one day be devised, but here and now, at any rate, is a package of systems which can and has (in various situations) delivered radical change in human society.

An interesting view of how the Wright brothers got airplanes to fly comes from James Webb, administrator of NASA's early years. He contrasts the earlier and unsuccessful attempts to design a stable airplane with the Wrights' decision to design an obviously *unstable* device which, however, was controllable. The Wrights added a coordinated control system to change attitude in three dimensions, requiring a man to guide the machine. The man thus added an efficient computerized guidance system—his head and his senses—to deal with environmental variables.

Similarly, in an organization that wants to change, we cannot hope to design a stable system to get from reality today to reality tomorrow. The situation has too many variables and a few unknown factors. But we can imitate the Wrights' example in dealing with variables and unknowns by building in a coordinated set of controls "to make the thing fly." A change system is a coordinated arrangement of controls and change forces. Men can use this set of controls to manipulate conditions and to deal with both variables and unknowns well enough to make radical change happen in their own organizations.

In focusing all the dynamics of change deliberately upon a single organization there is no doubt that considerable stress will be placed upon its participants and its present structure, but, after all, that's part of the point of the whole effort. Without such stress our current rigidities of thought, relationships, value systems, and organizations could never adequately respond to the imperatives of our time. We must get on with the job of deliberately introducing radical change into the organizations and institutions of society; no better route to large-scale improvements in social and economic profit exists. With a balanced humanist philosophy, a serious concern for intellectual assistance of the first order, and an open curiosity about experimentation with human systems we might do very well.

Knowledge about human organizations is expanding, but the questions still outweigh the answers at hand. Nevertheless, enough is known today to design a change system for most organizations with reasonable probabilities of success. In the same way, Orville and Wilbur Wright could see far enough into the problem of flight to open the age of aviation.

Sometimes, simple how-to-do-it instructions are more stimulating to useful action than a long theoretical exploration. Here is a simple beginning guide. More detailed ones will be presented later.

How to Conduct a Radical Change System

1. Decide what class of organization you have (pyramid, mosaic, etc.; see Chapter 2). Write this down.
2. Decide in what life cycle stage it is now (develop, standardize, etc.; see Chapter 4). Write that down.
3. Decide if an exciting, powerful, and possible goal does exist for your organization (see Chapter 4). Get others to agree. Listen to lower-level employees especially.
4. Conduct a full-scale change-feasibility study (see Chapter 5). Write down its final summation in one sentence.
5. Design and conduct a change-readiness program if needed (see Chapter 5). Encourage people to design their own.
6. Make your final goals decision.
7. Construct a change system to realize your goals on a time schedule.
8. Measure and display all programs in public (see Chapter 7). Let everyone see for himself what is going on in the organization.
9. Protect existing operational elements while the new system is being completed and tested for effectiveness.
10. Integrate the old elements into the newer, larger concept.

Another way to grasp the broad general movement of the change system process is to study Figure 6-1, a rough representation of its major elements. Again, we are merely seeking a broad sense of the

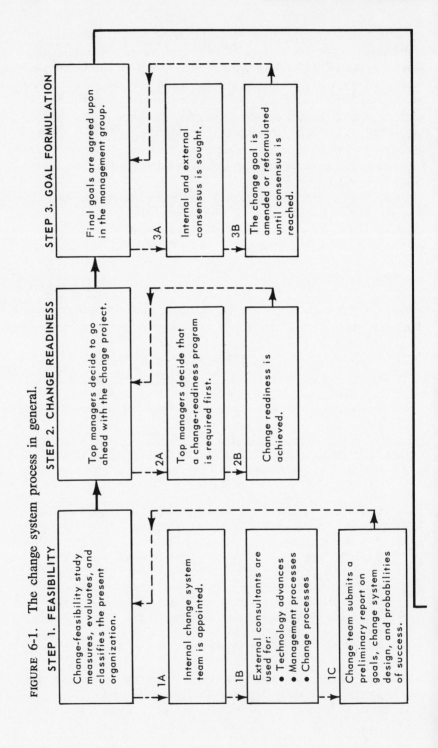

FIGURE 6-1. The change system process in general.

STEP 1. FEASIBILITY

Change-feasibility study measures, evaluates, and classifies the present organization.

1A

Internal change system team is appointed.

1B

External consultants are used for:
• Technology advances
• Management processes
• Change processes

1C

Change team submits a preliminary report on goals, change system design, and probabilities of success.

STEP 2. CHANGE READINESS

Top managers decide to go ahead with the change project.

2A

Top managers decide that a change-readiness program is required first.

2B

Change readiness is achieved.

STEP 3. GOAL FORMULATION

Final goals are agreed upon in the management group.

3A

Internal and external consensus is sought.

3B

The change goal is amended or reformulated until consensus is reached.

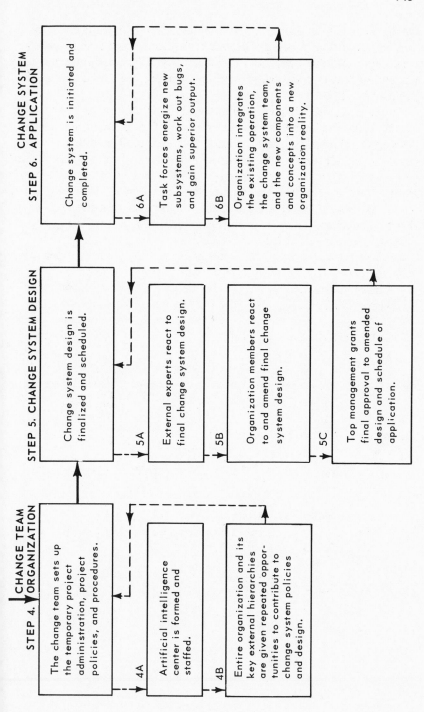

STEP 4. CHANGE TEAM ORGANIZATION

The change team sets up the temporary project administration, project policies, and procedures.

4A Artificial intelligence center is formed and staffed.

4B Entire organization and its key external hierarchies are given repeated opportunities to contribute to change system policies and design.

STEP 5. CHANGE SYSTEM DESIGN

Change system design is finalized and scheduled.

5A External experts react to final change system design.

5B Organization members react to and amend final change system design.

5C Top management grants final approval to amended design and schedule of application.

CHANGE SYSTEM
STEP 6. APPLICATION

Change system is initiated and completed.

6A Task forces energize new subsystems, work out bugs, and gain superior output.

6B Organization integrates the existing operation, the change system team, and the new components and concepts into a new organization reality.

change project's components and direction. Still another useful way to look at the change process defined here is demonstrated in Figure 6-2, which describes three general areas of activity: What the present organization does, what the change system team does, what the future organization will do.

In general, this chapter provides many ways for managers to look at and appraise the radical change process. This is necessary because designing a change system to control that process is complex and will be uniquely affected by the particular character of each organization and its environment. By considering the change system design process from several standpoints, the manager can better pick and choose what will work best to effect radical change in his own organization. Now that we have some familiarity with the overall process, we can ask what a change system is.

— A pragmatic answer is: A systematic and orderly way to get from where you are now to where you'd like to be.

— A more complicated answer is: A change system accepts your whole organization, analyzes its components and resources, designs a wholly new organization to make better use of the components, and, finally, installs the new reality and absorbs the old ones.

— An answer by analogy is: A change system is a garage to which you take your car when it begins to fail. When you arrive to pick it up, you find that the mechanics have reworked it into a jet airplane that changes your life forever.

FIGURE 6-2. General division of activities within a change system.

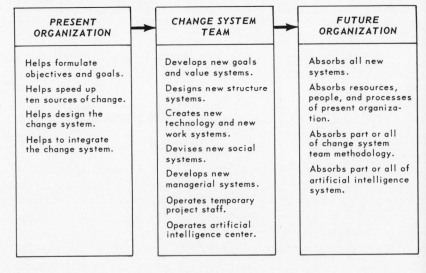

PRESENT ORGANIZATION	CHANGE SYSTEM TEAM	FUTURE ORGANIZATION
Helps formulate objectives and goals.	Develops new goals and value systems.	Absorbs all new systems.
Helps speed up ten sources of change.	Designs new structure systems.	Absorbs resources, people, and processes of present organization.
Helps design the change system.	Creates new technology and new work systems.	Absorbs part or all of change system team methodology.
Helps to integrate the change system.	Devises new social systems.	Absorbs part or all of artificial intelligence system.
	Develops new managerial systems.	
	Operates temporary project staff.	
	Operates artificial intelligence center.	

— A technical answer is: A change system speeds up dynamic processes of organizations within a general system whose goal is to discover and realize a major constructive transformation. (For management scientists, a more detailed description is in the appendix.)
— Another answer is: A change system is a systematic way to apply all that is known about changing organizations on a large scale.
— And finally: A change system is a temporary superstructure set up to transform an organization to the next higher state of which it is capable.

The Sources of Radical Change

From a 15-year review of the literature, in addition to my participation in and review of a large number of case histories of attempts to change, I have developed ten major sources of change in human organizations. The feasibility study's main task is to measure the status of these ten sources. The change-readiness program concentrates on accelerating each of them, and a change system requires that as components they operate at full speed ahead for several years. They are crucial to success. They are:

1. Radical change requires a major *innovation* in goals, products or services, markets, functions, or operations in the organization.

2. The organization's *technology* should reflect the growing edge of the state of the art because more radical change has been created by technology than by any other factor. In addition, the organization should be getting a flood of minor *work process improvements* from employees at all levels.

3. The full-scale introduction and implementation of *organization development* theory and practice is needed to open up the organization —to improve its interpersonal relationships, expand participative management, and enlarge day-to-day respect for the rights and human needs of the individual member.

4. A *futures forecasting* technique is needed as a homing device with which management can target and guide itself to change more flexibly and surely.

5. The fifth dynamic is a new and deeper understanding of the organization's *culture*—the many unspoken assumptions, behaviors, mores, and life-styles which have gradually combined to create "the way things and people are around here." Every change process must understand and adopt this reality as a base of strength.

6. Radical change requires an enormous increase in the amounts

and types of education and training given to each organization member. Wholly new situations can stimulate employees to acquire many new skills. *High-speed education,* using modern teaching methods, is a major change dynamic.

7. A key factor in all change processes is the saturation level of *symbolic, graphic, and rational communications* on change: its goals, the better future it can realize for each organization member, the values it represents, and why it is worth attaining.

8. Most attempts at change ignore the actual hierarchies which control or deeply affect the organization. Expanding *hierarchical cooperation* to include all pertinent internal and external leaderships is an essential core of all change system processes.

9. Most organizations assume omnipotence and rarely use outside experts even when they are well behind the state of their art. Conversely, too many outside experts do not know how to make their expertise valuable to operating organizations. A key element of radical change is the construction of a bridge to *many sources of outside expertise* across which employees and outside experts might easily and regularly traffic to update techniques in the management sciences, communications, technology, education, training, data networks, organization development, artificial intelligence assembly, and change process management.

10. To design, construct, and bring up to speed the many subsystems required to support a large-scale change system, a wide range of *interdepartmental task forces* will be needed. These horizontal committees with specific missions and task responsibility will bear the brunt of the effort to install a change system and make it pay off.

These ten dynamic factors of change in organizations fit together into a framework which is one of the several major supports of a change system. This five-part framework for the ten change dynamics is as follows. The numbers in brackets identify the dynamics of change as they are listed and discussed above.

    I. The change system goal involves large-scale innovation [1] that includes:
        A. Technological and work process improvements [2].
        B. Organization development [3].
    II. Management's guide, which operates as a "homing device" throughout this process, is the technique of forecasting future events and alternatives [4].
    III. The background for the entire change process is the composition and character of the organization's culture as well as the culture in which the organization is set. Understanding the realities of that

culture or cultures [5] is the foundation of the change edifice. Cultural description will include what managers see in their organization and a great deal more.

IV. The mechanisms which operate most powerfully and visibly in a change system are:

    A. The influence of high-speed education and training [6], which helps organization members to participate in and to adjust to the change process.

    B. The powerful, self-fulfilling effect of a generally shared vision of the future goal, which is disseminated to organization members by the evocative use of communications/graphics/symbols [7].

V. To execute the change system and maintain its momentum until it has completed its tasks, three primary dynamic factors are introduced:

    A. Every hierarchy pertinent to the organization, inside and out, is encouraged to cooperate in goal formulation and change system design and implementation. Hierarchical cooperation [8] insures acceptance of the many basic changes required by the change system.

    B. To obtain unusual intellectual inputs and sophisticated appraisals of goals and change system design, a wide range of outside experts [9] is used regularly.

    C. Finally, interdepartmental task forces [10] are set up to work out the specific plans, standards, controls, procedures, and policies necessary to integrate the new system elements into the organization structure.

Perhaps it would be useful to look at a case history of a change system which succeeded beyond the wildest dreams of its proponents and installers. The change process is defined in this example by using the terminology of the five-part framework and the ten dynamics of change, as indicated by corresponding numbers.

I. The innovative goal [1] was to create a free society under law, not under an arbitrary power, in which men would equally seek their happiness and be unhampered by traditions or authority. The managers created new technology and work process improvement [2] in the form of a democratic representative government and a written constitution of laws which were to be greater than the government. They then removed all powers from the ruler and gave them to the common citizen, separated the church and state, and provided for an increase of individual independence. In addition, they insisted that no state, legislature, power, or ruler could govern any group of men without its consent. As to the use of organization development theory [3], they created several useful unifying devices:

A. The Letters of Correspondence were established to share their thoughts and to better define the differences between them.
B. A Continental Congress enabled them to try their wings at design.
C. A Constitutional Convention helped them to hammer out consensus on key issues.
D. A final unified federal structure of government was devised to do the final job they wanted done.

These organization devices gradually expanded interpersonal relations and understanding across colonial (interdepartmental) lines, built up mutual trust among people in many hierarchies, and developed a general confidence in the new venture among the public.

II. The management guide to this process was gained through editorials, pamphlets, books, and the local press [4]. These media reported the immediate and long-range implications of events and negotiations with the rulers so that the logic of the ultimate goal of independence was perceived by the public as well as by the leaders (Federalist papers, writings of Franklin, Dickinson, the Adamses, and so on).

III. The cultural background [5] for this effort was that, in contrast to the culture of servants, lowly land serfs, obsequious tradesmen, and the lords and ladies of England, the local managers knew well the stubborn, Bible-reading independence of the American farmer who was the model for this culture. Managers like Franklin and Washington made sure that Tom Paine, Madison, Jay, and Tom Jefferson designed measures and systems to fit that typical American. They were well aware that the key facets of his character were his self-reliance and an inheritance of belief in individual and legislative rights.

IV. One mechanism of this change process was education [6], especially the unusual education of local leaders in the humanities and in government, the weekly education in revolution provided from pulpits throughout the territory, and the fairly widespread literacy of the public exercised mostly in reading the Bible and local rebel newspapers. These educating devices created an information pool from which a good system design could evolve. A repeated use of symbols (Don't tread on me, Yankee Doodle, Boston tea party, the shot heard round the world, no taxation without representation, the flag) created evocative and inspiring visions of individual liberty. The benefits each person could gain from the entire venture and the gifts of a free society were demonstrated in works like *Common Sense, The Crisis,* and *The Rights of Man* written by the remarkable Tom Paine. These self-fulfilling images

[7] were vitally necessary to motivate the weak, revolutionary venture over the long and arduous years it had to run.

V. The change process execution depended to a large degree on getting hierarchical cooperation [8] from the churches, the local governments, lawyers and judges, the rich landowners, and the business system, besides the leading and most respected local farmers. This was speeded by the written commitment of the core hierarchy, who risked their careers, their lives, and their fortunes on the success of the Declaration of Independence. Luckily, about thirty experts [9] in the history of governments, the decline and fall of many authoritarian regimes, and the new ideas of Hobbes, Locke, Hume, Needham, Bacon, and others were available and ready to design the new system (Jefferson, Franklin, John Hancock, Thomas Paine, James Wilson, Hamilton, John Dickinson, Daniel Dulany, Madison, Jay, Washington, the Adamses, and so on). The task forces [10] needed to install subsystems and complete the work were:

A. An army to fight the ruler's mercenaries.
B. A political group to keep the colonies in line and active in raising money.
C. A group to design the new government.
D. A group to communicate with and motivate the public will.
E. Several official bodies to iron out current operating problems (like money, help from other nations, shipping, and supply of the army and navy) while the new nation was being formed.

The entire change process worked out well. Almost 200 years later this general system design remains the most remarkably fair and efficient allocator and creator of social, cultural, and economic resources for human beings the world has ever seen. It is also remarkable that so many attempts to borrow this change model have been made by societal managers (Latin American and European "democracies") who refuse to or are unable to include all ten of the ingredients and processes required to make it work. Perhaps they should begin by studying the uniquenesses of their *own* cultures and then allow a government structure to grow *organically* out of their own particular natures. It could work as well as the American experiment.

For purposes of designing change systems which will work in modern organizations, however, it will be useful to consider each of the ten dynamics of change in detail. As he considers each change dynamic, the manager of change can be deciding how to energize it and gain its benefits within his own organization. Again, the bracketed numbers refer to the list of ten dynamics of change.

Innovation [1]

As we have seen in Chapter 2, some clockwork, mosaic, pyramidal, and conglomerate organizations have little or no room for innovation in any structurally important element of the system. Minor adaptive or homeostatic facets of operations, such as inventory control, data processing, public relations, product refinement, human relations, and sales techniques, can be improved, but only as long as no basic organization issue is raised. Thus the possibility of change is limited severely in these organizations. For roughly 90 percent of all organizations, then, internal innovation does not really exist in any meaningful sense. Executive conversation may be full of current innovative terminology, but organization realities today are much as they were five years ago unless some sector of the organization has deteriorated enough to go broke. For this reason, the quality and extent of any innovation in a change system will be a wholly new experience for most people in organizations today. Our objectives in stimulating large-scale innovation are:

1. To create a vision of the organization's future state worth seeking and realizing
2. To innovate new operational concepts for organization structure, function, and purpose
3. To create important technological advances or to innovatively apply existing advanced technology to operations on a large scale

These three processes will require a substantial effort from organization members as well as from consultants of many kinds.

There is really no way to stop the creation of new ideas by the people in an organization; it comes naturally to human beings with drive and intelligence. Mostly, however, organizations adopt methods to kill off or repress new ideas; occasionally, some will set up methods to appraise and implement innovation. Once management begins to reward innovation and innovative people (instead of rewarding stewards whose merit is in keeping things orderly, that is, in repressing new ideas), once it convinces its people that great innovative challenges exist, once it demonstrates a serious concern for innovation by constructing a fair and thorough innovation appraisal system, then it will be flooded with useful ideas from the employees and managers it now considers sterile.

Throughout the many phases of a change system, large-scale innovation is deliberately stimulated by direct investment, employee rewards, manager leadership and example, and outside expert contracts. The literature of creativity, imagination stimulation, and new concept building is utilized to provide manager and employee groups with many new skills in devising the major innovations needed and specified in the change system program. Aside from the standard sources of innovation —R&D groups, marketers, corporate planners, acquisitions executives, researchers, and product developers—innovation is especially sought in an organized program from all those many people inside an organization whose talents and capacities are usually ignored when this subject comes up.

Technological and Work Process Improvement [2]

Iron, steel, crockery, and bronze and the axe, wheel, lever, arch, plow, automobile, computer, and space platform bear witness to the fact that our organizations, our values, and indeed our lives are changed more by technology *than by all other factors combined.* For this reason, a change system bears down hard on every possible approach to a major technological improvement of the organization's purpose, nature, operations, and functions. Both interior and exterior clues must be explored with thoroughness and imagination to uncover or create a major technological advance if it is at all possible. No quicker or cheaper route to radical change exists, which is why so many organizations have traveled that way in history.

Skilled and astute observers of the change process [1] have allocated to technological improvements in how work is done an ability equal to that of behavioral science so far as changing people's attitudes and behavior is concerned. You can change a lot of negative behavior and poor attitudes by doing a better job of arranging how the work is done. People know a good deal about technological and managerial skill in modern production processes. When they are presented with poor planning, improper machinery, and a weak process technology that gives arbitrary and unpredictable results, there is almost no way to make them happy about their work. Thus technological and work process improvements hold tremendous promise for radical change.

Organization Development [3]

For twenty years the behavioral sciences have developed the field of organization development. Its benefits are:
— Improved relations between people, especially between employees and supervisors.
— A greater honesty and integrity in communication between individuals in groups, written records, memoranda, and confrontations.
— More openness and more willingness by managers and employees

to discuss sensitive issues, obscured realities, unspoken assumptions, failings, grievances, and inequalities.
— A greater participation at all levels in decision making, goal setting, problem solving, and policy making.
— Much greater concern for the rights and independence of others such as blacks, women, nationals of other countries, and suppliers and a stronger respect for each individual as a person.
— A stronger awareness of one's own influence or effect upon others, as for example, of a manager's image on his department's output.
— Greater sensitivity in group behavior (meetings and work groups) as to dominance/submission behavior, apathy, refusal to discuss interdepartment issues, adoption of unreasonable measures, refusal to share necessary information, hostility, gamesmanship, manipulation, deliberate distortion of events, and the alienation of members.

This arena has expanded in recent years to deal with blacks, Chicanos, children, parents, dope addicts, young couples, teachers, the professions, and many others. In all this ferment—from transactional analysis for personal reformation to game theory in international politics—we are busily reinspecting how we deal with one another and reaching for warmer, more honest, and more authentic human relationships. At the same time, many people are abandoning their former superficial, hypocritical, combative, and dishonest relationships, which they now suddenly reappraise as such due to new knowledge and new awareness of self.

Aside from its intrinsic value, organization development (OD) contributes to radical change in organizations. By establishing an atmosphere of openness and trust, it allows what is human about human beings to reassert itself. Thus, instead of encouraging mechanical cold structures in organizations, OD helps people to develop new, life-giving arrangements. This humanizing influence is vital. We must resist the overpowering mechanical and mathematical bureaucracies which by their nature attempt to crush out the last errant vestige of humanity in their employees. OD is both a set of new skills and an ideology running counter to that trend. It fits in perfectly with the transition to organic organizations of the growing plant and the human type described in Chapter 2.

Two good examples of combining organization development with work process improvements occurred in the General Foods and Procter & Gamble organizations. At a pet food factory in Topeka, Kansas, General Foods managers noticed an increase in infantile reactions—vandalism, graffiti on the walls, and so on—and decided to reorganize the operation around human needs instead of around the needs of the production process. They gave employees autonomy, removed specialist and administrative jobs, forgot about hours and rules, expanded the committee system to absorb specialist functions, allowed people to do many different jobs in one day, based their pay upon how much they learned, and allowed employees to hire and fire. One operator said, "I've been ill and come to work anyway because I know I'm needed. General Foods affords me happiness. If a man is happy in his work, he'll be happy at home . . . these people make me feel important. Two years ago I wouldn't have thought it possible to find these many people who took pride in their job." The results of all this have been outstanding performance by this plant, especially as to higher quality product and lower product costs.

Procter & Gamble's plant in Lima, Ohio, arrayed its highly automated production system around the needs of the people who work in it. There are no job classifications. Each individual continually adds to his skills; specialists take turns on operating tasks; and semiskilled laborers take on sophisticated problems of control and instrumentation design. Everyone is on straight salary; there are no time clocks or class distinctions; the employees set the pay scales and write the financial reports; and all are considered equal human beings. The overall results of this effort have been that costs in this plant are about half those of a conventional plant and quality is nearly perfect. These unique and proven examples of the effectiveness of the OD principle were presented by David Jenkins,[2] who says there is little recognition of the OD principle in America.

Futures Forecasting [4]

In addition to the broad, economic forecasts needed in the feasibility study, management needs, throughout the operation of a change process, the benefit of regular forecasts that display the future consequences of current actions and alternatives. Such information helps managers assess the long-term value of current alternatives. In recent years, the field of futures forecasting has exploded with new techniques and forecasting methods. It would not be appropriate to discuss the merits of each one here, but we can construct a general framework the manager can use to develop this expertise for his own organization's use during a change process.

Futures forecasting in a change system is a homing device which narrows down strategies to reach the change goal on schedule. As each alternate route to the change goal appears before them, change team members will inform the artificial intelligence center (described later in this chapter) to make appropriate forecasts of its value. The new alternative will be considered along with an estimate of its future value to the change process. Managers are already keenly aware that no magical system can tell them exactly what the future will bring; however, it is also true that we are greatly improving our abilities—through futures forecasting—to get some sound ideas about the future consequences of current choices. This strength is needed to keep the change process on track.

Some organizations will have personnel in their computer centers or in their economic analysis groups who are skilled in these methods; most will have to consult expert practitioners in the field to gain their help in training internal personnel and selecting a battery of logical forecasting methods. If a manager were to go exploring in central Africa, he would want the best guide possible; similarly, in future forecasting we'll have to scramble for good guides until the field becomes larger and its techniques are more fully integrated into day-to-day management procedures. Any change process worthy of the name will consistently forecast its future success, based on present data, analyzed by techniques such as the following:

Biological growth analogy	Dynamic forecasting/
Technology scanning	algorithms
Demand assessment	Possibility trees
Figures of merit	Theoretical limits test
Historical analogies	Delphi techniques
Substitution growth curves	Morphological analysis
Systems analysis	Hypothetical future conditions
Game theory analysis	Trend curves
Life cycle models	Technological mapping
Analyzing unique properties	Precursor event analysis
Impact studies	Technological changeover
Correlation and regression	phase
analysis	Envelope curve forecasting
Linear projections	Input/output tables
Expert panel consensus	Diffusion studies

Understanding a Culture [5]

Every organization that counts human beings as components naturally develops networks of symbols, relationships, traditions, and assumptions beyond all those interactions directly affecting the work itself. These networks are work-related, of course, and they take form and gain life in the working day. But they are not really under anyone's control; they are not planned for; and they can materially affect performance.

Many people and events inside and outside the organization contribute to the cultural setting in which the organization operates. Key events, beliefs, and characteristics of the people involved build comprehensive networks we can call culture. People do this because (1) they have minds, (2) minds do not like ambiguities, and (3) minds will quickly take bits and pieces of reality and experience that lie at hand in any situation and build some kind of mental framework in which they can fit, however awkwardly.

Some cultural characteristics of an organization will come from the location and others from the kinds of people employed, the technology used, the events of organization history, and the society in which the organization is set. Sociologists, social psychologists, and anthropologists specialize in studying cultures, ancient and modern. Here we claim that the same kind of study can be adapted to a single organization to good effect. Change system design should not be attempted without a new and much deeper understanding of the internal and external culture, that is, newer and deeper than was necessary to run the system as it was. From one floor of the headquarters building to another even the most naïve observer can feel the impact of different cultures. From the boardroom to a field maintenance crew is a long carry. These differences are not merely differences in power, authority, training, background, and income; they are differences in worlds, in reality.

Most management programs attempting change in organizations have ignored or glossed over cultural differences. Although that is particularly true in multinational corporations, it is true in local organizations as well. As a result, efforts to create radical change have failed. Some managers assume that they can decide what is to be done and then impose this change upon the organization. At times such action is called leadership, although this terminology is erroneous. The cult of leadership implies that two cultures and no more exist in the organization: one is the leader culture; the other is the follower culture. As has been shown in Chapter 2, such assumptions are much too primitive for managers to make unless they are managing very simple tasks in a primitive or near-Neolithic society.

A cultural analysis of any organization will be tailored by the professional to suit the needs and setting of each particular organization; however, to give managers some idea of the kinds of appraisals which might be included in such an effort, the accompanying preliminary checklist is offered. These kinds of analyses enable management and the change system team members to tune in to organization realities that are not often inventoried systematically. These cultural realities materially affect the process of radical change.

A Preliminary Checklist for
Organization Culture Appraisals

Depending upon the professional analyst's opinion after he is briefed on organization concerns and goals for radical change, the following might be included in a report.

1. Value systems prevalent in the organization
2. The status and rights of individuals at all levels
3. Intensive appraisal of the status of managers, specialists, officers
4. Repressed or unfulfilled job-related wants of employees and managers
5. Employee participation in community life
6. Employee participation in the dominant institutions of local society
7. Kinship networks if any are pertinent
8. Demographic data from personnel files supplemented by pertinent census tract data
9. Philosophic viewpoints:
   Views of self-purpose
   View of organization purpose
   Dominant religious view, if any
10. Past job mobility and present internal job mobility
11. Division of labor and status by sex, age, or other classification
12. Social interaction off the job
13. Participation in company sports, social events, and extra interest groups
14. Ethics displayed in current behavior patterns
15. Etiquette, manners, and styles of work relationships
16. Primary activities outside working day
17. Communication modes on the job:
    Nonverbal
    Meeting behavior
    Decision behavior
    Confrontation behavior
18. Attitude networks:
    Those based on preorganization experience
    Internal attitudes
    Specialist attitudes
19. Ideological systems:
    Economic understanding
    Social understanding
20. Key organization events and traditions

Education [6]

Education, historically one of the most liberalizing, humanizing forces in society, should be viewed by management also as one of its finest tools for change. Companies and other organizations which sequester or assign minor roles to their training centers or training policies are neglecting an important source of well-being. An organization commitment to continuous education of personnel at every level sharply divides advanced business organizations from all others. Not only does a fully rounded internal and external education program increase employee skill and effectiveness on the job, it also symbolizes:

1. That top management is not afraid to have its employees pick up new ideas and new concepts of how to do their work
2. That knowledge is more important than authority, position, or standard operating procedures
3. That self-renewal is an organization as well as a personal commitment
4. That continuous education is a natural component of life

Most organizations have no education policy. This means they do not know what skills and abilities their people should draw from the exploding world of knowledge in order to help the organization function better. It means they are not reaching out for new ideas or new concepts. It means they reject any need for intellect in their operations. I have met executives who admitted in plain language that their systems automatically reject intellect from operations in the same way reactionaries reject people with long hair or a different skin color.

A useful beginning assumption for managers is that, from top to bottom, your organization members do not have in their possession the specific knowledge and training needed to run a change system successfully. In any culture, large-scale change depends upon a massive increase in education for the participants.

By education, we do not mean the boring, dehumanizing, stultifying process that passes for an educational experience in most schools— indeed, in most colleges. Education is here defined as a ready resource of people, a set of self-paced techniques and devices which can deliver skills or facts whenever a motivated person steps up and says, "I want to learn that."

Education has too high a price when it operates—as it does in many organization training centers—on the basis of threat: "You must learn this to keep your job." Very few company or organization training centers avoid the open or implied use of crude threats to employees. Perhaps we became used to this idea in public schools wherein society says to the student: "Go to our boring school and mind your manners five days of the week or go to jail." Some light on what goes on today in the educational institutions we were once so proud of can be gained from this passage from John Holt's *Freedom and Beyond:* [3]

As one college student put it, we are trained to sell our learning for grades so that later we will sell our work for money. Worse, we learn to think not only that work is what we do for money, out of fear, envy or greed, but also that work is what we would never do *except* for money, that there could be no other reason for work, that anyone who talks about meaningful work must be the wildest kind of romantic dreamer and crackpot. We learn [in school] to take it as natural, right, and inevitable that our work should be boring, meaningless, hateful.

In a change system program, large numbers of people will have a substantial reeducation problem to face as they adjust to radical change. Education available to help them must be so varied in nature, capable of either private or group experiences, and adjusted to all the cultural and ego variables of the group involved that it becomes a truly pleasurable and rewarding process. Above all, conditions in which people can themselves seek the training they need must be devised.

Neither the change team nor its education consultants or managers should hesitate to design new methodology that makes information and skill available to those who seek it. The systematic development of an environment in which incentives and awards accrue to those who achieve self-education will stimulate and intrigue the rest of the work force.

In some emergency situations mandatory procedures will be necessary, but again the price of power applied to people to force their learning is very high. Education imposed from a power center lowers the self-respect of the participants. In the United States, public education in the 1970s—despite its previous excellence—has done more to lower the self-respect of children than all the inept parents in the country. Organizations want and need self-respecting, self-responsible people in their employ, particularly when they venture out on the seas of radical change. Such people respond poorly to arbitrary power.

A radical change process places great burdens upon all organization members. Those responsible for its vital training aspects really have no other choice than to design better and more flexible training choices with the faith that employees will in time realize what they must learn to play their part in the venture. To do this, educational program design must begin with the people and what *they* think rather than with the knowledge and how it is to be taught. Over and over again, we set up schools that slice knowledge into categories easiest for teachers to teach and then try to stuff them into students' craniums. John Holt looks at this task quite differently:

The world and human experience are one whole. There are no dotted lines in it separating History from Geography, or Mathematics from Science, or Chemistry from Physics. In fact, *out there* there are no such things as History or Geography or Chemistry or Physics. Out there is—out there. . . . Different ways of looking at reality should not make us forget that it is all one piece, and that from any one place in it we can get to all the other places.

The United States society is moving away from its present over-institutionalized school system—with full appreciation of its utility in the past—toward a wide-open pluralistic lifetime learning commitment. This arena, in which present institutions will find shrinking support and a shrinking market, will be a several billion dollar market for education entrepreneurs to consider. More important to the manager of change in an organization is that the more successful he is in developing conditions in which employees consistently enlarge their skill and knowledge, the more certain he can be that they are becoming receptive to radical change.

In the design of a change system, sets of specifications are developed for each dynamic of change. For example, in education, at timed phases of the change process, specifications will set forth the need for certain new skills, knowledge, and training among particular employee and manager groups. These will be made public in the organization, and it will be clear exactly why and how they will be vital to the success of the change process. This education schedule never assumes that people must abide by it; instead it trusts that they will want to fulfill its expectations. As previously stated, manipulation or command is of little value in this process. To guarantee employee participation, managers can rely only upon inspiration, a sense of community of purpose, and an exciting vision of what is to be gained by all in the future.

The delivery of specific knowledge and skill into a given number of bodies indifferent to crude threats is well beyond the capacity of most professional educator techniques. Too many educators have abandoned the idea of delivering measurable quantities of education in favor of vague generalities and a system which never measures its output. New and more democratic education systems are sure to replace much of what we are afflicted with now. In this area, many serious and concerned educators are already pushing hard within the system to gain its reform; but, as has been illustrated earlier, in a clockwork or mosaic organization reform and radical change are usually imposed from without by society itself. Dynamic new educational systems are springing up in the adult education field, which most professional educators ignore as being beneath them. In this area—and in companies and other organizations —there is much room to ask how the student can most quickly and efficiently gain the learning he wants. Business managers and their training staffs can and should freely take part in experimentation that fits education to people's needs instead of trying to fit people into some elitist concept of education.

Much time will be saved in business and industrial organizations by following the lead of those few advanced companies that have already developed internal and external education as a major capital resource. These organizations—IBM, Procter & Gamble, General Foods, Xerox, and so on—can teach us all a great deal about this problem and can help realize high-speed education techniques as a major internal dynamic of change.

Communications/Symbols/Graphics [7]

A change system requires that a powerful, graphic, understandable vision of the *end result,* the beneficial and exciting future state, should be the magnet toward which all activities can trend. There is no easy way to change a modern organization operating in a relatively free society without a powerful vision of its future.

President Kennedy provided a sharply defined goal of this nature when he said "We will send a man to the moon and bring him back before the decade is out." From then on NASA and the nation had a clear objective, and progress toward it was rapid. Any system does a great deal better with understandable objectives that square with its values than it does with muddy ones that conflict; for example, contrast the United States public's behavior in the Vietnam and Korean conflicts with the wholehearted dedication it displayed in World Wars I and II.

When it comes to talking about change in an organization, each manager and communicator should have a really good answer to the question, "Change for what and for whom?" The answer that is fitting will create a reaction like, "Ah, *that* is really worthwhile. *That* is worth going after." Because each organization has so many different kinds of people, each with varying values, only a truly broad and powerful vision of the future can have some meaning for all of them. A change goal lacking that quality will fail.

This section has concentrated thus far on the content of change communications—much of which is established by the quality of goal formulation described in Chapter 4—because content is so crucial to communications effectiveness. If the change objective actually possesses enough magic, excitement, anticipation of treasure trove, and satisfaction for the noblest aspirations of man, it will tend to self-fulfill. The people most directly concerned will want it to happen so badly that they will bring it into being. As a result, there is every reason for management to deliberate hard and long on the *end result* of change and to consider its communications potential carefully.

Once a clear, sharp vision is set for the change system to realize, basic communications methods can be used to hammer it home and to keep it alive throughout the process. Some of these are:

1. Find many ways to explain in simple terms exactly how each affected person will benefit from realization of the goal.
2. Use simple basic language and simple graphic symbols.
3. Maintain excitement, dramatize; invoke the cultural values of the organization and its key groups.
4. Repeat messages regularly and gain their acceptance into every form of message sending used in the organization.
5. Invest seriously in communications as a vital necessity.
6. Plan for feedback from all levels of the organization so that you can measure as much of your communications effectiveness as possible.

Communications specialists will be of value in devising the communication methods and determining the form of messages which reinforce the ethos and goal of the radical change system. Nothing should be left to chance in this sector of a change process. Full provisions must be made for clear message sending as well as for a wide and honest variety of techniques for getting feedback—discussion groups, surveys, question processing, and so on. Organization members need to acquire enough confidence to reveal their thoughts and to be put into a situation in which they can feel comfortable to talk about the pros and cons of any change measure. People need easy channels to present complaints and objections, ask for more information, and react to the primary, secondary, and tertiary effects they see in the change system goal. Such provisions should continue, throughout the change system schedule, to operate at a fever pitch when large-scale changes are actually being tested or introduced into the system.

Because it has been tried already, and because some organizations will be tempted again, the manager of change is reminded that he cannot merely communicate a future vision, hire a few consultants, and embark upon a radical change without *installing* the full change system machinery. Only when people know for a fact that a vast, well-thought-out venture is afoot will they pay special attention to communications about its potential for them. If there is no string of concrete decisions and events which demonstrate beyond doubt that management is committed to a radical change, no communications effort claiming such standing can be effective for long.

Hierarchical Cooperation [8]

Allied to the appraisals of cultures within and without an organization is the task of gaining and holding the active, involved participation and cooperation of an organization's hierarchies. As the following list indicates, there are many hierarchies inside and outside the organization that deeply affect organizational activities and performance:

External Hierarchies	Internal Hierarchies
Union	Operations and line management
Public media	
Political and governmental bodies	Research and development
	Finance and acquisition
Banks and credit services	Maintenance systems
Users, clients, customers	Marketing
Suppliers	Stockholders and owners
Communities	Personnel

A radical change system approaches these hierarchies from the earliest possible point in a change-feasibility study in order to (1) Inform them of what is going on. (2) Solicit their counsel, their ideas, and their aid in (a) setting change goals, (b) designing a change system, (c) making the change system work, and (d) dealing with secondary and tertiary effects of the change. (3) Gain their wholehearted approval as to the value and the merit of the change venture when it is appraised within *their* organizations.

Considerable effort, sincerity, redesign, and an abandonment of manipulative methods will be needed from managers before hierarchies will grant their cooperation over long periods of time to the change system.

Inside the organization the fact that a change system allocates scarce resources and management attention to its activities over several years raises competitive situations within internal hierarchies. As Chapter 3 on obstacles to change demonstrated, none of these internal hierarchies has an obvious and vested interest in radical change; quite the opposite is true. Change team members cannot afford to lose sight of the natural reasons why such groups lose interest in radical change, especially when the going gets rough. Yet, without their dedicated cooperation, the change venture cannot succeed. No more difficult area in which to maintain momentum and commitment exists in the entire change process. All hierarchies inside and out tend to split off or to build walls around themselves so quickly that herculean effort will be needed, using all the tools available, to continue to *earn* their support.

The Use of Experts [9]

Organizations frequently gain a mixed bag of experience with outside experts. There is the problem of adequately briefing the expert in organization realities, on the one hand, and there is the difficulty experts sometimes have in escaping their disciplinary narrowness, on the other. As a patient, the organization is extremely complex and unruly; as a doctor, the expert tends to treat the diseases he knows best rather than those he finds. Either factor can be the cause of a poor fit. And when management insists on dealing with the problem that concerns it at the moment and the expert sees that problem as no more than an effect of a deeper trouble, again a poor fit results. Aside from these difficulties and all the human failings likely on both sides, the need for expert outside counsel and appraisal in a change process is acute. It is a logical contradiction for any organization to try to change itself radically by using the skills it now uses to run its system. Most management and organization procedures are designed to resist change, and not to create it. To get radical change, many new things must be added to the mix. Outside experts can help add them.

New concepts and new technology can come from the acknowledged leaders of research and development in the field of technology in which the organization's operations lie. New knowledge and breakthroughs are created constantly throughout society, but most organizations lag behind the state of their art by 15 to 20 years. Catching up is one reason to use outside experts; moving ahead of the pack is another.

The change system team will begin to use outside experts during the feasibility study and in the change-readiness program. Then, in the change system itself, the regular interdisciplinary use of unique outside perspectives is a mandatory requirement for success. The construction of a temporary project management team called the change system team requires that it innovate an entirely *new* system to utilize the organization's resources. This difficult task needs a great deal of high-quality intellectual effort consistently applied over a long period of time.

Three groups of experts have a particular importance in the earlier phases of the change process. One is composed of outside experts in the field of technology with which the organization is most directly concerned. These people are expected to update pertinent technology, provide clues to critical growing areas of technology, recommend future product or service alternatives, and make prognostications of major technological events likely in the field (technology forecasting). The results of this contribution will be to directly enrich and challenge the technological base which relates to the setting of new organizational goals.

The second important group is composed of management scientists —those who are concerned with organization structure, people's behavior in groups, and other aspects of organization development. They are expected to contribute an evaluation of the obstacles to radical change in the current organization's formal organization, an appraisal of contradictions in organization structure, ideas for structures to implement the new strategy of change when it is developed, and to suggest ways to redesign of structure based on the probable needs of society in the future.

After the feasibility study results in a decision by management to install a change system, these management scientists will again be asked to review final change system design, change team policies, stability protection devices, and technological implications for organization structure. Such deliberate second-guessing and active participation by outside experts will help to insure that half-baked or behaviorally impractical ventures will not be substituted for the sound, organic development of a major organization advance. Among the quotes opening this chapter was one from Harold Laski in which he said, "We don't get naval disarmament when admirals confer." The point here is that if only inside managers confer on radical change, the odds are against their creating it. Raising the odds for success consists of deliberately organizing for massive outside contributions and extending the internal discussions of basic issues of change to every employee level.

The change system team is the third group of experts important to the entire change process. In a company of about 1,000 employees, the team would look something like this:

Internal Members:
1. Administrator—an executive vice president, who assumes direct responsibility for the entire program and its results
2. The corporate planner
3. Personnel vice president or organization specialist

External Members:
4. The change system adviser, who assumes responsibility for the selection and testing of all change technology
5. The change system designer
6. A communications specialist (or artificial intelligence specialist)

This team of four to seven members is assembled first to steward the change-feasibility study. Later, after management's decision to go ahead, it will lead and direct the entire change system over a period of three to five years. Team responsibilities include:

Change-feasibility study preparation and final report
Change-readiness program design and completion
Change system design, budget control, and operation
All internal and external liaison
Control of project managers and task forces which apply change subsystems
The maintenance of a time schedule for radical change completion
Final delivery of the desired results to management

The change system team members are line managers and consultants at the same time, which is a difficult position. They operate a huge temporary project, the change system; at the same time they work with everyone in the existing organization and its supplemental hierarchies to help them prepare for and adapt to the new "becoming" reality. Needless to say, with the stakes involved, the members of this team should be the finest top management can commandeer. Other experts will be involved from time to time in the change process, but these three groups—the technology experts, the management scientists, and the change system team—are the most important to the entire change process.

Managers may wonder how to find outside experts who are willing to join in the radical change process. Admittedly a considerable search process is in the cards, but some guidelines now may help.

— Really superb minds—the best in any field—are relatively unused. They may be quite busy in low-challenge tasks, but you may be certain that very few organizations can offer a strong intellect much to interest it. Again, if your change goal is really worthwhile, the best brains will help you.

— Package your requests and time them so that they fit the expert's life, travel and other habits, schedule of duties, and interests.

— Start with an expert you know well and can confide in; then build your network of experts with his help.

Finally, because each manager knows that he will have to live with experts for several years while he is dealing with crucial and controversial issues, it is obviously important to seek those who possess a reasonable balance of health, wisdom, emotional maturity, stability in personal lives, and sound philosophy in addition, of course, to their technological skills.

Task Forces [10]

To implement the fifteen or so new subsystems of a major change system, as well as to evaluate old systems and discuss the design of new ones, is the assignment for specific internal task forces. Carrying out the interdisciplinary aspect of the change team's structure, each task force will be an interdepartmental group assembled as a logical response to the needs of the subsystem it is working with. For example, a major redesign of a production line, which might be involved in a change process, would bring together line managers, R&D people, line supervisors, union representatives, supply, quality control, maintenance, and marketing people. Representatives from the logically involved entities and a change team member would decide how to fit the production line redesign into current operations as well as how to get it up to speed once it is installed. At the same time, each task force member has legitimate interests in the decision, the plan to implement it, and the effects it might have upon his own area of responsibility. The best rule is: "Get everybody in the act as early as possible."

Throughout the change process, these interdepartmental task forces will bear the brunt of the effort. They will concentrate realistic counsel and appraisal from operating elements of the organization to go along with what is being gleaned from the outside, from specialized staff groups, and from the change team itself. Once final plans are agreed upon, the task force can fit them into the organization and make them work better than any management edict could.

The task force procedure is recommended at every level to break down interdepartmental walls at least temporarily and to allow new concepts and programs to be thoroughly evaluated. It also greatly increases the number of organization members who have a direct stake in the successful outcome of a change system.

An Interim Review

We have now arrived at another level from which to consider the radical change process. To review the book thus far, it has (1) described why radical change is necessary and desirable in almost all organizations today, (2) explained how little radical change occurs in organizations and focused on the primitive nature of present organization design, (3) defined the obstacles to change, (4) illustrated how to formulate radical change goals that are worthwhile, (5) described the feasibility study phase of the project, and (6) described the ten sources of change and how they work together as part of the change system.

Now we can discuss in more detail how the change system works on and with the organization structure. To do so, we will have to cover three additional areas: (1) temporary project systems, (2) artificial intelligence, and (3) organization variables. Before starting those discussions, an overview of the relationships between these elements can be gained from Figure 6-3.

Temporary Project Systems

In constructing an oil refinery, a space vehicle, a dam, or any major building complex, engineering and construction firms habitually establish temporary project systems. The parent firm supplies management, talent, and process technology to a project management team, which utilizes the client's resources to deliver a large finished construction to the client organization. The concept is not new. Some very large business, government, and industrial organizations follow the same idea when they mount major ventures. Examples in business are major foreign expansions, new product or service market development, or a new process development; examples in industry are the construction of new mines, mills, factories, or industrial complexes in remote areas; examples in government are the Manhattan Project, Voice of America, Atomic Energy Commission, and the Marshall Plan.

The temporary project concept is recommended for application in the change system. The change system team will find it needs to set up specific new operations to prove them out. R&D implications of the change process may also require an operational test of efficacy. In the case of business, new marketing systems will require an operating test. To accomplish such tasks, the change team can use its own personnel up to a point; but as subsystems multiply, it will find it must put together management groups for many assignments. For almost all operating tests of subsystems it is recommended that internal personnel be

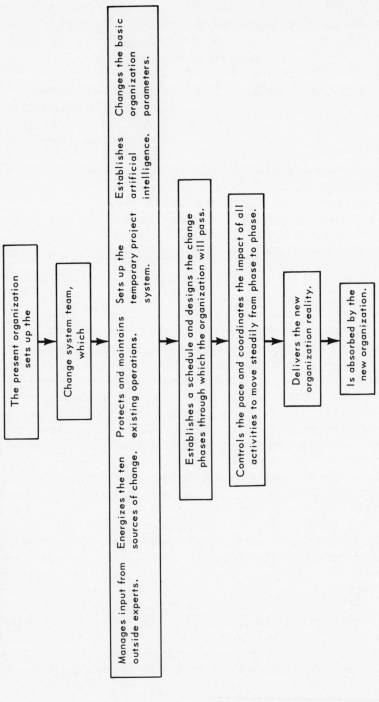

FIGURE 6-3. Change system activities.

used; only in the case of unusually sophisticated applications should the project team include outside experts. These activities provide the organization's personnel with an excellent opportunity to become familiar with and to internalize the new procedures which are very likely to be adopted later by the entire organization. In addition, the contributions of experienced internal personnel may create the final adaptations which will make any subsystem work really well in the organization. In the largest sense, the entire change system venture is a temporary project system designed to do a particular job and then be reabsorbed by the parent organization.

James Webb describes the early days of NASA, when the Russians were crowing over their successes and our rockets were exploding and burning on the pad in full view of the world, as a time in which many hearts were sick with disappointment over and worry about this nation's technological capacities. In those days, says Webb, the people of NASA "had to take a caterpillar and make it into a butterfly when we had never seen a butterfly." This is a rather provocative way to look at a large-scale endeavor such as a change system. In each organization wherein radical change is attempted, the exact nature of the final state cannot be known fully in advance. Each change system team will develop goals, set up procedures to realize them, and then hope that, like NASA, it can achieve them 100 percent, but there are uncertainties in the process.

To change most organizations will not often be an effort on the scale of NASA's but it will certainly be large and drastic to the participants. Consider the characteristics of large-scale endeavors, as experienced by Webb in NASA and in the Manhattan Project. Webb's thoughts about the common aspects of large-scale endeavors are paraphrased as follows:[4]

1. They begin as a result of a significant change in the environment.
2. They need detailed monitoring and feedback from the environment they deal with.
3. The prime key to their success lies in organization and not in technology.
4. Innovation in organization is not as important as the managing skill of the leadership group.
5. Systematically open communication is required.
6. Encapsulation (protection and support when in trouble) is needed.[5]
7. Setting clear specifications for breakthroughs in R&D gets results.
8. Negative side effects must be minimized, and positive side ef-

fects should be supported both inside and outside the organization.

9. Violent opposition should be expected and provided for.

10. Organization members must be trained and prepared to operate in the limelight of public inspection, wherein their failures and successes are well known.

These counsels from the man who was administrator of the largest and most completely successful temporary project system of our time are worth study by every manager of radical change.

Artificial Intelligence

Artificial intelligence is a component of the most advanced organizations. Most organizations are mechanistic systems with static, mindless, mechanical components. It is a contradiction in terms to expect these clocklike creations to become organic, like a human being or a flower, or to acquire the ability to think.

A chief mission of the change system is to operate upon the static components of the organization and transform them into organic components whose dynamic properties can in time give rise to an organization consciousness. This group mind, this consciousness, is the artificial intelligence we have been discussing. It creates in the organization the adaptive, responsive behavior needed to deal with today's dynamic and conflicting environmental conditions.

Earlier the thought was advanced that our best and most effective organizations—the few truly advanced companies on the U.S. scene—would achieve their next great development by "putting a head on their shoulders." This is another way of saying, "Turn mechanical components into organic ones, start an artificial intelligence system, and create an organization consciousness."

The reason all managers should seriously consider moving away from mechanistic organization structures [6] is that such structures were best suited to eras in which slow or medium rates of change were effective. We no longer live in such an era, nor are we likely to for another hundred years if ever. *Mechanistic* management systems involve sharply defined specialization of tasks, a strict hierarchical structure ruled at the top, a great need for loyalty, obedience, and submission to the commanders, and an inward-looking management that claims omniscience.

In contrast, *organic* management systems include adoption of new information and new skills, the spread of commitment and responsibility in a network, the development of goals through horizontal interaction, a commitment to excellence with knowledge gained "outside" necessary to being skilled at your job, and an outward-looking management that self-actualizes its people.

Change systems will frequently try to abandon mechanistic organization arrangements for organic ones. These attempts must be designed, related to both the change goal and present organization realities, tested, and then installed. No easy task. After that, the next step is to devise the concept of an artificial intelligence that is the development of a central perception, memory, imagination, reason, and motivation.* These factors will operate day to day as an *organization consciousness*. Developing the workings of these group minds will give managers and management scientists more than enough to do for the next hundred years. Consciousness will give organizations the capacity they need to deal with their whole internal and external environment, that is, to manage radical change.

This leads logically to a reconsideration of the complaints made in our society about the failures of our organizations to deal with our times. How can we pour out book after book that deprecates these poor, primitive mechanistic organizations which we and our forebears created but forgot to equip with any intelligence? No wonder these social and economic devices created so many unintelligent consequences in today's society!

In contrast to the wails of doomsday criers, all that man really faces is a redesign job involving higher goals for his organizations. Other than the obviously exploitative forms of organizations such as dictatorships, socialist states, and monarchies, the human organizations which constitute the free world need no more than redesign. No ill of society, in short, will resist a redesign of the organizations operating in that area. Whether the area is the steel industry or child welfare, ocean resources or inflation, change systems that redesign our existing organizations around greater goals are the main highway out of our difficulties and into a much better world. Some observers, usually elitists, prefer that the world should plunge into complete social destruction and chaos. Later they propose to rebuild society on their own terms. The author prefers to trust in people's present wisdom and intelligence to deal with their own organizations. All that they require is a new battery of change techniques, and these are here made available to all.

* See the appendix for more detail on artificial intelligence concepts.

Aspects of Artificial Intelligence

For an organization undergoing change, an artificial intelligence system can be set up very simply. Consider it first as a room or a place that updates, gathers together, and displays the key information being created to guide and describe the change process as it goes on. It could be thought of as a war room, a place for plans with wall maps that outline the territory in dispute and a place to make strategic decisions; but again, the win-lose aspects of this idea are really inappropriate to the change process. We can also think of the intelligence center as a file or a library which collects, assembles, and displays factual and trend information so that top managers, change team members, and interested employees can find out what they want and need to know to carry on the change process.

When the flood of change data rises as programs and subsystems are designed and installed in large organizations, then in contrast to the simpler arrangements suitable for smaller organizations, the monitoring, learning, reporting, storing, tracking, and public display of change trends and data will require computerization, remote terminals, and modern display systems. In very large organizations, a complete nervous system and brain will need to be constructed to bring pertinent data and information in large amounts to a wide range of organization members embroiled in change processes continuously.

A key facet of this intelligence center and network on a small or a large scale is its openness. Anyone who wants information on what is going on in the organization's change system can come here to get it, get it from a remote terminal, or get it through some open channel. Probably no other factor will be as helpful in maintaining the cooperation of hierarchies inside and outside the organization as to allow them access to this network in which any question can be answered without screening by management.

What About Security?

Because radical change deals with the most important issues, skills, technologies, and strategies of an organization, it will inevitably bring up the issue of security. In some few fields of human activity this will be a real issue, but for 95 percent of human activity it is ephemeral. We suggest that a security system like that of your local public library is the best possible protection against competitors who might seek to learn of your plans to change. The public library makes everything available to anyone. It dispenses tons of information which cover a large share of all the knowledge the world has thus far gleaned, but how many wise men have you met in your life? With all this information fully available—the output of the greatest minds—why do so few absorb it? There is your security system.

A well-designed change system will have such depth and extent that all kinds of data about it can be spread to an industry of competitors, but they will not know what to do with it. Nor will they be ready or organized, nor will your change system fit their situation. Forget security and operate in the open.

Organization Variables

For the purpose of designing specific change systems we have defined 12 key organization parameters.* These parameters are operated upon by the 10 dynamic sources of change to create a transformation. The 12 organization parameters and the subsystems they fit into are as follows:

Organization Parameters	*Fit Into*
1. Goals and values	I. Goal
2. Technology	II. Technology
3. Differentiation of structure	III. Structure
4. Integration of structure	Structure
5. Communication patterns	Structure
6. Roles	IV. Psychosocial subsystems
7. Organized groups	Psychosocial subsystems
8. Influence relationships	Psychosocial subsystems
9. Informal organization	Psychosocial subsystems
10. Decision making	V. Managerial subsystem
11. Planning	Managerial subsystem
12. Control	Managerial subsystem

As defined earlier, the chief force for change in an organization is technological innovation, which might be expressed in new products or services, new marketing concepts, new financing arrangements, or other radically different ventures. A necessary spin-off of innovations in the technology of the organization will be the new forms of internal organization they require. As Alfred D. Chandler, Jr.,[7] made clear in his study of large-scale changes in major United States business organiza-

* Primarily the work of Gary Chism, a designer of change systems at Change Systems Corporation in San Francisco.

tions, a new *structure* follows a basic change in *strategy*. Aided by its intelligence center, the change system team will devise and install new structural networks for the organization. It does this by deliberately rearranging and reshaping organization variables. In short, a major component of the change process is its eventual planned effect upon the organization parameters listed in the preceding table. When large-scale innovation finally gets expressed in changes of organization parameters, a transformation of identity has occurred within the organization.

Management Considerations

As managers consider the value and scope of the goals and the complexity of change system application, some sense of tactical considerations is necessary. The following guidelines should prove useful in installing a change system.

1. Provide the change system with an official, authoritative policy, a commitment of resources, and a wise and respected key executive as administrator.

2. As initially organized, the change team should include the organization components directly related to its work such as the corporate planning office, organization specialists, economists, management information systems group, R&D, training center, and acquisitions specialists. Put your knowledge specialists together in this task.

3. A wide-open public commitment to the goals is needed among employees, stockholders, suppliers, clients or customers, and other involved hierarchies to convince the organization it can change itself.

4. Begin with and maintain an interdisciplinary approach to all change system activities in order to avoid one-sided strategies.

5. Do not overdesign the change team's organization. Prepare all its participants for redesign and for changes of both course and structure so that a flexible response is built into this group.

6. Plan for the maximum internal visibility of all change processes, even to putting change team meetings on closed-circuit TV. The change of a whole organization cannot be buried in some department or executive suite. It can succeed only out in the open as an obsession everyone shares.

7. Delegate authority *and* responsibility to operate a subproject only *after* it is designed. To initiate a subproject, delegate responsibility for design to one or several and then require the change team to share the authority to decide upon a choice.

8. Ask the change team to measure and chart the record of all activities and their condition monthly. Require a review for top management and directors each quarter. Annually review and appraise the entire project for internal and external hierarchies and, in particular, for all employees. Maintain weekly public fever charts of key change indicators (as described in Chapter 7) and post them in the organization's offices, factories, and lunchrooms.

9. Require the change team administrator to continually upgrade and maintain his key trusted personnel to perform to the highest standards with work habits that reflect a sincere dedication to the change goal.

10. The prime duty of the top members of the change team is to concentrate on the whole change process rather than to be buried in details of managing a component subsystem.

Now that a reasonable understanding of change systems is shared, budgets and schedules should be considered. To review earlier thoughts, we can run the system as it is and hope for the best, we can spend some money adapting the system to a few of its external or internal dislocations, or we can reach out for radical change with the goal of large-scale improvement and large-scale increase of economic and social profits.

If a manager decides to reach for radical change—and many managers will—he should be given a view of the commitment that is as accurate as possible. We have covered other commitments to some degree; now we should discuss schedules and budgets.

Schedules

As organizations become more complex and deal globally with a more and more complex world, managers have become accustomed to schedules and programs stretching 5 to 15 years ahead. A change system is in this category. In quite small organizations, or if change readiness has already been achieved, a three- to five-year schedule can be realistically projected; but for the rest a longer effort is mandatory as far as the present state of the art is concerned.

Such considerations will stimulate some managers to forget about radical change and to hope either for luck, another war, population growth, or a failure of their competitors to save their bacon. Many will choose to delay, but the most forward-looking managements will explore the radical change option now. Table 6-1 presents time schedules that apply to most organizations.

Large-scale organization activities extending over relatively long

TABLE 6-1. Estimated time schedules for change systems completion (in months).

NUMBER OF EMPLOYEES	FEASIBILITY STUDY	CHANGE-READINESS PROGRAM	CHANGE SYSTEM	TOTAL
100–500	3–4	8–12	24–36	35–52
501–1,000	4–9	12–16	36–48	52–73
1,001–10,000	9–12	16–24	48–60	73–96
10,001–50,000	12–16	24–36	60–72	96–124
50,001–100,000	16–36	36–60	72–144	124–240

periods of time are expensive, although a change system does not require much investment in hardware or plant. Most of its expense consists of the time of present employees, who are asked to perform change system tasks in addition to their present duties. It is believed that most of our organizations can afford large quantities of such time, but it will be unavailable unless employees are motivated and inspired by the change process and its goal. For that reason, all these budgets have

TABLE 6-2. Budget estimates (in 1974 dollars).

NUMBER OF EMPLOYEES	INTERNAL BUDGET *	EXTERNAL BUDGET	TOTAL INVESTMENT	AVERAGE COST PER YEAR
For a 3-Year Change System				
100	$ 225,000	$ 150,000	$ 375,000	$ 125,000
500	900,000	535,000	1,435,000	478,333
1,000	1,650,000	605,000	2,255,000	751,666
For a 6-Year Change System				
5,000	$ 6,400,000	$ 1,600,000	$ 8,000,000	$1,333,333
10,000	11,000,000	3,000,000	14,000,000	2,333,333
50,000	16,000,000	8,000,000	24,000,000	4,000,000
For a 12-Year Change System				
100,000	$60,000,000	$12,000,000	$72,000,000	$6,000,000

* Estimates include all internal time charges incurred by presently employed organization members. In most organizations, 30 to 60 percent of the internal costs need not be incurred as new expenses because of overstaffing and underworking situations that have become traditional. For example, the average cost per year for a 1,000-employee-operation change system is likely to be near $370,000 instead of $751,666 as shown in the last column.

TABLE 6-3. Budget estimates for a 3-year change system in an organization of 1,000 employees.

Major Cost Elements	Year 1 Costs *		Year 2 Costs		Year 3 Costs		Activity Totals
	Inside	Outside	Inside	Outside	Inside	Outside	
1. Change project staff management	$100,000	$100,000	$100,000	$100,000	$100,000	$100,000	$600,000
2. Artificial intelligence center	80,000	20,000	80,000	5,000	100,000	0	285,000
3. Change communications	40,000	5,000	60,000	5,000	75,000	0	185,000
4. Management science experts	10,000	20,000	10,000	10,000	10,000	0	60,000
5. Technology experts	0	20,000	0	10,000	0	0	30,000
6. R&D	100,000	5,000	50,000	0	0	0	155,000
7. Education system	50,000	5,000	50,000	5,000	50,000	5,000	165,000
8. Innovation system	50,000	50,000	100,000	50,000	100,000	20,000	370,000
9. Task force operation	25,000	5,000	100,000	25,000	100,000	20,000	275,000
10. Change measurement	30,000	10,000	50,000	10,000	30,000	0	130,000
Subtotals	$485,000	$240,000	$600,000	$220,000	$565,000	$145,000	$2,255,000 *
Yearly totals	$725,000		$820,000		$710,000		

* Estimates include *all* internal costs, meeting times, costs of services, travel, and other components. In most organizations operating at "normal" levels, 30 to 60 percent of the inside costs shown above need not be incurred as new expenses. For example, in a low-workload bureaucracy—government agency, school system, monopoly enterprise—the total outlay shown as $2,255,000 would more likely be $1,500,000. In a few cases only external costs need be considered; that is, a $605,000 total instead of the $2,255,000 total shown.

TABLE 6-4. The change system process.

I SEEK OUT ROUTES, PREPARE SYSTEMS *Measure and prepare internal capacities for change.*	II DEVELOP SPECIFIC PLANS *Develop the skills needed to plan large-scale change.*

INFORMATION DEVELOPMENT PROGRAM

In-house records	Model needs
Computer sources	Forecasting
Internal surveys	needs
External surveys	Need to com-
Change commu-	plete key
nications net-	studies from
work design	feasibility
	study

START EXPERTS ON PRELIMINARY GOAL, PROBLEM, AND ROUTE DEVELOPMENT
Technology experts
Management science experts
Change process experts

ORGANIZATION DEVELOPMENT PROGRAM
Initial evaluation of gaps between the present status and change goals
Top management group process program
Manager and supervisor training program
Employee training program
Change-readiness enhancement program

TECHNOLOGICAL DECISIONS
Set specifications for innovations needed for the change program
Start R&D groups on basic explorations that are pertinent
Expand the innovation network to include the entire organization

STABILITY MAINTENANCE PROGRAM
Initiate discussions with finance, marketing, and production groups

PRELIMINARY GOAL AGREEMENT
Develop subsidiary goal chain
Plan to entrench change goal in existing cultures
Forecast the effects of goal attainment to organization members

GOAL EVALUATION
Among internal hierarchies
Among external hierarchies
Among outside experts

PRELIMINARY CHANGE SYSTEM DESIGN
Operational consequences
Marketing program
Financial analyses
Personnel needs

CHANGE COMMUNICATION PROGRAM
State goals with evocative imagery
Design goal graphics
Develop complete communications program internally and externally
Design an open feedback loop to evaluate effectiveness

EDUCATION PROGRAM
Set education specifications for each phase of change system
Design systems for on- and off-job availabilities of training
Plan education motivation

TABLE 6-4 (Continued).

III DESIGN THE CHANGE SYSTEM	IV MANAGE RADICAL CHANGE
Agree on the final change system design.	*Start and manage the change processes in all subsystems.*

DESIGN STABILITY MAINTENANCE PROGRAM
Operating, financial, and marketing groups approve final strategy

CHANGE SYSTEM DESIGN

Administration	Policies
Plans, programs	Methods, proce-
Goals, subgoals	dures
Schedules and	Budgets
controls	Forecasts

CHANGE MEASUREMENT SYSTEMS
Technological advances
Organization behavior
Economic improvements
Marketing targets
Change dynamics

CHANGE COMMUNICATIONS
Dramatic events
Open channels
Reinforcement
Goal-switching inhibition

ARTIFICIAL INTELLIGENCE CENTER
Open feedback display on all change processes and activities
Management tracking of progress
Performance measures and ratios
Environmental factors
Social indicators

CHANGE SYSTEM APPRAISAL
Outside experts appraise entire change system design
Top managers review design
Organization members review design

INITIATE TASK FORCES
Implement all new subsystems
Test innovations in the field
Adjust horizontal conflicts
Maintain momentum of change processes
Keep to schedules

FUTURES FORECASTING
Expand self-fulfilling forces by revealing consequences of current behaviors
Inform top management of major crossroads
Adjust targets of change
Evaluate surprise developments

SHARPEN CONTROL SYSTEMS
Develop budget performance
Refine departmental goals
Expand public display of measures
Record in full detail the final achievement of the goal

PROJECT CONCLUSION MEASURES
Stabilize and adapt to new realities
Disband task forces as needed
Absorb change team and artificial intelligence center skills
Standardize operations to implement previously frustrated homeostatic drives among people

charged internal time (already paid for in most instances) to the change system budget. This inflates overall costs, yet from a strict view, it is appropriate. In Table 6-2 are examples of 3-, 6-, and 12-year budgets. So you will better understand these budgets for change systems, a year-by-year breakdown of a 3-year budget is offered to demonstrate the nature of the investment; see Table 6-3.

A Project Layout

A manufacturing organization of about 2,000 employees has been selected as the general subject of Table 6-4, which lays out the entire change process. Not all factors are included because of space restrictions, but enough are displayed to give managers a clear idea of the workings of a change system. Similar plans, when spun out of the internal realities of each organization, will deliver radical change to large and small organizations.

How a Change System Overcomes Resistance

In Chapter 3 the obstacles to change were set forth, and it was made apparent that formidable obstacles to radical change exist naturally in every organization. Also in Chapter 3 change systems were advanced as a reasonable and effective device to overcome these obstacles and create constructive, profitable, beneficial change in large organizations. Now that the structure of a change system has been made clear, it is appropriate to consider exactly how such a change effort would contain or eliminate the obstacles to change. Figure 6-4 provides some answers. In the right-hand column the obstacles to change are listed with the numbers or letters of the change forces which can and will deal with them.

For example, one of the obstacles to change in organizations is the tendency of groups within the company to reject outsiders. This is listed in Figure 6-4 as the fourth item under II, Obstacles to Change in Group Behavior. Notice that after the words "rejection of outsiders" there appear (8, 9, A). To decode the parenthesis, check the left-hand box:

8. "Hierarchical cooperation" suggests that the members of the group that rejected outsiders can gain a larger view through experiences in hierarchical cooperation at many levels in and outside the company.

9. "Use of experts" means that fear of outside experts is likely to erode as a considerable and regular number of experts move in and out of the organization's affairs. Familiarity removes fear.

A. "Temporary project system" suggests that in a large temporary project system in which everyone is welcome to participate with members of other groups, fears and lack of trust are likely to fade with experience.

None of these processes work automatically. Managers and employees will need both skill and motivation to make them work, but here are specific channels that increase management's options and raise the odds for success.

FIGURE 6-4.   How change systems overcome the obstacles to change.

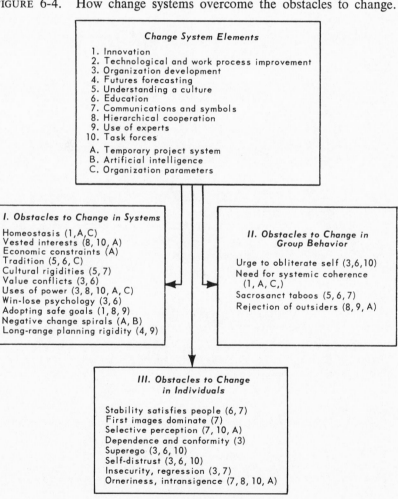

<table>
<tr><td colspan="2">

Change System Elements

1. Innovation
2. Technological and work process improvement
3. Organization development
4. Futures forecasting
5. Understanding a culture
6. Education
7. Communications and symbols
8. Hierarchical cooperation
9. Use of experts
10. Task forces

A. Temporary project system
B. Artificial intelligence
C. Organization parameters

</td></tr>
</table>

I. Obstacles to Change in Systems

Homeostasis (1, A, C)
Vested interests (8, 10, A)
Economic constraints (A)
Tradition (5, 6, C)
Cultural rigidities (5, 7)
Value conflicts (3, 6)
Uses of power (3, 8, 10, A, C)
Win-lose psychology (3, 6)
Adopting safe goals (1, 8, 9)
Negative change spirals (A, B)
Long-range planning rigidity (4, 9)

*II. Obstacles to Change in
Group Behavior*

Urge to obliterate self (3, 6, 10)
Need for systemic coherence
(1, A, C,)
Sacrosanct taboos (5, 6, 7)
Rejection of outsiders (8, 9, A)

*III. Obstacles to Change
in Individuals*

Stability satisfies people (6, 7)
First images dominate (7)
Selective perception (7, 10, A)
Dependence and conformity (3)
Superego (3, 6, 10)
Self-distrust (3, 6, 10)
Insecurity, regression (3, 7)
Orneriness, intransigence (7, 8, 10, A)

NOTE: *The change system element which works to eliminate or contain an obstacle in listed by number or letter in parentheses.*

Because measurement of an organization before, during, and after a change process is vital to the organization's success, the following chapter is devoted to change measurement systems. Managers who have the courage and sense of adventure necessary to attempt radical change in their organizations will find that the day-to-day visibility of progress in each of many change measurements will be a great source of encouragement. When we can measure progress and target our efforts to a goal, we have some assurance that we are going to succeed. This is now the case for radical change. *It can be achieved.*

References

James E. Webb's quotation is from *Space Age Management* (New York: McGraw-Hill, 1969); that of Eric Hoffer from *The Ordeal of Change* (New York: Harper & Row, 1952). Harold J. Laski's quote is taken from his article "The Limitations of the Expert," *Harper's Magazine,* December 1930. See *Environment and Change* (Bloomington, Ind.: Indiana University Press, 1968) for Pierre Bertaux.

1. Robert Guest, *Organization Change: The Effects of Leadership* (Homewood, Ill.: Irwin, 1962).
2. David Jenkins, "Democracy in the Factory," *The Atlantic,* April 1973.
3. From *Freedom and Beyond* by John Holt. Copyright © 1972 by John Holt. Published by E. P. Dutton & Co., Inc., and used with their permission.
4. James E. Webb, *Space Age Management* (New York: McGraw-Hill, 1969).
5. Verified by Robert Guest (see reference 1).
6. Acknowledgment is made to the debt these items owe to an unusual book: Tom Burns and G. M. Stalker, *The Management of Innovation* (London: Tavistock, 1961), pp. 119–125.
7. Alfred D. Chandler, Jr., *Strategy and Structure* (Cambridge, Mass.: MIT Press, 1962).

CHAPTER SEVEN

Rate-of-Change Measurement Systems

Executive secrecy obscures great issues of public policy and permits sustained masking of blunders.

HAROLD WILENSKY

It is a good general rule that governments only begin to do something about problems when they learn to measure them.

DANIEL P. MOYNIHAN

A class of facts relating to the environment in which the corporation operates is what is really required by top management.

ROBERT L. JOHNSON and IRWIN H. DERMAN

One technical manager and his deputy thought that their colleagues must be spending 70 percent of their time on current production problems. . . . (It was actually) 12 percent.

TOM BURNS

The UNESCO team members looked at one another in silence. The latrines they had built in the village a year ago stood unused. "All that effort to explain about flies and diseases has gone to waste," they thought. The only change in the South Seas village was that the women did use the water out of the new one-inch pipe instead of walking a mile to the stream. Everything else—the feces in the streets, the flies, the sick children, the fresh, small graves—were just the same.

The message had not gotten through despite a lot of smiles, nods of agreements, and long hours of exhortation and palaver with the chiefs. They realized they had to start all over. How do you get a whole society to practice sanitation and use a latrine when it has no conviction the effort is worthwhile?

In six months the streets were clean, flies were rare, disease was dropping steadily, and the village was very pleased with itself. What had happened?

It was a lesson in the people problems of achieving change. First, in backtracking their assumptions, the UNESCO team discovered they were dealing with the wrong hierarchy. *This* society handled problems involving life-styles through the oldest female, usually a great-aunt, in every family. The chief's authority did not extend to these areas. So the UNESCO team got together with the ladies and the air began to clear. The women finally grasped that the UNESCO team wanted to help them save the children. This goal had been obscure before; now it was an evocative image of the attainable future. Next, with the ladies' help, the UNESCO team interested the very young children in a daily contest to catch flies and put them in bottles that killed them. Each youngster brought in his bottle and stood by while his flies were counted. A score was put opposite his name for all to see. The scores were generally higher each week of the contest.

Next, older boys were given a street to police for "night soil." How many times had anyone defecated in his street or around his house since yesterday? A score was put up every day for each street. Neighborhoods began competing with each other to lower their scores. The boys' efforts soon resulted in social pressures on grandfathers, children, busy mothers—indeed, everyone. Without pressure from "foreigners" or from the wrong hierarchy, the right conversation began. Rather than make the boys shovel and lose face with a poor score, villagers began using the latrines regularly.

And so it all worked out by invoking some of the basic dynamics of radical change:

— New technological elements from the UNESCO team—fresh water, latrines, and knowledge of the disease carriers.

— Hierarchical procedures—a bow to the chiefs but direct negotiations only with the older ladies.

— Measurement of the right variables—dead flies and unsoiled streets with scores posted for all to see. The villagers concentrated on improving the scores instead of preaching to one another.

— A natural buildup of group pressure to improve the scores.

— Reinforcing procedures—contests that ran long enough to build personal habits.

— Pride in accomplishment as the goal became reachable, especially when it became clear that each villager's personal habits could help improve the health of the children they all loved. The prophecy "we can save the children" had found a way to self-fulfill.

When the chiefs of the next village got word of this remarkable improvement in the health of the young people, they asked the UNESCO team to come over and do the same job for them. The team members looked at each other and just smiled. Later, when it was easy, they went to talk to the ladies in the other village.

This story of change has probably suggested many applications to managers who frequently have the same problem, namely, they cannot get people to do what is obviously in their best interests. Maybe it's time to drop unworkable approaches to cultural groups and look at the situation with new eyes that can discern the handholds to change.

Did the UNESCO people become better manipulators? I think not. They became better students, better human beings, better social scientists who were less likely to project their own assumptions upon another culture and who devoted themselves to a constructive goal instead of attempting to win an argument. Most of all, they finally found and used the right systems to create change.

The Arts of Measurement

We reveal a great deal about ourselves and our organizations when we list what we measure. An organization which measures no more than hours worked, years employed, dollars earned, infractions of rules recorded, and days spent surely has a strange view of the real life, blood and guts people it employs. A retail business that concentrates on bills paid versus bills unpaid makes clear its meager interest in its customers. A bank whose record of contacts with its depositors is greatest when they have recurrent financial difficulties and lowest when they have none should wonder at its purpose.

Manufacturers who dwell on lost time, accident rates, down time, employee turnover, and output per day should occasionally wonder if they are measuring the key events in their organizations. Which measures have anything to do with change? Or with organization health? Or with people? Should we count only negatives or cash flows or other impersonal events? Are all positive and meaningful organization behaviors uncountable? This is not likely. What measures will spark up an entire workforce? *Change what you measure and you may change all.*

A change team worth its salt will spend long hours in deciding what to measure in its organization's cultures. These decisions are crucial to success. The following are the elements of a powerful and pertinent measure of organizational events:

1. The events must be in fairly large numbers.
2. The events must be easy to count.
3. The events should be considered appropriate things to measure.
4. Scores, as between groups or individuals, must be intelligible and should reveal varying behaviors from positive to negative.
5. Events should relate directly to some change goal.
6. Simple measures are best; such abstractions as honesty and quality require great ingenuity to measure publicly.
7. Some easily available scoreboard is needed so that those who determine scores are regularly aware of them.
8. Procedures to quick-cure negative spirals must be ready.
9. Measures should not require uniform behavior from people.
10. Considerable thought must go into deciding whether it is better to score positive (desired) events or negative (unwanted) events or both.

While these guidelines are practical and useful, they are not meant to oversimplify the basic problem of measurement which obsesses management scientists. Ongoing research should continually supply improvements to these thoughts. For example, in a campaign which needs employee innovations as a component, it would be foolish to measure hours worked on innovations or hours conducting library research. The employee could be on the job and in a stupor or trance, but he would get a perfect score. Scores should relate to goals, not to pious assumptions about people's behavior in an organization or to contributory activities.

The South Seas village example provides an elegant solution to the measurement question. The measurement system reinforced desired behaviors, increased social pressure in the right direction, created involvement naturally, and helped the prophecy "we can save the children" to self-fulfill. That's the art of measurement we seek in every change system.

Negative Spirals

Many sales managers are at times dismayed when carefully planned sales contests create sales records that spiral down instead of up. A few negative events can impair the morale of a sales crew, particularly if the selling tasks are difficult, and will reinforce natural fears of failure instead of desires for success. Change, like all human activities, can be positive or negative. People can fulfill whatever condition they think is most likely, including organization disaster. For these reasons, a measurement system that commits an organization to placing its daily performance on public view must have available some procedures to stop-loss the possible downward spirals, which are as likely to occur as the upward ones. This is particularly true during the period of uncertainty when new beginnings are attempted.

How can change team managers prevent downward spirals from plaguing their change measurements? In each organization, hard mental effort will be needed to develop many procedures for this purpose. Here are a few suggestions:

1. Make all first steps of the process easy to take.

2. Keep goals close to existing situations so that slight improvements can push scores up. Time enough later on to raise your sights.

3. Before any public attempt, provide information on how people in other organizations have done well by using similar measures.

4. Eliminate threat from the situation; it tends to make people realize the worst results.

5. Initiate marathon communications procedures on the change goal: how much it will do for everyone, its social importance, its ability to distribute economic benefits, its attainability, how it will work, and how it might be achieved. This will give people a clearer idea of *why* the goal and its measurements are important.

6. If downward spiraling persists, break up all normal activities—perhaps for special training purposes—and engage in wholly new and unusual programs briefly to spark attention and awareness. After the diversion, allow only a few people—the most positive—to return to measured activities; then, as their results are recorded positively, bring back the whole group slowly.

7. If all else fails, bring in new people to do the same work and insulate them from the group while they record improved scores. As a last resort, change leadership or group structure.

From these comments it should be clear that negative spirals are a risk continually present in all organizations and visible in measurement systems. Shaking any organization out of its sleepy low-performance normalcy makes life uncertain. We will never run short of people whose perversity impels them to destructive behavior whenever they are disturbed from their usual rut. Change team members will be on their guard to maneuver out of these situations with specific programs and actions once the situations start to deteriorate.

Upward Spirals

Because humans and human organizations are normally constructive, upward spirals will be relatively frequent; most measurement systems will be dealing regularly with upward spirals and rarely with downward ones. By the time any organization has weathered the first one-third of a change process, negative spirals will be out of the picture except as a result of exterior disaster. A variety of conditions affect measurements of upward spirals, and change system managers should watch for them. Some examples follow.

1. Fascination with scoring devices of any kind can impel group members to realize continually improving scores by sacrificing secondary restraints. This happens when throughput of products goes up but quality and appearance go down. In recent years both American and foreign-made automobiles have suffered from situations in which cars rolled off the assembly lines with far too many manufacturing flaws that were not quickly visible. This illustrates the operation of a typical device: it records the numbers required by management and then a bit more to gain praise, but it passes through products which others must finish, repair, or refit. Many a car or tractor dealer has had to finish the assembly line job for which the production crew has taken misplaced credit.

The integrity of individuals, groups, divisions, and managements is necessary to any measurement system. Ways can be found to cut down or reverse scores for ignored or omitted secondary values in any process and thereby make clear that everyone is really measuring *the whole performance*.

2. The second issue is who is measuring whom and why. Measurements of employees by management soon deteriorate into games of getting even. If, however, a group and its *own* leaders decide to get somewhere and realize that only by measuring several key variables can they find out if they are moving in the right direction, then measurements go into the group mores and are *theirs*. Remember the flies and the clean streets of the South Seas village? Those were their flies, their clean streets, their children, and their pride in the results.

To answer the why question with some arbitrary management reason is also self-defeating. "Why" must be to attain a goal everyone in the group would *like* to achieve. Once the South Seas villagers found the proper procedures, nothing could stand against the power of the goal: to save the children.

3. There are very few scoring systems of any human activity, from football to golf to net profits to income taxes, in which people generally have perfect confidence. In far too many cases we can see people warp, twist, gloss over, or in one way or another prejudice the scoring results. As a result, change system teams have an uphill road to travel in gaining credence for their measures by either organization components or top managers.

We have had good cause for cynicism about the score, particularly where managements of organizations can influence the outcome in private. In the United States integrity of scoring in any activity from gambling to time cards is far more prevalent than in many other cultures. Even here, however, there is a long way to go in improving public confidence. Chapter 5 presented some examples of measurement systems of communications. For the benefit of change team members concerned about what to measure, a detailed discussion of unique scoring systems follows.

Innovation Events Score

The innovative capacities of an organization are rarely measured or even allowed to flower. Assuming that a change goal is great enough that it cannot be accomplished without the help of a hotly innovative organization, how does one proceed to score innovativeness?

First, the welcome mat must be spread for innovation by all types of employees in all job classifications. It will not do to allow innovations to emerge *only* from R&D or any other staff groups. This welcome mat program should exchange innovation for cash, promotion, recognition, responsible evaluation, and implementation. The literature of innovation research should provide managers with guidance on these issues. The record of people who have left organizations to implement their valuable innovations elsewhere should be reason enough for concern about these procedures.

Second, because most innovations which people think up are not truly useful, a way must be found to contrast innovation development with both necessary and unnecessary innovation elimination. This is not easy.

FIGURE 7-1.   Quantity of innovation events; totals per month.

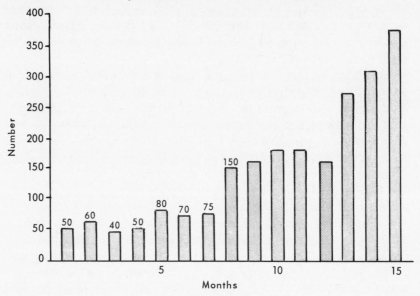

FIGURE 7-2.   Innovation acceptance versus rejection.

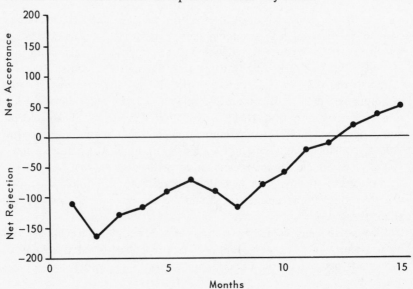

A scoring system that establishes simple rules of classification for innovations might be useful to portray the extent of an organization's development of this skill. To resolve issues of quality, the rules might be that each innovation turned in by an employee or group of employees will be counted publicly only if it gains the endorsement of at least two out of five screening agents. These scores might be set up by managers selected from R&D, long-range planning, marketing, personnel, top management, engineering, or immediate supervision.

Each innovation could be described and submitted by the innovator to all five screening agents. Once the innovation received a general endorsement from at least two out of five screeners, the innovator could turn in his idea to be scored by the change team, as well as to be processed and considered as an innovation. Thus measurement of scores could be plotted and look like the steadily improving situation in Figure 7-1. A measure of organization capacity to innovate could thus be established.

Obviously, an increase in the number of innovations, even with some screening by experienced managers, is not enough to reveal the whole story of organization behavior regarding innovations. The next measure helps bring the story home to everyone in the organization. Here the change system team records the number of already screened innovations that are actually adopted in contrast to those that are finally rejected. Pending items are ignored unless they are so high a proportion of the total that they constitute a finding in and of themselves. To get a total score for each month, the change system team scores innovations rejected as minus items and innovations accepted as plus items. The resulting plus or minus total can be graphed, as in Figure 7-2, to display another facet of organization acceptance of new ideas.

Managers will quickly discern ways to beat the scoring mechanisms, as by turning in strings of minor but useful innovations, but such factors can be dealt with by the change team and by serious-minded employees. After all, the true purpose must be clung to with determination. Figure 7-3 shows how one might quickly lay bare an attempt to beat the system by turning in volumes of minor innovations. Here the dollar value —it could be time value—of each innovation is charted. When it is observed that, for example, most innovations cluster at lower levels, managers can decide to eliminate from future consideration all innovations whose potential effect is less than $100,000 per annum. These can be handled elsewhere and thus maintain organization focus on the large breakthroughs needed. By such means and by superior ones which astute managers will devise, the organization can focus on activities which

directly relate to its capacities for radical change as well as its basic
health.

Obstacle Removal Rate

Another useful measure can come from the summary of obstacles to
change which organization members perceive and describe in an organization survey. This could produce a total of, say, 500 obstacles. The
measurement system would then deal with the rate of removal of internal obstacles as seen by those immediately involved. Obstacles could
be such hurdles to change as:

Unrealistic quality controls
Outmoded machinery
Uneducated supervisors
Militant unionism
Narrow management policies
Manager secretiveness
Mistrust of employees
Symbolic division of rank
Manager insistence on unquestioning obedience

The change team would accept the total as defined by the organization's members. Once individual programs were set up to attack each
area, the change team or any other group could decide the time had
come to measure whether the obstacle had been removed by these efforts. A brief local opinion survey of those directly affected could obtain a vote on the issue. Two-thirds yes could define an obstacle as
removed. As these processes went on—somewhat laboriously because
obstacles to change built up brick by brick over the years are hard to

FIGURE 7-3.   Innovation potential for production savings.

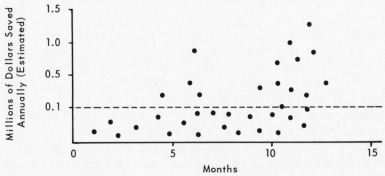

FIGURE 7-4.   Change obstacle removal record.

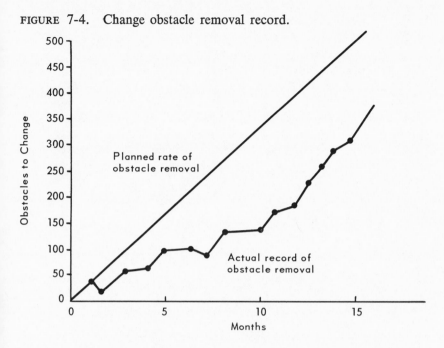

tear down—the time would come when the scoring system would look like Figure 7-4. Organization members, knowing the difficulty of the process, could derive great satisfaction from seeing these records.

Adoption of Change Goals

As change processes continue in any organization, the issue of acceptance/rejection by work groups of process goals and conditions will become more acute. In a company seeking a new organization structure, group and individual defenses of the old structures will increase as their demise becomes evident. Nothing is so hard to lose as an unworkable but familiar tradition.

In trying to develop new organization patterns, change team members should remember the beggar from Benares. He cursed the medical team that cured the sores he had been using to ply his trade. They removed his life pattern by removing his sores, and they had no way to give him another means of support. The moral is: Never remove an organization element without having its replacement ready to bear the load. This factor relates to the rate of adoption of organization change goals and procedures, and so also do the dissemination of information, the presence of new technology, a change in location, and other changes going on in the organization.

In measuring change adoption, our first assumption is that there are many levels of compliance well short of wholehearted cooperation. We seek the emergence of consensus, group by group. An organization may consist of 300 work groups, levels, or regional components. As for a particular change goal plus the procedure to attain it, the change team may perceive that it needs a minimum of 75 percent adoption. How to measure this? Rather than enter into the ramifications of content, it is suggested that adoption of a given goal be evaluated as follows by each group member.

Select One

1. Our group rejects this goal for good reason.   ( )
2. Our group has some problems with this goal.   ( )
3. Our group is indifferent to this goal.   ( )
4. Our group generally favors this goal.   ( )
5. Our group is committed 100 percent to realize   ( )
   this goal

The approach is to have each work group member—say, a personnel office staff or a production line group that works together—rate itself on the single change goal issue. Once 50 percent of a group scores 4 and 5 on the preceding list, the group can be considered to have

FIGURE 7-5.   Change goal A adoption record.

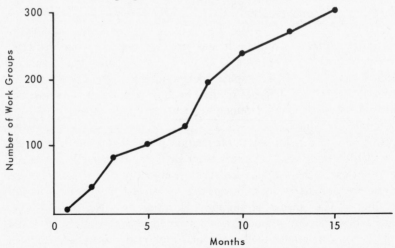

adopted the goal. When 225 (75 percent) or more of the 300 work groups fall into this category, the change team can legitimately state to management that the organization has adopted the goal. Managers will quickly recognize from the initially low scores of this measure that far more than a set of arbitrary orders or long-range plans from top management is necessary to penetrate the thinking of a 75 percent majority of work groups in this fashion. Note Figure 7-5.

Major Work Process Improvements

Any radical change goal of substance might well contain cost reduction programs of 20 to 30 percent or production rate improvements of 30 to 40 percent. Normally such increases are simply not available to an organization's steady state mode of operations. Managers can usually feel very happy with consistent 2 or 3 percent per annum improvements in these areas. Increases of 20 or 30 percent are usually considered impossible, and in fact they are unless radical change is attempted or extraordinary good luck occurs.

How does radical change occur? In small, steady increments or in large chunks of progress? If we focus on small increments, do we eliminate the possibilities of major breakthroughs because our risk taking is too meager? A manager's experience tells him that improvements come slowly and painfully. Must we deny him his experience?

The message here is that small increments are not truly the steps to a change process. They are the grist of the adaptation process discussed in Chapter 1 and the normal straining to do well inherent in any steady state condition. This is not to deny that if large-scale changes take place in an organization, a tremendous amount of filling in with smaller changes is necessary to solidify gains. The main effort, however, must be to increase the large-scale breakthroughs.

How, then, do we measure major work process improvements in a change process? What will we measure? One answer is to use futures forecasting and change system planning techniques to uncover the eight to ten key breakthroughs now unrevealed but necessary to the change process. Achieving these becomes the work process improvement objective; scoring is a matter of deciding upon appropriate steps in the process of attaining these goals. Figure 7-6 illustrates this situation for a private college seeking transformation from its current status to a lifetime learning institution fitted for tomorrow's world. These work process goals of an education institution could be achieved only within

FIGURE 7-6. Work process improvements.

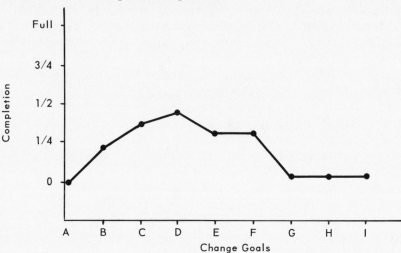

A. Establish competing faculties.

B. Eliminate official groupings by age.

C. Establish 18-hour-a-day, 7 day-a-week operation.

D. Establish a 12-month year.

E. Automate two-thirds of all courses.

F. Eliminate tenure and all other rigidities that affect ability to educate.

G. Obtain sufficient capital to conduct operations and create cash flow.

H. Eliminate all degrees.

I. Sell off buildings.

a radical change system dedicated to tomorrow's needs for education as a pervasive, lifetime learning element of society instead of its present limited role. At any point college management could fairly easily assess its own progress in these areas.

Change Goal Gap Reduction

A basic principle affecting the change process is that once any goal has been fully adopted, an organization and all the groups and individuals within it will tend to reduce the gap—the unsatisfied tension—between where they are now, their present state, and where they would be if the goals were realized, their future state. The precept is, "When a future state is strongly desired, a multitude of forces will tend toward its realization." When change goals are truly adopted and understood at all levels, considerable useful pressure and movement can be generated in any organization by the display of goal gaps.

Other Organization Variables

Without exhausting the list, three measurable organization variables are suggested here as relatively easy to measure and score by the change system team.

1. *Span of control.* This measure involves simple walk-through interviews with supervisors and managers to find the number of persons who report to each one directly. The findings are plotted to display span of control variations in the organization. Comparison can then be made with top manager preferences, the needs of the change process, and the discussions of what is good and bad in this respect in management literature.

2. *Ratio of administrative to production employees.* In any work unit, department, or division of an organization, this measure can be obtained from a study of manning tables plus on-the-ground inspection of work behavior. These data can then be plotted as ratios. Management and employees will need to consider the future needs of the changed organization carefully to decide what a desirable ratio is.

3. *Interdepartmental interactions.* A simple self-administered record of the number of times employees and supervisors interact for any reason with employees and supervisors of other departments over a two-week period will create data for this score. It measures horizontal as well as vertical interactions and can be very useful in portraying either closed or open organization structures.

Measurement Can Be Positive Reinforcement

As the various factors in the change process improve, a public scoreboard provides positive reinforcement to all employees. People see things getting better and thus tend to enhance the positive behaviors that raise the score and restrain the negative behaviors that would reduce the score. A good example of this in the area of normal work improvements is reported by the Emery Air Freight Corporation.[1] A performance improvement program has saved the company an estimated $2 million over a three-year period. The program involves:

— Self-paced programmed learning for salesmen. (Sales jumped from $62.4 to $79.8 million in a year.)

— Self-recording of customer service events that more than tripled the speed of services.

— Profitability ratings that let employees know which operations were profitable and which were not. For example, containerized shipments jumped from 45 to 95 percent, sometimes in a single day.

— A specific commitment to let *each employee* know every day how he is doing on what counts most in his job.

Composite Indices

The complexity of organization change requires that top managers combine the kinds of single measures presented earlier, which may be quite useful as positive reinforcement on the plant floor, with other measures. As J. J. O'Connell [2] has pointed out, behavior data and economic performance data must be combined to construct composite indices that are meaningful to top management. Designing a monitoring system for change processes involves many such subtle considerations and requires that we examine the system in many dimensions to fully understand what is going on. This does not mean that we should become lost in the complex considerations of measurement by which experts sometimes prove that nothing can be measured; it does mean that top managers will want to concentrate closely on what is measured and how it is measured. As stated earlier, change what you measure and you may change all.

New ideas for measurement will come from our ambitions to seek radical change. The next chapter suggests that, when we consider the twenty-first century, we can be sure that what we measure in our organizations then will be very different from what we measure now.

References

The quotation of Harold Wilensky is from *Organizational Intelligence* (New York: Basic Books, 1967); that of Daniel P. Moynihan is from *Toward Balanced Growth: Quantity with Quality*. A Report of the National Goals Research Staff (Washington, D.C.: GPO, 1970); that of Robert L. Johnson and Irwin H. Derman is from "How Intelligent Is Your MIS?" *Business Horizons,* February 1970; and that of Tom Burns is from *Methods of Organizational Research* (Pittsburgh: University of Pittsburgh Press, 1967).

1. "New Tool: Reinforcement for Good Work," *Psychology Today,* April 1972.
2. J. J. O'Connell, *Managing Organizational Innovation* (Homewood, Ill.: Irwin, 1968).

PART THREE

Organizations
Tomorrow

CHAPTER EIGHT

21st Century Requirements of 20th Century Organizations

Our civilization is running out of control, overwhelmed by its own resources and opportunities, as well as its superabundant fecundity.

LEWIS MUMFORD

The end of acquiescence poses challenges to all societies.

ROBERT L. HEILBRONER

When watching men of power in action, it must be always kept in mind that, whether they know it or not, their main purpose is the elimination or neutralization of the independent individual—the independent voter, consumer, worker, owner, thinker—and that every device they employ aims at turning man into a manipulatable "animated instrument," which is Aristotle's definition of a slave.

ERIC HOFFER

Many of our institutions have performed very well the tasks which we set for them a few decades ago. However, in so doing they have created unanticipated problems with which we must now deal.

NATIONAL GOALS RESEARCH STAFF

Those who have been awed by the magnitude, the complexity, and the cost of an organization attempting a change system to transform itself must at times wonder what vast global emergency could demand such paroxysms of activity from our organizations and institutions, indeed from whole societies.

The emergency already exists, as well-informed persons are aware. Despite widespread admiration of economic development, there is a general breakdown of confidence among informed leadership all over the world in the industrial society and the values upon which it was built. Many among our leaders see continued industrialization and growth as inadvertently destroying life on this planet. Men devoted their lives to what they thought was the constructive and useful development of great industries, great cities, or great transportation networks and are appalled that, having been built, these systems should so quickly plague their communities with smog, noise, defeatism, dirt, unemployment, moral degradation, ugly habitations, and a sharply lowered quality of life.

What went wrong? We thought we were building a better world; we know that by industrial growth we improved the jobs, the incomes, and the welfare of millions of people around the world who now live more comfortably because of our effort. Why is that not enough? Why are revolution and change a daily topic for discussion? Why are so many people deeply dissatisfied? There are two things to keep in mind when we look for an answer: (1) Nobody planned it that way. (2) It has happened before.

Now let us examine what responsible analysts forecast for our society in the twenty-first century. In one estimate for the year 2000, the problems created by the inadvertent side effects of market economy growth that seem so cataclysmic today will be solved in large part. The heat will have gone out of them, and the growth of business and industrial enterprises will continue much as it does today.

In another, equally likely forecast we will resist most demands for change and thereby plunge ourselves into several decades of drastic, violent, internal revolution and guerrilla warfare. The society which emerges from that chaos will be either freer and more wholesome or far more rigidly controlled—a collectivist state which buries our greatest human potentials for many decades if not forever.

No business, government, or institutional planner can much longer ignore these widely variant possibilities of the society he serves. When the corporate planner spells out a long-range plan for the board of directors of his organization to consider, he is projecting into an extremely cloudy and dangerous future in the last third of the twentieth century.

Too few organization planners account for anything beyond economics or technology.

As we all know, it is perfectly possible to be presented with a major societal challenge and to ignore it in planning or in any other management function, but not for long. To provide each manager with a sharp realization of how unusually great a change in his thinking and behavior, both personal and organizational, our times seem to demand of him, consider Albert Speer's tragedy. Speer lived his most productive years as an architect designing giant projects for the Nazi government. He was part of Adolf Hitler's inner circle. In his memoirs [1] he says:

> One of the purposes of these memoirs is to reveal some of the premises which almost inevitably led to the disasters in which that period culminated. I have sought to show what came of one man's holding unrestricted power in his hands and also to clarify the nature of this man. In court at Nuremberg I said that if Hitler had had any friends, I would have been his friend. I owe to him the enthusiasms and the glory of my youth as well as belated horror and guilt.

Today, in our media, many commentators anxious to avert such "belated horror and guilt" are sounding off about the human damage caused by our market economy working through our organizations in our society on our fellow Americans. They are not alarmists. Neither is Speer when he wonders how an upper-middle-class professional such as he was could have been so blind and indifferent to the great human outrages going on around him. He says:

> Quite often even the most important step in a man's life, his choice of vocation, is taken quite frivolously. He does not bother to find out enough about the basis and the various aspects of that vocation. Once he has chosen it, he is inclined to switch off his critical awareness and to fit himself wholly into the predetermined career.
>
> My decision to enter Hitler's party was no less frivolous. Why, for example, was I willing to abide by the almost hypnotic impression Hitler's speech had made upon me? Why did I not undertake a thorough, systematic investigation of, say, the value or worthlessness of the ideologies of *all* the parties? Why did I not read the various party programs, or at least Hitler's *Mein Kampf* and Rosenberg's *Myth of the Twentieth Century?*

We must ask Speer's questions of ourselves. Why do we not question the honor, integrity, and goals of our organizations and their leaders? How can we commit so much of our lives to groups or people we never question? Is there enough money to buy such obedient blindness? Speer goes on to discuss organization behavior which one can see every day in "modern" organizations wherein men avoid any inquiry on the basic issues.

Had I only wanted to, I could have found out even then that Hitler was proclaiming expansion of the Reich to the east; that he was a rank anti-Semite; that he was committed to a system of authoritarian rule; that after attaining power he intended to eliminate democratic procedures and would thereafter yield only to force. Not to have worked that out for myself; not, given my education, to have read books, magazines, and newspapers of various viewpoints; not to have tried to see through the whole apparatus of mystification was already criminal. At this initial stage my guilt was as grave as, at the end, my work for Hitler. *For being in a position to know and nevertheless shunning knowledge creates direct responsibility for the consequences—from the very beginning.* (Italics added)

In trying to explain to himself how he could have acquired habits of thought or attitudes which permitted him to join in one of the world's most monstrous and vicious errors, Speer said that in his schooling there was no room for criticism of courses or subject matter, let alone of the ruling powers in the state. "Unconditional faith in the authority of the school was required. It never even occurred to us to doubt the order of things, for as students we were subjected to the dictates of a virtually absolutist system."

Many government agencies, churches, schools, and even companies now operate under exactly that kind of rigidity of thought control around the world and even in our own "open" society. Will they be able to stomach its bitter fruit? Speer reports that the drive that moved him was his need for a way to ply his profession. He was up against an era of general business malaise, and he wanted to build buildings. He saw he was manipulated by Hitler, who gave him buildings to build as the price for his soul. He admitted, "For the commission to do a great building, I would have sold my soul like Faust. Now I had found my Mephistopheles. He seemed no less engaging than Goethe's."

No one can read this book of honest and courageous confession, or many other books on Nazi Germany, and not realize that the men and women who perpetrated or acquiesced in those vast social outrages were identical with you and me. These were our brothers on this planet, and what was in them then is in you and me. When our young people say, "We have met the enemy and they are us," they demonstrate that they fully understand this bitter reality.

It is terrible to contemplate how well-meaning people like Speer (or like you and me) would go on with their work in an organization and ignore the brutish smashing of civilization and people going on around them. In painful honesty, Speer admitted his leadership had found a useful way to manipulate him. They paid his price. Is someone paying yours? It is a device much used today by businesses, institutions, and governments all over the world. It is used in *your* organization. Speer also says:

> The ordinary party member was being taught that grand policy was much too complex for him to judge it. Consequently, one felt one was being *represented*, never called upon to take personal responsibility. The whole structure of the system was aimed at preventing conflicts of conscience from even arising. The result was the total sterility of all conversations and discussions among these like-minded persons. It was boring for people to confirm one another in their uniform opinions.
>
> Worse still was the restriction of responsibility to one's own field. That was explicitly demanded. Everyone kept to his own group—of architects, physicians, jurists, technicians, soldiers, or farmers. The professional organizations to which everyone had to belong were called chambers (Physicians' Chamber, Art Chamber), and this term aptly described the way people were immured in isolated, closed-off areas of life. The longer Hitler's system lasted, the more people's minds moved within such isolated chambers.

We can think of this every time we allow groups to isolate themselves in phony professionalism or we wall them off from others by the arrangements we make in our organizations. Are we again fiddling while Rome burns? If we fail to develop new ways to cooperate as equal human beings in the resolving of socially destructive forces in society, we make ourselves as guilty for what will come as Albert Speer was for the tragedy of Nazi Germany.

Therefore, we can be sure that those who follow us after the year 2000 and for the next several millennia have a direct claim on our conscience and on our behavior today. They will have to live with major decisions we make or allow to be made. We can very easily leave them an utterly rigid, centrally controlled dictatorship much like the government that China, Cuba, or Russia intends today. The business-as-usual policy has led to that before. Some of our leading writers, media commentators, politicians, young people, and academics actually want that to happen and are working toward that end. In contrast, we may decide to open the door to the next great flowering of civilization wherein all human beings will have found new ways to be free, independent individuals within a much more effective societal system.

It would be pleasant, perhaps, to look forward to an era of stability, but almost all the signs of our times point to radical transitions in the years ahead. There is no escape from this condition no matter how many drugs, diversions, or amusements we occupy our minds with, nor does it matter how many blinders we put on to avoid looking at the consequences of our "time of transition." After World War II our technologies and markets roared ahead to satisfy pent-up demands. Most people got their share of goodies. Then the unwanted side effects of an exploding, not completely aware technology expressed in business, industry, government, and education organizations began a sickening fallout from the clouds of euphoria in which we lived.

Our times now combine (1) vast, unsatisfied social demands, (2) technological side effects from a worldwide market economy, (3) a huge, new, hard-to-understand technology for postindustrialism and fractured organizations and institutions much too frail for these loads. Add instant worldwide communications to this and you have completed the formula for high-speed social transition. But what do some of the wisest observers of our times say? Let us look at a series of quotations describing several alternative futures for the United States, and by projection, for the whole world.

First, let me say that although there are many "the world is coming to an end" forecasters among us, most are best avoided. The track record of doom-crying soothsayers is poor. Despite the superb tapestry of change painted by Alvin Toffler in *Future Shock,* more victims of automobile accidents will go into physical shock than our times will send into future shock. We're a resilient species, despite all our serious problems. In facing the realities of our problems this work reflects a convinced optimism that mankind can meet and overcome any "doom" except a stellar explosion in our vicinity.

Future 1-A

The Hudson Institute and Herman Kahn define a basic surprise-free and largely business-as-usual projection. This is their "Hudson Standard World 1-A Basic Projection for the next decade or two, i.e., the world of 1990." [2] Our times are fortunate to have a Hudson Institute at work among us. Their work does not shrink from unpleasant truths. This projection suggests a world very much like the one we live in. The following is a description of what World 1-A will be like. Kahn envisions:

1. Some revival, some evolutionary development, and some erosion of "La Deuxième Belle Epoque." [Kahn's phrase for the decades im-

mediately following World War II]. A general but irregular movement toward a multipolar but economically unified half of the world (the half or so of the world's people which participate intensely in the world economy) but with countervailing tendencies toward anarchy as well as order. The nation-state system is largely maintained with about 15 large nations (see below) and more than 100 small nations.

2. This *politically increasingly multipolar* world should see in the 70s the "end" of the "post WW II" era (including an effective political settlement of that war) and the following "consequences."

A. Rise of Japan as an economic, financial, and technological superstate (and possibly political and/or military superpower).

B. Rise of France to the largest national economy (at least nominally in terms of GNP) in Western Europe.

C. Almost full reemergence of both Germanies (but some political disabilities are likely to remain).

D. As indicated in the list below, an emergence (or increased independence and assertiveness) of new regional and large powers.

E. U.S.-Soviet strategic equality—or possibly even Soviet superiority —accompanied by a relative decline of both superpowers in power, prestige, and influence.

F. An enlarged EEC, with perhaps *a new role for France* as the "leading nation" of the community—also possibility of a breakup of the current enlarged EEC.

G. Possible creation of an *Eastern European EEC*.

H. At least ad hoc creation and perhaps self-conscious advancement of a very dynamic (economically) Pacific Hemisphere Trading/ Investment Area (PAHTIA).

I. Many other new possibilities: e.g., new alliances, new arms races, politically unified Europe, intensely isolationist U.S., etc.

3. Some acceleration, some continuation but also some selective topping off of *multifold trend* (and perhaps some temporary reversals).

A. Further intensification of many issues associated with a *1985 technological crisis;* growing need for worldwide (but probably ad hoc) "zoning ordinances" and other environmental and social controls.

B. Other problems in coping with sheer numbers, size, and bigness.

C. With important exceptions, erosion of (*12*) *traditional societal levers;* a *search for meaning and purpose, some cultural confusion, polarization, conflict.*

D. Increasingly "revisionist" *Communism, Capitalism* and *Christianity* in Europe and the Western Hemisphere; perhaps a "Crisis in Liberalism"—some persistence and even eruption of the counterculture.

E. *Populist, conservative, backlash,* and/or "counter-reformation" movements.

F. Increasing problem (worldwide) of *educated incapacity* and/or illusioned, irrelevant, or ideological argumentation—greater explicit emphasis on feeling and emotion.

4. *Emergence of various styles of postindustrial culture* for nations with about 20 percent of world's population and in enclaves elsewhere characterized by:

A. *New political milieus:* Rise of "humanist left," "responsible center" confrontation in at least high culture of developed nations (but in particular in the U.S. and northwest tier of Europe).

B. Emergence of *"mosaic cultures"* (at least in U.S.) incorporating esoteric, deviant, communal, and/or experimental life-styles. Some increase in anarchistic behavior and movements—ideological and political development of the counterculture.

C. Possible successful synthesis between old and new in France, Japan, Scandinavia, northwest tier, or elsewhere.

5. Above sets context for *further development of a unified* but multipolar and (partially) competitive (half) global economy.

A. A general understanding of the process and techniques for *sustained economic development.*

B. A worldwide *"green revolution";* also a worldwide capability for modern industry and technology.

C. Growing importance of MNC's as *innovators of economic activity and engines of rapid growth.*

D. High (3–15 percent) GNP almost everywhere—five especially dynamic areas.

E. Sustained *growth in trade, communications, travel.*

F. Increasing *unity from technology, private industry, commercial and financial institutions,* but relatively little by international legal and political institutions.

G. Some development of *year 2000* (and/or compound interest) *ideologies.*

H. Little or no long-term overall catastrophic difficulties with environment, pollution, or scarcity of resources, though there will be many temporary crises and doubtless some limited catastrophies.

6. Thus a relatively anarchic but also relatively orderly and unified world with *new issues of international control:*

A. Continuing growth in *discretionary behavior,* corresponding worldwide (foreign and domestic) *"Law and Order"* issues. Some growth in violence, deviant, or criminal behavior.

B. Probably increase in terror, violence, subversion, unilateral changes of international rules, etc.

7. *Some important but "nonsignificant" surprises* and perhaps some significant ones as well.

In this Hudson Institute projection we sail a rocking boat but we sail on. At the White House Conference, Kahn also presented a projection of the world's gross national product for the 1980s.

Likely GNP of the 15 or so Large Nations in 1980
(Trillions of 1970 $)

1.5	United States
0.9	U.S.S.R.
0.5	Japan
0.25	France, West Germany
0.1–0.2	China, United Kingdom, Italy, Canada, India
0.05–0.1	(perhaps Brazil, Australia, East Germany, Mexico, Sweden, Poland, and/or Argentina or Indonesia)

Managers of large organizations and institutions can take comfort in these projections because, in view of current conditions and recent experience, they certainly "feel right." In addition, most Americans have not lost confidence in our ability to deal with huge problems and to master them. It may be useful to contemplate the "large problems" which Hudson Institute realistically sets down and suggests we shall have mastered if World 1-A comes to pass in 1990. Calculate for yourself if our society, its government, its businesses, and its social structures can overcome these "special technological dangers."

1985 Technological Crises—Hudson Institute
Areas Likely to Give Rise to Special Technological Dangers

I. Intrinsically Dangerous Technology
    A. Modern means of mass destruction.
    B. Nuclear reactors—fission or fusion.
    C. Nuclear explosives, high-speed gas centrifuges, etc.
    D. Research missiles, satellite launchers, commercial aircraft, etc.
    E. Biological and chemical "progress."
    F. Molecular biology and genetics.
    G. "Mind control."
    H. New techniques for insurgency, crime, terror, or ordinary violence.
    I. New techniques for counterinsurgency or imposition of order.
    J. New "serendipities" and "synergisms."
II. Gradual Worldwide and/or National Contamination
or Degradation of the Environment
    A. Radioactive debris from various peaceful nuclear uses.
    B. Possible greenhouse or other effects from increased CO_2 in the atmosphere, or new ice age because of dust in stratosphere, etc.

C. Other special dangerous wastes—methyl mercury, DDT, etc.

D. Waste heat.

E. Other less dangerous but environment-degrading wastes such as debris and garbage.

F. Noise, ugliness, and other annoying byproducts of many modern activities.

G. Excessive urbanization.

H. Excessive overcrowding.

I. Excessive tourism.

J. Insecticides, fertilizers, growth "chemicals," food additives, plastic containers, etc.

III. Spectacular and/or Multinational Contamination or Degradation of the Environment

A. Nuclear war.

B. Nuclear testing.

C. Bacteriological and chemical war or accident.

D. Artificial moons.

E. Projects West Ford, Storm Fury, etc.

F. Supersonic transportation (shock waves).

G. Weather control.

H. Big "geomorphological" projects.

I. Million-ton tankers (Torry Canyon was only 111,825 tons) and million-pound planes.

J. Other enterprises or mechanisms of "excessive" size.

IV. Dangerous Internal Political Issues

A. Computerized records.

B. Other computerized surveillance.

C. Other advanced techniques for surveillance.

D. Excessively degradable (or unreliably reassuring) centralized capabilities.

E. Improved knowledge of (and techniques for) agitprop and other methods of creating disturbances and disruption.

F. Improved knowledge of, and techniques for, preventing disturbances.

G. Complex or critical governmental issues leading to either "technocracy" or "caesarism."

H. Nuclear weapons affecting internal politics.

I. Excessively illusioned attitudes.

J. Other dangerous attitudes.

V. Upsetting International Consequences

A. Both new and "traditional" demonstration effects.

B. Technological obsolescence of "unskilled" labor.

C. New synthetics or processes—e.g., coffee, oil from shale, etc.

D. Forced modernization.

    E. Growing guilt feelings by many in wealthy nations—particularly among the alienated or young.

    F. Inexpensive and widely available "realistic" communications and physical travel.

    G. Accelerated "brain drains."

    H. Cheap (synthetic?) food.

    I. Cheap education.

    J. Control and exploitation of the oceans, space, moon.

VI. Dangerous Personal Choices

    A. Sex determination.

    B. Other genetic engineering.

    C. Psychedelic and mood-affecting drugs.

    D. Electronic stimulation of pleasure centers.

    E. Other methods of sensual satisfaction.

    F. Excessive permissiveness and indulgence.

    G. Dropping out and other alienation.

    H. Excessive narcissism or other self-regard.

    I. Super-cosmetology.

    J. Lengthy hibernation.

VII. Bizarre Issues

    A. Generational changes, e.g., extended longevity.

    B. Mechanically dependent humans, e.g., pacemakers.

    C. Life and death for an individual, e.g., artificial kidneys, etc.

    D. New forms of humanity, e.g., "live" computers.

    E. "Compulsory" birth control for "impossible" groups.

    F. Other external controls or influence on what should be personal or even institutionally private choices.

    G. Life and death sanctions or other control of "outlaw" societies which have not yet committed any traditional crime.

    H. Even the continuation of the nation-state system.

    I. Controlling and limiting change and innovation.

    J. Radical ecological changes on a planetary scale.

    K. Interplanetary contamination.

That Hudson Institute list should convince the reader that our organizations and social structures will shortly go through the wringer.

Another participant at the White House Conference was Willis W. Harman, distinguished futurist and director of the Center for the Study of Social Policy, Stanford Research Institute. Harman [3] says that

technically advanced societies like the United States are undergoing a major historical transformation to some sort of postindustrial age characterized by diminishing dominance of industrial production as a social function, by increased prominence of service activities, and by increased concern with value questions related to quality of life. Opinions are more varied on the matter of how rapid and extreme this change will be in values, perceptions, and institutions. I shall summarize the case, based on a number of systematic and historical analyses, that the shift is likely to be *rapid, extreme, and hazardous.*

This forecast is in distinct contrast to the view that the available alternative futures comprise modest deviations from a "long-term multifold trend," with slow changes in social institutions and cultural values. I am keenly aware that it is not possible at this time to demonstrate whether one view or the other is the more correct. Five years from now the situation may be clearer; at this point both views are held by groups of reasonable men.

Thus I want to examine with you the arguments suggesting that forces toward an abrupt and drastic modification of the "long-term, multifold trend" may eventuate in a revolutionary social change within the next two decades. . . . History gives us little reason . . . to think we can escape without . . . economic decline . . . disruption of social processes considerably greater than anything we have experienced or care to imagine.

Harman goes on to say that

the industrialized world may be experiencing the beginning phase of a sociocultural revolution as profound and pervasive in its effects on all segments of the society as the Industrial Revolution, the Reformation, or the Fall of Rome. I hasten to add that I am not speaking of "The Greening of America" nor of the achieving of any of the popularly promoted Utopias. The shape of the future will no more be patterned after the hippie movement and the Youth Revolution than the industrial age could have been inferred from the "new-age values of the Anabaptists."

In describing the society we now have in the United States and in most highly industrialized societies, Harman stresses five supports for the framework or paradigm of the "industrial state":

1. Development and application of scientific method; wedding of scientific and technological advance.
2. Industrialization through organization and division of labor, machine replacement of human labor.
3. Acquisitive materialism; work ethic; economic-man image; belief in unlimited material progress and technological and economic growth.
4. Man seeking control over nature; positivistic theory of knowledge; manipulative rationality as a dominant theme.
5. Individual responsibility for own destiny; freedom and equality as fundamental rights; nihilistic value perspective, individual determination of the "good"; society an aggregate of individuals pursuing their own interests.

In his well-reasoned statement, Dr. Harman presents a list of the factors which history has taught us will lead to revolutionary change. The reader can judge for himself whether the following list of lead indicators of revolutionary change [4] pretty well describes our times.

- Decreased sense of community.
- Increased sense of alienation and purposelessness.
- Increased occurrence of violent crime.
- Increased frequency of personal disorders and mental illness.
- Increased frequency and severity of social disruptions.
- Increased use of police to control behavior.
- Increased public acceptance of hedonistic behavior.
- Increase in amount of noninstitutionalized religious activities.

Believing that the conditions for radical change are here, Harman suggests that the rigid, collectivist, big-government society so many seem to want today may not be a good choice. He sees great difficulties in a return to our recent and current view of entrepreneurial capitalism but advocates a forward-looking redefinition of that system to what he calls humanistic capitalism.

Throughout his statement, Dr. Harman stresses the basic task of reorienting our society's value structures and doing this job in one organization or institution after another. He says:

Requirements for effective functioning of large complex systems naturally support such values as personal honesty, openness (to ensure accurate information flow); responsibility (hence self-actualization); and cooperative trust. The values required in the team that puts a man on the moon and gets him back are a far cry from those that suffice for operation of a used-car lot. Thus as the production and service tasks of the society become more complex, humane values become not only moral but functional imperatives.

An excellent review of how our times might affect the structure of corporations is provided by Roy Amara,[5] president of the Institute for the Future. He describes "some possible inputs of societal trends in the corporation" as we move out of one phase into another, as follows:

Societal or Organization Value Change
Which Moves from Economic Toward Social Emphasis

As Expressed by:
Shareholders: Encourage corporate social involvement but retain largely economic concept of profit.
Employees: Seek meaningful work. Seek less-structured work environment.

Consumers: Press for useful, safe, reliable products that serve genuine consumer needs.

Government: Reexamine and reformulate national goals to reflect public-sector priorities. Provide legislative guidelines and financial incentives to stimulate private initiative in public-sector areas.

The Public: Seek redefinitions of corporate objectives to reflect increasing role in social goals.

Value Change Which Moves from
Industrial Toward Post-Industrial Emphasis

As Expressed by:

Shareholders: Encourage gains in productivity through application of information-related technologies.

Employees: Seek voice in corporate affairs. Seek shorter work week and increased fringe benefits.

Consumers: Demand publication and dissemination of product data. Seek voice in corporate affairs.

Government: Revamp manpower planning programs for retraining, for midcareer changes, and so forth. Encourage productivity gains.

The Public: Seek mechanisms for greater public involvement in corporate boards.

Value Change Which Moves
from Technological Toward Post-Technological Emphasis

As Expressed by:

Shareholders: Seek mechanisms for sharing costs with government for development of new technologies.

Employees: Seek means for hedging against delays, uncertainties, and additional costs of new technologies.

Consumers: Insist on thorough assessments of new technologies affecting consumer.

Government: Encourage balanced development of new technology.

The Public: Demand that corporations understand environmental effects of new technologies.

Value Change Which Moves
from National Toward International Emphasis

As Expressed by:

Shareholders: Encourage development of new technology to meet foreign competition. Look to multinational investment opportunities.

Employees: Seek mechanisms for easing dislocations to employees from foreign competition.
Consumers: Encourage trade measures for reducing costs of consumer products.
Government: Facilitate international trade.
The Public: Support measures for balanced development of international trade.

Another set of projections presented at the 1972 White House Conference on the Industrial World Ahead was prepared by The Conference Board. In his introduction, president Alexander B. Trowbridge states:

[The] findings [of the report] reflect a decision . . . to assume that the basic social structure within which the U.S. economy develops over the next two decades will not be altered radically. . . . This assumption, a part of the conventional methodology of long-term projection, leaves room for evolution of the social structure as in the past.
 . . . At the same time, it should be clear to the reader that the rate of social change can vary. . . . Broad new examinations of goals for the system as a whole are under way in both the private and public sectors. It is altogether possible that structural innovations designed to meet new priorities for the seventies and eighties will greatly alter the outcomes projected here. The findings of the report should thus be treated as representing *one* among a wide range of outcomes for the American economy of 1990, depending on the social ends we choose to seek, and the means by which we pursue them.

A prudent policy for managers in business would probably be to accept the imminent likelihood of radical change in the United States and in most of the industrialized societies around the world. In essence, the twenty-first century presents each manager and informed citizen with this choice:
Either take an active part in the radical changes our times demand, starting with your *own* organization, *or* accept the domination and restructuring of society and business as imposed by either revolutionaries from our countercultures, regulation from backlash reactionaries, or government from other limited-wisdom political/economic power centers.
The book *Things to Come* [6] provides a perspective which relates well to some of our problems today and tomorrow:

There are many historical precedents for a counterreformation. In the late Middle Ages, the people, especially intellectuals, rulers, and educated persons, were largely abandoning the traditional religious emphasis of life in Europe. People, particularly educated people, were much less interested in religion and in the condition of their souls, but seemed to be principally devoted to the improvement of their lives on earth and the enjoyment of the blessings of the material world. This mood came to a screeching halt when Martin Luther nailed his Ninety-Five Theses on the church door at Wittenberg in 1517. For the next 150 years the intellectuals, princes, and commoners of Europe were concerned and convulsed with the questions of religion.

A similar but perhaps less studied turn took place at the end of the first third of the last century. Early nineteenth century England, called "Regency England," was a notoriously materialistic, hedonistic, secular, skeptical, and corrupt society. This was the age of Beau Brummell, scurrilous journalism, and cynical politicians. The English Prime Minister, Lord Melbourne, was a cheerful skeptic. A duchess of this time described her nieces approvingly as "comfortable girls who enjoy a dirty joke." But within a few years there was an almost complete reversal of the moral tone of British society. The British ruling classes soon became staid, serious-minded, religious, and at least outwardly chaste. "Victorian" morality appeared from within a fairly sensate society. There was a time when the older members of the House of Lords had to be careful with their language lest they shock their younger peers. We really do not know what made this happen. We can identify certain harbingers of it in the form of a Romantic counterculture which grew within the bosom of Regency society. Perhaps one explanation is that the corrupt upper classes of England were deeply frightened by the revolutionary upheavals which shook their country—most notably the Chartist movement—and recognized that they had better shape up or they would go the way of their French cousins a generation before.

An even more recent example is that of Stalinist Russia. The triumph of Bolshevism in Russia was accompanied at first by many "liberated" manifestations in personal and social morality, as well as in art and other forms of general culture. These flourished in Russia during the 1920s, but Stalin put an end to them. Today the public and private morality of Soviet Russia resembles that of Victorian England.

Going even further back into history, there was a very serious and important reform movement in Athens after the defeat in the Peloponnesian War. At that time, there were certain subversive teachers abroad who were undercutting traditional religion and morality among the elite youth of the day. One of these subversives, Socrates, was put to death by a democratic "ideological renewal" government.

From these comments we can understand that the counterculture in any era has its roots in a search among both young and old for the meaning and purpose of life when all around them they see fracturing and disillusionment in organizations and institutions. Kahn and Bruce-Briggs do not duck this hard issue; in fact they give it structure:

Historically, the twelve societal levers (listed below) have moved Western man or, to use the contemporary cliche, provided "meaning and purpose to life." One of the most widely publicized and discussed phenomena of the 1960s was the startling change among upper- and upper-middle-class young people in the United States, in much of Western Europe, in such Latin American countries as Mexico, Venezuela, Chile, and Colombia, and (before August 1968) in parts of Eastern Europe such as Czechoslovakia and to some degree even in Japan. In these upper and upper-middle classes there was a substantial waning of these levers.

The 12 Traditional Societal Levers
(i.e., traditional sources of "reality testing,"
social integration, and/or meaning and purpose)

1. Religion, tradition, and authority.
2. Biology and physics (e.g., pressures and stresses of the physical environment, the more tragic aspects of the human condition, etc.).
3. Earning a living.
4. Defense of frontiers (territoriality).
5. Defense of vital strategic and economic interests.
6. Defense of vital political, moral, and morale interests.
7. The "martial" virtues such as duty, patriotism, honor, heroism, glory, courage, etc.
8. The manly emphasis—in adolescence: team sports, heroic figures, aggressive and competitive activities, rebellion against "female roles"; in adulthood: playing an adult male role; similarly a womanly emphasis.
9. The Puritan ethic (deferred gratification, work orientation, achievement orientation, advancement orientation, sublimation of sexual desires, etc.).
10. A high degree (perhaps almost total) of loyalty, commitment, and/or identification with nation, state, city, clan, village, extended family, secret society and/or other large grouping.
11. Other sublimation and/or repression of sexual, aggressive, aesthetic, and/or other instincts.
12. Other irrational and/or restricting taboos, rituals, totems, myths, customs, and charismas.

The eroding or disappearing of these levers from many current lifestyles—particularly among upper and upper-middle-class members of societies which feel they get their "security for free"—may make an enormous difference in events by 1985. Indeed, it seems a reasonable generalization that much of the New Left and many "dropouts," in almost all countries, come from upper-middle-class homes where these levers have been almost fully eroded.

Enough has been presented here of society's demand for radical change to make the demand clear, but a much greater problem looms on the horizon of the twenty-first century. An era of unprecedented growth and expansion in the industrial nations has been followed by a wide variety of comfortable settlings down.

Our organizations—in particular the larger ones—are behaving as though their size, power, markets, and general status will endure forever. A basic strategic decision has been made: "All we need do is keep on doing what we are doing, with only slight alterations, as new processes, techniques, products, or services come into demand."

It is time to puncture this balloon not only because it is not admirable in itself but because it is leading modern civilization to a disaster comparable to that which befell the civilizations preceding ours. The strategic problem is basic and pervasive. Business and industry have settled on long-range policy which includes the reduction of income-creating systems, the increase of income-dissipating systems—government, services, amusements, and bureaucracies of all kinds—and a reliance on technologies of production which steadily exhaust planetary resources.

When all these factors spin out from today's decisions by managers of business and industry, as well as managers in all other institutions, we will have a civilization which steadily increases the indirect and direct tax cost of government and services until the production machinery can no longer bear it and the entire structure collapses. Already the welfare demands of segments of the population which the world of work freezes out or discards are so high that we can see what will happen.

In short, in our business societies the basic strategic decision today is to allow social demands to expand through government and not through markets. Instead of satisfying emerging needs, we insist on business as usual and thus allow politics to explode. In this way we have made government, union, and educational bureaucracies the largest employers in the country. Such uneconomic employment will triple in a few decades.

Our currency is deflated around the world because of our profligate, immature social behavior. We throw away our prime resources—our ability to produce, to sell, to create new and better lives for people— and then wonder why the world questions the American strategy. When the day comes that our taxes confiscate 50 cents out of every open-market dollar, there will no longer be many options for radical change as likely as revolution and riot. The better options are here and now, while there is still time and some profit to work with in business enterprises. Too soon, if we deliberately encourage the costly rise of parasitic bureaucracies throughout society, profits will be rare indeed.

All of our business institutions can become employment agencies—as many are already—hanging on to terminal conditions, hoping only to meet the payroll and the tax bill, forgetting the days when a profit worth talking about could be made. Without profits of all kinds in businesses and social profits in other institutions, the engines of change lack fuel. If we continue as we are in the 1970s, early in the twenty-first century our present policies might eliminate profits and with them the free enterprise system which has proved to be the most efficient creator and allocator of value man has ever seen.

Despite this dismal possibility, some say a probability, a strong commitment *now* to radical change among our major business, government, and education leaderships can prevent this bleak future from being our legacy to the twenty-first century. Rapid, large-scale change is needed in a great many industries, activities, and, in fact, most of the organizations of man. To accomplish such changes we will need managers who have added a new dimension to their skills—the ability to be a manager of change. The new managers of change will apply all that we have thus far learned about our organizations and their potentials and will go beyond that to create new codes, new manager styles, and a new managerial philosophy adequate to the challenge. Some of this promise is presented in Chapter 9.

References

The quotation of Lewis Mumford is from *The City in History* (New York: Harcourt, Brace, 1961). Robert L. Heilbroner's quotation is from "Capitalism Alive or Dead," *World Magazine,* September 1972. Eric Hoffer's remarks are from *The Ordeal of Change* (New York: Harper & Row, 1952). The quotation of the National Goals Research Staff is from *Toward Balanced Growth: Quantity with Quality* (Washington, D.C.: GPO, 1970).

1. *Inside the Third Reich* by Albert Speer. Copyright © 1969 by Verlag Ullstein GMBH. Copyright © 1970 by The Macmillan Company.
2. *Things to Come* by Herman Kahn and B. Bruce-Briggs (New York: Macmillan, 1972). Copyright © 1972 by The Hudson Institute, Inc.
3. *A Look at Business in 1990: A Summary of the White House Conference on the Industrial World Ahead,* February 7–9, 1972 (Washington, D.C.: GPO, 1972).

4. Based on N. B. McEachron, "Forces for Societal Transformation in the U.S. 1950–2000," Stanford Research Institute Report.

5. Presented at the White House Conference on the Industrial World Ahead, February 7–9, 1972.

6. *Things to Come* by Herman Kahn and B. Bruce-Briggs (New York: Macmillan, 1972). Copyright © 1972 by The Hudson Institute, Inc.

CHAPTER NINE

Managerial Codes and Styles

We find . . . that despite the help we may get from thinking systematically about organizational behavior, we still have to deal with the fact that we who are trying to understand other humans in action are, ourselves, human, with a lot of feelings about what we observe. We cannot escape this humanness, even if we wanted to. All we can do is try to be aware of it, take its likelihood into account as we review what we think we understand about events around us, be somewhat suspicious of ourselves, and try being as systematic as we can in the process of carrying on our diagnoses.

JOHN A. SEILER

Unlike the traditional specialist, the new systems manager will be a super-generalist.

PETER P. SCHODERBEK

Very few of our most prominent people take a really large view of the leadership assignments. Most of them are simply tending the machinery of that part of society to which they belong.

JOHN GARDNER

As managers we delve deeply into the who, what, where, when, how, and why of our organization's input/output processes. We acquire ideas about how we *should* act as managers and how our organization *should* work. Yet as John A. Seiler of Harvard said in the opening of his book, *Systems Analysis in Organizational Behavior,* "Our experiences indicate that while some actions we take produce the effects we want, others do not. Furthermore, when we are dealing with situations in which human beings play a large part, the proportion of undesirable or surprising effects seems to rise." [1]

It is quite possible that human organizations continue to escape our "complete" understanding because they are no more than what organization members and observers think they are. It is also possible or even probable that, if large numbers of organization members change their view of the organization from state A to state B, the organization is changing. Perhaps no matter what clothing we hang on the body of organization in the form of factories, offices, people, markets, products, technologies, and services, the organization remains no more than what we think it is. Perhaps to change it is no more than to set up a continuing process which provides real and symbolic encouragement to most organization members to think differently about it. Certainly we know that, if and when the members do think differently, the organization will operate differently and affect other systems differently; it will have changed.

Managers are well aware that the image a manager holds of himself and the images he perceives among his fellow managers deeply affect performance. There is no end to the description of managerial types. A few are listed below. They vary by degree of involvement, philosophy, a sense of traditionally approved behaviors, mental sets, and the uses of power. It may be useful to each manager to contemplate these manager styles and to try to match them to real people, including himself, whom he knows as managers:

Rule setter	Organization analyst
Manipulator	Elitist
Neurocrat	Management scientist
Authoritarian	Organization designer
Politician	Emancipator
Change agent	Production specialist
Exploiter	Profits builder
Forgiver-participant	Self-protector
Problem solver	Group defender
Constraint remover	Peacemaker

Innovator	Generalist
Asset liquidator	Educator
Alienated specialist	Systems builder
Technology expert	Coordinator

As the list indicates, there are many roles we can play in our organizations as managers. Far more choices are open to us than we sometimes realize.

Many people feel that the complex problems of living in organizations would vanish if people would just behave differently toward one another. Others—and the author is one of them—see organizations and their futures as a problem in systems conception, analysis, and reshaping. Neither view has all the answers; indeed, there are many other views. For example, Howard H. Pattee summarizes the application of hierarchy theory to management by pointing out why the role of manager can be completely obscure to the man who has it. Pattee says:

> The manager of any complex organization must clearly appreciate the distinction between the structural levels and the descriptive levels of the system and must know how they interact . . . otherwise, even though he is called the manager of the system, he may not have control over it. This we know from experience is often the case with administrators of large social, business, and political organizations.[2]

Several able theoreticians, such as Pattee, can distinguish large gaps in our knowledge of organizations whose components are humans, resources, networks, and technologies, yet these are the real but tenuous systems we actually face every day as managers. Within the limits of current comprehension, then, we still must act. Thus, to act as wisely and effectively as possible on the challenge of creating large-scale change in organizations, the following pages set forth some general guidelines for manager behavior during change-feasibility studies, change-readiness programs, and change system operations.

A Manager's Code for the Feasibility Study Phase

Do's

1. Challenge all of your organization's basic assumptions with a steady faith that they need the challenge.
2. Require yourself to look at your operations through the eyes of professionals in many different but pertinent disciplines. Tune in to the

fact that people in your organization do not experience the organization as you do.

3. Look at the ingredients of a change-feasibility investigation and plan a series of briefings for yourself by these experts so that you personally understand what they are doing and how to evaluate their effort.

4. Establish your change team procedures, operations, ethics, and goals on the highest levels to earn the greatest amount of natural hierarchical respect possible in the situation.

5. Treat all persons in the appraisal process as your equals.

6. Find ways to dissipate or neutralize the campaigns of those with power or privilege to block constructive change.

7. Maintain a reasonable objectivity; do not become convinced that change is either practical or impractical before you have a solid case constructed by many investigators.

8. Insist that the uncertainty of the outcome be maintained until the final change team appraisal. The removal of uncertainty stops most minds from thinking.

Don'ts

1. Don't allow "experts" to dominate the change appraisal process. Avoid elitism.

2. Don't fail to establish and maintain trust, equality, and open communications at all levels and especially at lower levels of the organization. This can insure your success in ways not immediately apparent.

3. Don't use power, authority, or any hierarchical muscle to gain compliance with your requests.

4. Don't permit gatekeepers to inform you and thereby protect their enclaves with selected information. As a rule, go to original sources for your data.

5. Don't avoid the probability that your assigned change goals are inadequate. Open wide the goal formulation process to deal with the entire reality of your circumstances.

6. Don't forget it takes ten times more skill, knowledge, and ingenuity to change an organization's structures than to run the organization the way it is now.

7. Don't allow small uncertainties and objections to grow into large obstructions.

8. Don't manipulate people. Deal squarely.

These do's and don't's simplify and codify many of the principles and conditions described in detail earlier in this book. They cannot guarantee success, but they will help maintain the integrity of the change-feasibility appraisal.

A Manager's Code for a Change-Readiness Program

Do's

1. Concentrate on creating objective, exciting measures of key organization events.
2. Develop new, high-speed, self-education techniques so that people can take the initiative to educate themselves on and off company time. Make training widely available and expected of everyone.
3. Develop communications excitement on overall objectives, progress toward goals, measures of change readiness, and the development of radical change skills.
4. Stress organization development (OD) principles. Use OD consultants early in the game.
5. Respect the many different cultures in your organization. Do not design a single program or policy to fit them all. They differ.
6. Remember that in this stage you lack any top management commitment to a truly powerful change goal to stimulate improvement and cooperation. Go softly.
7. Devise concrete rewards to distribute to those who cooperate in increasing change readiness.
8. Use top-level people to demonstrate to the entire organization management's seriousness about the change-readiness program.

Don'ts

1. Don't allow negative spirals to get far before you check them.
2. Don't surprise work groups with requests or events they have not planned for.
3. Don't fail to check in advance with every hierarchy or power center involved in your activities.
4. Don't start at the bottom or middle of the organization. Let everyone know that a wide-open, tough investigation began at the top.
5. Don't allow a backlog of pet programs to funnel through your activities.

Change-readiness programs have a difficult stance; they are preparations for change without the benefit of a clear management commitment to make a specific change. As such, they can easily fall into the weak positions shared by all do-gooder programs within an organization. These might be indulged in by personnel because of general goodwill toward managers, but they lack the bite of an activity conducted to gain promotion, a raise in pay, or job protection.

In contrast, once a change system is committed by top management, if all the internal considerations have been dealt with, everyone in the organization has some idea that large undertakings are afoot. Then adventure, risk, identification with worthy causes, and the excitement of seeking out unknown territory combine to heighten individual awareness and commitment.

A Manager's Code for Change System Operation

Do's

1. Select the outside experts you will work with for many years with an eye to their personal integrity, balance, wisdom, intellectual strength, and depth of experience, as well as their professional skills.

2. Make it clear that the organization is committed to attain a specific change goal by a specific date.

3. Inform all manager/supervisory and staff personnel of the change team's progress in creating an artificial intelligence to help guide the change system.

4. Inform everyone that the organization has embarked on a journey to a distant goal for which no adequate road maps yet exist. Express confidence that extraordinary efforts by each individual will help reveal the route. Make it clear that your present standard operating practices fall far short of this need.

5. For organizational stability, separate the entire change team and its artificial intelligence group from ongoing operating responsibilities. Make certain that both operating people and change team personnel can and do move back and forth regularly; that is, construct a temporary project system much like the engineering/construction force that builds a new refinery.

6. Start with small changes close to people's interests.

7. Treat most of the organization information, counsel, and data created early in the change process as probably superficial. Organizations under stress tend to throw up erroneous data to substantiate nonchange. Press for breakthroughs in this natural barrier.

8. Plan direct routes to goals and subgoals, but prepare to achieve most of your important objectives by indirection, that is, in surprising ways.

9. Rely on organization health and high levels of change readiness to effect more real progress than your overall change system plan, but do not fail to plan seriously and in detail to create momentum.

10. Continue to expand the number of people undergoing intensive self-improvement allied to tasks of innovation.

11. Remember to cultivate systems thinking, orientation, and innovation.

12. Remember that, by change-readiness improvements, you prepare the soil; with the momentum of a change system you plant the tree. In good time it will bring forth the fruits of radical change.

Don'ts

1. Don't forget that superior technology, that is, improving by wide margins how the work is done, changes more organizations and attitudes than any other force.

2. Don't threaten people with the elimination of their jobs.

3. Don't be satisfied with minimum levels of change readiness lest you increase the risk of failure.

4. Don't discourage people from suggesting new concepts. Provide them with fair machinery for evaluation and continue to stimulate idea production at all levels.

5. Don't make the most common errors of selecting goals too soon, selecting routes too soon, or building organization structures too soon. Allow uncertainty enough time to incubate superior alternatives. Resist those who court failure by snap decisions; NASA did not get to the moon by snap decisions. A quick decision is *not* better than no decision at all.

6. Don't avoid or complain about legitimate constraints. If the organization cannot afford to invest more than $1 million over four years in a change system, do not insist on $5 million. Whatever handicaps exist, the job of the change team is to overcome them.

7. Don't forget to listen hard for the clues to success. At first they are usually faint. The change process may well uncover hundreds of alternatives; your task is to isolate the few almost sure to work and then to select one to run with.

These do's and don't's for a change system manager are not far from intelligent behavior in any field. What is new is the scope of the investigative/decision-making/structure-creating network in which managers will be involved for relatively long periods of time.

The Systems View of the World

The nature of reality is that all matter and energy organizes itself in systems. As Ervin Laszlo says, nature creates systems; it does not "distribute matter evenly or condense it into featureless blobs." [3] Starting 3.5 billion years ago with viruslike life forms, all that is alive today emerged, most of it more and more complex. Structure, form, and thus system are everywhere in nature from the form of the atom to the routes of the exploding galaxies. Ludwig von Bertalanffy, the father of general systems theory, once exclaimed, "Systems everywhere!" As for man, we must recognize ourselves as living or *natural* systems in which there is (1) differentiation of function among parts, (2) hierarchy, (3) structure, and (4) harmony. The natural system called man interacts with the hierarchy of nature's systems and with that of man's culture systems.

But man is not a mechanical part of the scheme of things, nor is his role in life predetermined from birth. Man has developed a rare and unusual attribute thus far discovered nowhere else in the universe of systems. *He thinks and knows that he thinks.* Thus we are the only system which can discern the nature of what is around us and attempt to uncover its meaning. As far as testable knowledge goes, we alone can ask, "What is the meaning of all this?" Neither the ape, the dog, the dolphin, nor the whale asks anything like that.

This rare attribute not only has made us the master of other species and, indeed, to some degree of the planet and its satellite moon, but now enables us to determine our own evolution if we so choose. We can decide our number and our form. These awesome powers are coupled with similarly heavy obligations to act as the steward of all the life forms and, in our organizations and institutions, as emancipators of our brothers and ourselves.

If in 3.5 billion years we have come from the simplest structures—the hydrogen and carbon atoms and the ylem from which the first viruslike wriggle of life emerged—who can predict how extraordinarily far our journeys might take us? To the stars to some degree—yes, in time —but certainly here and now on earth to organizations which by our own efforts we can restructure to better fit the human condition and allow its nobler elements to emerge. In this highly civilized process, change systems should prove useful to managers who seek the greatest achievement of their profession: the radical change of their own organizations to the next higher level of which they are capable consistent with the vision of emancipation for mankind.

References

The quotation of John A. Seiler is from *Systems Analysis in Organizational Behavior* (Homewood, Ill.: Irwin, 1967); that of Peter P. Schoderbek is from *Management Systems* (New York: Wiley, 1971); and that of John Gardner is from the 1965 Annual Report of the Carnegie Corporation of New York.

1. John A. Seiler, *Systems Analysis in Organizational Behavior* (Homewood, Ill.: Irwin, 1967).

2. Howard H. Pattee, *Hierarchy Theory* (New York: Braziller, 1973).

3. Ervin Laszlo, *The Systems View of the World* (New York: Braziller, 1972).

Theoretical Considerations

This synthesis was written for the management scientist. In combining concepts from a wide variety of sources in organization theory and management science, we felt it would be helpful to reference as many as possible for purposes of clarity. The precise reader with access to a management library will find that page references have also been included for the source of each concept.

The first segment discusses the ten sources of change in the context of the organizational change project itself. The second segment summarizes our general systems view of formal human organizations. The third integrates the first two by relating the sources of change to the major concepts of the general systems model of organizations; that is, it locates change systems theory within the comprehensive discipline of general systems theory. The fourth segment elaborates the principle of artificial intelligence or consciousness in organizations. It argues the crucial importance of artificial intelligence for the survival of complex organizations in the highly unstable environments of modern technological societies. At the end of this discussion we have listed the references which specifically apply to it.

I would like to acknowledge that Gary Chism, a designer of change systems at Change Systems Corporation in San Francisco, made a substantial contribution, especially in developing logical coherence and in introducing new elements to the use of artificial intelligence subsystems. Most of the theoretical discussion is the result of his efforts.

1. Structure and Definition of the Ten Sources of Radical Change

The theory of organizational change systems may be summarized by ten sources of change:

1. Innovation
2. Technological and work process improvement
3. Organization development
4. Forecasting future events
5. Understanding a culture
6. Education
7. Communications/symbols
8. Hierarchical cooperation
9. Use of experts
10. Task forces

The relationship among these ten sources of change is indicated by the following outline, which subsumes the ten sources under five headings. Together, these five headings describe a theoretical framework for the process of radical change.

  I. Goal—innovation [1]:
   A. Technological and work process improvement [2]
   B. Organization development [3]
 II. Guide—forecasting future events [4]
III. Background—understanding a culture [5]
 IV. Mechanisms:
   A. Education [6]
   B. Communications/symbols [7]
  V. Execution:
   A. Hierarchical cooperation [8]
   B. Use of experts [9]
   C. Task forces [10]

What follows is an explication of this outline and the framework it represents, together with a brief discussion of each of the ten sources of change as they appear in this framework.

I. *Goal.* The goal of the change effort is large-scale organizational innovation. This refers not to minor modifications in current practices, but rather to a radical transformation of the operation which elevates it to a new and distinctly superior level of performance. The organization in fact maintains its identity only by virtue of the continuity of current resources in the transformed operation. In other words, a change system functions by putting the organization's present resources to better use. In terms of structure and process, the original organization may scarcely be recognizable after the change effort has been completed. An apt analog might be the metamorphosis of a caterpillar into a butterfly.

Innovation may be of two types. Technological and work process improvement concentrates upon the way the work is performed, that is, the mechanics or logic of current operations. This involves the *technology* of organizational procedures. Contrasted with this type of innovation is that described as organization development. Here the focus is upon *the human element.* Role structures and authority relationships may be redefined; the organization chart may assume a new shape. Subtle psychological factors enter into this phase of innovation.

II. *Guide.* The guide to the change effort is accurate forecasts of future outcomes and events. The initial forecasts are those which motivate the change enterprise itself. These are the broad economic, ecological, or social prognoses which signal the inadequacy of the current operation. Methods which have sufficed in the past may no longer support growth or survival in an environment of accelerated change, new value systems, and intensified competition. Once an organization's change system is under way, further predictions become necessary. At each stage of the change process, alternative courses of action must be compared and choices made among them. Because the outcome of given modifications in the structure or function of current operations cannot usually be anticipated with certainty, one must employ such forecasting techniques as simulations in order to evaluate alternatives in advance.

III. *Background.* The background to the change effort is the underlying culture of the organization. In every social environment there are unspoken values and norms. (These are not to be confused with formally prescribed organizational roles.) Such values and norms arise "unofficially" in the course of human interactions among members of the organization but are in fact indispensable to the functioning of the formal operation. No change effort can succeed without taking these forces into account.

Cultural values and norms are not the *object* of the change enterprise. Radical change must be effected within the context of these stable influences, which act as constraints upon the whole undertaking. Because these forces in the culture arise so gradually and are so subtle in character, there is little hope of including them among the organizational variables to be adjusted in the change effort.

IV. *Mechanisms.* The mechanisms of the change effort are education and the motivational forces of communication and symbolism. All personnel in the organization, from the chief executive to the lowliest clerical assistants, will require continual education and reeducation during the change process and subsequently. This training must first attend particularly to the adaptive problems that organizational personnel experience as they try to reorient themselves within a transformed operation.

Once the main phase of transition in the organization has passed, further reeducation on a regular basis will insure that initial gains are not lost through obsolescence of skills. In fact, this process of continual renewal may be considered the principal influence in achieving long-range benefits through the organizational change enterprise. Education in this phase has less to do with adaptive problems than with the retooling of skills and enlargement of knowledge as the technological state of the art advances in the environment of the organization.

A second mechanism of the change effort has a largely motivational value. Whereas education feeds the intellects of personnel in the organization, the provocative use of communication and symbolism stokes their hearts and spirits against the rigors of the change enterprise ahead. At the inception of the change process, all members of the organization must appreciate the benefits to be had from change; otherwise, natural forces of fear and resistance will rapidly emerge to eliminate the effort. Thus the personnel involved must acquire the imagery of progress and growth that influenced top management in its decision to approve the change project in the first place. Most effective to that end is a thorough and lucid description to all organizational personnel of the steps to be taken, together with logical arguments and explanations which make it apparent how benefits will accrue from the process.

V. *Execution.* The execution of the change effort entails hierarchical cooperation, the use of experts, and the formation of task forces in the development of a temporary change system which will eventually be wholly or partially absorbed into the organization itself. Hierarchical cooperation refers to the coordinated efforts of personnel from the top to the bottom of the organization ranks, as well as the collaboration of environmental groups. Thus hierarchical cooperation implies a strong internal and external dedication to the organization's mission of radical change and emphasizes the scope and intensity of this enterprise.

Specialists and experts from both within and without the organization must bring their respective skills to bear upon the change effort. A venture of this scope requires unusual intellectual input and guidance. Three categories of experts are involved. On the one hand, experts in the organization's technology are needed to evaluate present operations, propose major improvements, and second-guess the recommendations of the change team. These technology experts are contrasted to the second cadre of experts, the management scientists composed of organization theorists who utilize data from the change team to develop alternative organizational designs in accordance with precise normative standards. The third group is the core change team which counsels the entire organization on change processes.

Finally, special task forces composed of personnel drawn from both within and without the organization will collaborate on the execution of the change effort. The formation of such task forces represents the integration of the specialized skills and talents described above. Only through the coordination of such skills and talents can a unified change enterprise be conducted. The harmonious interplay of these specialties is critical to the success of the complex, multifaceted undertaking that the organizational change project represents. An important function of the task forces is to surmount the artificial departmental divisions of the organization as they install new systems. Although departmental walls are often practical at a time of steady state operation of the organization, these divisions tend to fragment the radical change process if they are not breached deliberately.

The change system process described above organizes itself into a temporary project system. The elements of hierarchical cooperation, the use of experts, and the formation of task forces are applied to the development of a temporary project denoted by the author as a *change system*. This change system is superimposed on the organization and functions in symbiosis with it in order to perform the transformation which elevates the organization to a superior level of performance. The change system is required while this transformation is in progress, since any thought of self-transformation of an organization through its own resources would involve logical contradictions and unrealistic assumptions. The change system is an unusually capable agent developed from internal and external resources to effect a major reprogramming in order that a wholly new state may be realized while the internal functions are preserved sufficiently to insure survival.

Yet the change system is only a temporary device which must in large part be absorbed by the organization once a higher level of performance has been attained. Its absorption represents the internalization by the organization of those very capacities of the change system which enabled the latter to transform the organization to its present state of operation. By absorbing the change system, the organization therefore insures its own ability to perpetuate that higher level of performance which the change system has brought about.

2. A General Systems View of Organizations

Organization: An open system in its environment. Organizations are open systems. This means that a human organization receives inputs from its external environment and transforms them into outputs which are released to this environment. All inputs are in the form of either material, energy, or information. Organizational processes can be directly related to this function of transforming inputs into outputs while influenced by an overall environment.*

Subsystems of the organization. Trist and others at the Tavistock Institute of Human Relations in London have formulated the conception of the organization as a structured sociotechnical system. Kast and Rosenzweig extended this concept to consider all of the organization subsystems and their interaction. According to this view, the organization as a system comprises five subsystems: (1) goals and values, (2) technology, (3) structure, (4) psychosocial factors, and (5) management. Goals and values of course lie at the source of the organizational enterprise as its *raison d'être*. Technology includes not only machine technology but also the knowledge of techniques required to perform organizational tasks. Structure has the function of integrating the technology of the organization with its fourth subsystem, the psychosocial factors which define the relationships among the personnel in the organization. Finally, management has the role of coordinating the first four subsystems within the environmental context of the organization.

In the following sections the subsystems of the organization are employed as a framework for a discussion of the human organization from a general systems point of view.

* In both structure and content, this section relies heavily upon F. E. Kast and J. E. Rosenzweig, *Organization and Management* (New York: McGraw-Hill, 1970).

Technology and Structure

Technology and Organization

Technology defined. "Technology" is a term of somewhat broader significance than that frequently applied to it. Technology includes the machinery employed to produce goods and services and the tangible mechanical equipment which one might see on a shop floor; it also entails the knowledge, skills, and methods which enter into the processes that convert inputs to outputs.

Classification of technical systems. Thompson classifies organizational technologies as follows:

1. Long-linked technology such as the mass production assembly line.
2. Mediating technology, which joins clients who are independents.
3. Intensive technology, which treats a specific problem.

This scheme is applicable to all kinds of human organizations, not only those in the industrial sector. Organizations in the public sector may be classified in this way as well.

Impact of the technical system. One may examine the influences that the technical system exerts upon each of the other subsystems of the organization. Research has revealed that the following structural characteristics correspond closely to the technical sophistication of an operation: the length of the line of command; the span of control of the chief executive; the percent of total turnover allocated to the payment of wages and salaries; and the ratios of managers to total personnel, of clerical and administrative staff to manual workers, of direct to indirect labor, and of graduate to nongraduate supervision in production departments. In addition, a certain organizational structure seems to be most conducive to successful operations in a particular category of technological systems. Finally, the presence of technological change itself in an organization tends to require that horizontal structure relationships replace hierarchical vertical relationships.

Technology also affects the psychosocial subsystem in many ways. It influences the network of social relations among personnel in the organization. Job-related emotional problems often ensue after technological changes. Changes in the organization must accommodate the psychosocial subsystem, or else the newly designed technical system will fail to be adopted. Several alternative designs of social interaction may be consistent with a single technical system. Some will offer greater personal satisfaction than others and lead indirectly to higher worker productivity.

Technology impinges upon the managerial subsystem by creating the need for highly trained systems analysts and other specialists in management techniques. In addition, middle line managers must coordinate the efforts of ever more staff personnel as technology advances. Problems of integration increase. Rapid technological change demands a management system which differs markedly in character from that suited to stable conditions.

Such a fluctuating environment favors a system with loosely defined roles and tasks, a network pattern of control and communication, the dominance of lateral over vertical interactions among personnel, and the broad diffusion of authority according to one's personal qualifications for task performance rather than one's entrenched status in a power structure.

Organization Structure

Definition of structure. One may define the structure of a human organization as the fixed configuration of relationships among the parts of the organization. The significance of structure is further elucidated by contrasting it with the processes of an organization. Whereas structure refers to the static properties of a system, processes describe its dynamic behavior over time. Though the well-known "organization chart" contributes to one's understanding of structure in a given organization, it serves only to outline the overall pattern of formal organizational structure. Not only does it omit the details of this formal structure, but it completely overlooks the informal pattern of interactions and relationships which emerges with time in a specific group of individuals and which acquires crucial importance in determining organizational behavior.

Differentiation of organizational activities. Differentiation refers to the segmentation of the organizational system into subsystems. Vertical differentiation describes the hierarchical managerial structure; horizontal differentiation corresponds to the departmentalization of operations in the organization.

Integration of organizational activities. Although tasks and responsibilities must be parceled out in complex organizations according to some pattern of differentiation, the overall integrity of the organizational effort requires that the several subsystems so defined be integrated or coordinated. Without integration, only the local tasks and responsibilities of each subsystem could be accomplished; the broad, overriding objectives of the system as a whole could not be served.

Litterer suggests three primary mechanisms for achieving coordination: the hierarchy, the administrative system, and voluntary activities. Hierarchical coordination implies the establishment of a central authority over the various activities. In the administrative system formal procedures serve to coordinate the more routine functions of the organization in its daily activities. Finally, voluntary coordination requires that the individual in an organization exercise his own independent initiative to integrate his own activities with those of others about him.

Horizontal and diagonal relationships. Organization charts tend to stress vertical interactions in the organization, yet horizontal flows are a critical variable in the dynamics of the system. Horizontal relationships have to do with the functional division of labor; thus, coordination or integration must operate both vertically and horizontally. The informal organization by itself is inadequate to achieve the task of horizontal integration. Formal methods are required as well.

The Psychosocial System

Role Systems

Role defined. A role defines the behavior expected of an individual who occupies a specific position in an organization. Thus one's role depends only upon his position and not at all upon his personal identity.

Role systems. Human organizations may be regarded as role systems. This conception highlights the importance of activities in describing an organization, since a role in fact embraces a set of prescribed activities. Because an individual often occupies several roles at once, each corresponding to his membership in a particular institutional situation, a complex configuration of multiple roles results. This multiplicity of roles admits the possibility of conflicting role behaviors. In complex organizations an individual may even confront several distinct roles within a single organizational setting alone.

Role conflict. Role conflict is of four types: (1) person role, (2) interrole, (3) intersender, and (4) intrasender. Person role conflict entails a contradiction between the requirements of the role and the needs or abilities of the individual invested with the role. Interrole conflict occurs when an individual's simultaneous membership in more than one organization compels him to respond to contradictory role expectations from the several distinct organizations. Intersender conflict differs from interrole conflict in that all the contradictory expectations originate in a single organization to which the individual belongs. In this case different persons in the organization have expressed distinct and contradictory expectations of the individual. Finally, intrasender conflict results when the individual faces contradictory role expectations from a single other person in a single organization to which he belongs.

Group Dynamics

Group defined. A small group is a body of persons, numbering between two and perhaps twenty people, who remain together over a period of time in pursuit of certain activities and purposes. Groups may endure for varying lengths of time. They may be either closed in membership or open with a flow of members into and out of the group. In a primary group the members deal regularly with each other on a face-to-face basis. In a secondary group they have little direct interaction among themselves. Finally, a group may exist either with reference to external tasks to be served or merely in order to satisfy the emotional needs of the participants.

Groups and organizations. An organized group is a social group with rather permanent relationships among the members. A distinguishing feature is the repetition of interactions among individuals. Positions exist in the group, and these positions are independent of the individuals who may fill them at a particular time. Thus organized groups have a structure. Small groups in organizations serve in part to link the individual with the organization as a whole.

Communication. Communication, broadly defined, comprises the totality of group interactions and thus has a crucial place in the analysis of group dynamics. Formal communication patterns are often established in organizations. An informal leader frequently emerges in the process of communication, due to his central position in the flow of interactions. Both technical and semantic difficulties operate to complicate the vital process of communication in small groups.

Group conflict. Conflict is not a purely destructive force in organizations and groups. Informed decision making in groups may necessitate the competition of opposing views in order that each may be evaluated relative to the others and the best choice made among them. Some authorities in the study of group dynamics have argued that conflict is in fact imperative to the formation and survival of a group.

Influence Systems and Leadership

Influence systems. Influence refers broadly to any interpersonal transaction which affects behavior. Thus it includes coercion, persuasion, suggestion, and emulation. One may define an interaction-influence system as the totality of influence relationships between pairs of individuals in an organization. Power is the ability to influence behavior; in organizations it is often institutionalized in the form of authority. Yet knowledge or expertise sometimes bestows effective power upon personnel who enjoy very little official authority. The exercise of influence is called leadership.

Leadership styles. At least five modes of leadership may be distinguished. In authoritarian leadership, a single individual dictates policy arbitrarily. In democratic leadership the group discusses each matter and reaches a decision with only the guidance of the leader. In laissez faire leadership the group is left completely on its own without even the advice of the leader. Bureaucratic leadership in effect substitutes a rule book for an autocratic leader. Decisions are dictated not by the leader, but rather by a formal code of regulations and procedures. Finally, neurocratic leadership refers to an autocratic mode wherein the leader acts from a neurotic compulsion to lead.

Organizational environment. Fiedler indicates three environmental forces which contribute to leadership effectiveness: (1) the leader's position power, (2) the structure of the task, and (3) the interpersonal relations between leader and members. Position power is the formal authority which the leader enjoys in an organization due to his position there. A highly structured task facilitates leadership to the extent that the instructions inherent in the task substitute for explicit direction by the leader himself. Finally, sound interpersonal relations, implying good rapport between leader and led, are the most decisive factor of all in determining leadership effectiveness in human organizations.

The Managerial System

Managerial Information-Decision Systems

The managerial system. Management is the process of integrating human and material resources into a total system for objective accomplishment. The managerial system coordinates the other subsystems of the organization—technology, structure, and the psychosocial system. It is possible to analyze managerial processes into the three functions of planning, organizing, and controlling. Similarly, one may subdivide the managerial system into the technical, organizational, and institutional subsystems. The technical subsystem relates to the operational concerns of the organization as it transforms inputs to outputs. The institutional subsystem attends to the problems of the organization in relation to its environment. The organizational subsystem has as its task the coordination of the first two subsystems.

The decision-making process. Six elements are common to all decisions: (1) the state of nature, (2) the decision maker, (3) the goals sought, (4) the alternative choices of action, (5) a relation which serves to order the alternatives by preference, and (6) the choice itself from among the alternatives. From these six elements follow the steps in the decision-making process: (1) searching the environment for conditions that call for a decision, (2) developing and evaluating alternative courses of action, and (3) selecting a course of action from among the alternatives. These three steps may be denoted as intelligence, design, and choice activity, respectively.

The problem-solving or decision-making process entails first a recognition of relevant factors in the environment of the organization. It is necessary to predict the probable effects of each alternative course of action. Next one must assess the importance of each such effect. By balancing these effects according to their relative probability and importance, one is enabled to make a choice or decision.

This elaborate process of decision making pertains only to nonprogrammed, that is, nonroutine, decision-making problems. There are often very many programmed or routine, repetitive problems which one may attack according to standard formulas or procedures which the organization has evolved in the course of experience.

Information flow and organization. Managers need information in order to execute their responsibilities of planning, organizing, and controlling operations. Unless this information has already been stored away, additional information must be obtained through communication systems in the organization. In a communication system, a transmitter conveys a message in coded form to a receiver, which decodes the message for its recipient. Typically, the channel contains noise in one form or another, which introduces some measure of distortion into the message.

Organizational structure greatly influences the pattern of communications in an organization. However, formal structure is not decisive in this regard, since informal channels of communication also emerge.

One can gain much understanding of an organization by studying the organization as a communication network. This conception acquires even greater potential if one interprets the decision process as an extension of the communication process by defining a decision point in the organization as an information-processing unit.

Information-decision systems. Decisions to be made in an organization furnish the impetus to the development of information and to the flow of information through the communication system. The overall information flow constitutes a system with a complex configuration of elements and subsystems. The information-decision system exerts a pivotal influence on the managerial functions of planning and control.

In a complex organization, management first gathers data both internally and from the environment in order to set overall objectives. Management plans evolve over time as a wide variety of knowledge accumulates. Plans flow both to the operating system and to the control system, where they will be compared with subsequent results for the purpose of modification and improvement. The operating system also absorbs detailed instructions for day-to-day organizational activities. Feedback flows of information serve the control function, which is concerned with corrective and adaptive actions and with innovation.

Computational Decision-Making Techniques

Rationality. Rational decision making emphasizes the use of objective, logical methods as opposed to subjective intuition. Classical economic theory specifies three assumptions for rational behavior:
1. Complete knowledge of relevant environmental factors
2. Ability to order preferences according to a measure of utility
3. Ability to choose the alternative which maximizes utility

Typically, applications of rational decision-making techniques require the use of a closed decision model, since an open model would introduce far more variables than can be managed by present-day techniques. This oversimplification is a major shortcoming of these techniques.

It should be noted that organization objectives rarely coincide with the personal aims of individuals in the organization, so that one must distinguish organizational from individual rationality. Moreover, the rationality of a given decision can be determined only in relation to the decision maker's state of knowledge at the time. Decisions which are rational when first conceived may no longer be rational once additional information comes to light in connection with the problem. Finally, rationality depends critically on the value system employed.

Quantification. Rational decision making involves the construction of a model for the problem under investigation. Though models may be either qualitative or quantitative, there are important advantages to quantification of a model. Communication problems are reduced; precision is increased; and the model's predictive value becomes amenable to measurement. Finally, mathematical models can be computerized.

Models may be either deterministic or probabilistic. In deterministic models parameters are fully defined and the outcome of given courses of action are certain; in probabilistic models such is not the case. There are several classes of techniques for rational decision making in the context of quantitative models. Algorithmic techniques are step-by-step procedures suitable for clearly defined, closed-system problems. Heuristic techniques entail trial and error and the use of personal judgment, and they may be required for complex, open-system problems. Analytical techniques yield a unique solution through mathematical deduction. Numerical techniques approach a solution by successive approximations, and so they are suited to more complex problems and are useful in testing alternative policy decisions.

Behavioral Aspects of Decision Making

Complexity. Closed decision models are applicable to only the simpler, smaller-scale problems of complex organizations. Major policy decisions necessitate explicit attention to political considerations and value judgments in the context of an open system, in which quantification may not be feasible. In these situations even the objectives themselves may be ambiguous or multifaceted. Rationality becomes a gross oversimplification of decision making in open-system problems.

Open-system decision model. An open decision model allows for human involvement in the process and takes into account the presence of numerous environmental factors. Assumptions of complete knowledge and strict logic are abandoned. The role of feedback flows and adaptive decision making finds recognition in the model. Satisficing, or the determination of "acceptable" solutions, replaces optimization, the computation of "best" solutions. The full complexity of the search phenomenon in seeking solutions is better appreciated than in closed decision models.

Value systems. Value judgments are of obvious importance in decision making, especially with regard to major policy decision in a human organization. Leys has proposed a scheme of six moral standards which explicitly acknowledges the existence of ethical pluralism in society. These standards include harmony, happiness, loyalty, survival, lawfulness, and integrity. The overlaps and contradictions among these six standards serve to reveal the complexity of value judgments in the decision-making process. It is always necessary to balance the several principles among themselves in reaching a clear judgment as the basis for a decision.

Managerial Planning

Planning defined. A plan is a predetermined course of action. Long-range planning receives special attention in modern organizations. It involves determining objectives, together with strategies for their attainment. It further entails the elaboration of detailed operational programs for carrying out the plans. Planning is related to decision making. It is the continuous process of making decisions systematically, organizing the execution of these decisions, and evaluating the decisions through feedback after their outcomes can be observed. Forecasting is crucial to long-range planning.

Planning dimensions. Single-use plans are those designed for nonrepetitive problems. Standing plans are used over and over again. They pertain to recurrent everyday problems of an organization. Standing plans include policies, the general guides to organizational behavior. Methods and procedures are standing plans to direct technical activities.

The time dimension is significant in planning. Long-range plans set the framework for medium-range plans, which in turn set the framework for short-range plans. It should be noted that time spans are relative; thus what is long-range planning for one organization may be only medium-range planning for another.

One may speak of scope in planning. Branch has distinguished three categories of planning. Functional planning refers to the planning of a component in a larger endeavor. Project planning embraces an entire enterprise of some kind. Finally, comprehensive planning is the most extensive in scope: it envelops all internal and external aspects of some grand, overall undertaking.

Planning occurs at several levels as well. First, the organization must establish plans for achieving its overall objectives. These plans in turn dictate further plans for the various subsystems of the organization, each of which has its own contribution to make to the broad objectives. The plans for each subsystem dictate further plans for the sub-subsystems of the organization, and so forth. There results a hierarchy of plans which corresponds to a means-ends chain in the organization. This chain describes the manner in which the means employed at one level to achieve the goals of this level become the ends or goals of the next level below.

Steps in the planning process. Logically, one may define the following sequence of stages in any planning process:

1. Appraising the future environment
2. Visualizing the desired role of the organization in this environment
3. Perceiving needs of the clients or beneficiaries of the organization
4. Determining changes in the needs of other interested groups
5. Providing a system of communication so that organization personnel may participate in planning
6. Developing overall goals and plans
7. Translating this broad planning into more detailed functional efforts
8. Developing even more detailed plans within each functional area

Integration of planning and control. Planning and control are closely related processes in an organization. A complete operating cycle for the organization would include six phases: (1) objective setting, (2) planning, (3) action, (4) accomplishment, (5) feedback, and (6) control. Anthony has formulated a unified framework for planning and control systems which involves three key concepts:

1. Strategic planning—the process of deciding on objectives, resources, and policies
2. Management control—the process by which managers obtain and use resources to accomplish organizational objectives
3. Operational control—the process of executing specific tasks

These three concepts coincide, respectively, with the institutional, organizational, and technical levels of the managerial system in an organization.

Organizational Control

Control defined. The control function can be defined as that phase of the managerial process which maintains organization activity within allowable limits as measured from expectations. Stability of output is obtained through continual feedback of past output to influence future input. Organizations exhibit a dynamic equilibrium. That is, control has dual functions: to maintain the system in a viable form and to facilitate adaptive responses to environmental change. Control processes operate through the comparison of the performance obtained with the standard which planning provides.

Elements of control. Any control system in a human organization contains four principal features. First, there is a measurable and controllable characteristic for which standards are known. There is also a sensory device which measures the characteristic. There must be a comparator to evaluate the discrepancy between the actual performance of the system and the standard sought. Finally, an effector serves to adjust the performance of the system toward the standard sought. These four elements are linked sequentially in a cycle to create the control process.

Control in the organization takes place at several levels, which correspond to the hierarchy of planning levels. Control processes may adjust not only the means employed to attain present goals but even the goals themselves.

Economics of control. Organizational control systems entail obvious costs of design and operation. Control is a relative process in that precise achievement of the standard applied to performance can never be expected. Some allowable margin of error is implicit in any control system. A key consideration in determining this margin is the greater cost of more precise control mechanisms. Thus the margin must be so narrow that the gains obtained from the system are offset by its cost.

3. A General Systems Analysis of Radical Organization Change

From the preceding section, A General Systems View of Organizations, one may derive 12 key organizational parameters which together serve to characterize a particular organization rather thoroughly, though only at a certain level of specificity. These 12 parameters are listed below, subsumed beneath five categories which correspond to the five major subsystems of the human organization which were designated in the preceding section.

  I.   Goals and values [1]
 II.   Technology [2]
III.   Structure
       A. Differentiation [3]
       B. Integration [4]
       C. Communication patterns [5]
 IV.   Psychosocial subsystem
       A. Roles [6]
       B. Organized groups [7]
       C. Influence relationships [8]
       D. Informal organization [9]
  V.   Managerial subsystem
       A. Decision making [10]
       B. Planning [11]
       C. Control [12]

A change system, the output of a temporary project group, is established to transform the present organization to a new state which functions at a level of performance distinctly superior to that at which the organization functioned originally. Because the change system is designed specifically for this single purpose, it possesses a special capacity. This capacity may be termed an artificial intelligence by virtue of its chief characteristic, which is the simulation of those faculties inherent in the intellect of the individual human being. It is this intelligent capacity which enables the change system to achieve its unique transformation function for the organization. The system "thinks it through."

The operation of the change system can be represented in general terms by the diagram of Figure A-1, which describes the interactions between the ten sources of change (discussed in the first section, The Ten Sources of Radical Change) and the twelve key organizational parameters. *Technological and work process improvement* involves both the organizational technology and the division of labor as expressed by horizontal differentiation. *Organization development* refers to modifications in the psychosocial subsystem of the organization. Broad economic and social *forecasts* are a critical phase of planning in organizations; smaller-scale forecasting methods such as simulations assist short-run decision making. The *culture* of an organization arises from that community of social relationships known as the informal organization. *Education* must attend at first to the difficulties of personnel as they attempt to adapt to radically different roles than those originally prescribed for them in the organization. Continuing educational efforts serve to maintain technological know-how at a current status as advances are achieved in the environment. *Communications and symbols* function to motivate acceptance of new goals and values throughout the organization. *Hierarchical cooperation* includes (among other things) the thorough integration of all subsystems at every level of authority in the organization so that a concerted effort may be realized. *Experts* required in

FIGURE A-1.   The logic of the change system.

Ten Sources of Change	Organization Parameter	Effective Change Source
1. Innovation	I. Goals and values	(7)
2. Technological and work process improvement	II. Technology	(2,9,6)
	III. Structure	
3. Organization development	A. Differentiation	(2)
	B. Integration	(8)
4. Futures forecasting	C. Communication patterns	(10)
5. Understanding a culture	IV. Psychosocial subsystem	
6. Education	A. Roles	(3,6)
7. Communications and symbols	B. Organized groups	(3,10)
	C. Influence relationships	(3,8)
8. Hierarchical cooperation	D. Informal organizations	(3,5)
9. Use of experts	V. Managerial subsystem	
10. Task forces	A. Decision making	(4)
	B. Planning	(4,10,8)
	C. Control	(3,10)

TABLE A-1. Artificial intelligence and organization variables.

Artificial Intelligence \ Organizational Variables	Span of Control	Ratio of Administrative to Production Personnel	Time Span Over Which Employee Can Commit Resources	Degree of Centralization in Decision Making
Organizational Perception	A large span of control enlarges a supervisor's breadth of view and thereby increases his perception.	A high ratio increases the number of personnel responsible for overseeing the work of others and thereby augments perception.		Decentralized decision making causes personnel throughout the organization to involve themselves in decision problems and thereby encourages perception among these personnel.
Organizational Memory	A wide span of control enlarges a supervisor's scope of concern and thereby involves him in a larger body of data and increases his memory.	A high ratio increases the number of personnel entrusted with broad data and thereby enlarges memory.		Decentralized decision making forces personnel throughout organization to store data for future decision problems and thereby enlarges memory.
Organizational Reason		A high ratio increases the number of personnel concerned with decision making and thereby augments reason.		Decentralized decision making brings more minds into decision-making processes and thereby augments reasoning capacity in in the organization.
Organizational Imagination		A high ratio increases the number of personnel employed to generate new ideas and thereby enlarges imagination.	A long time span allows employees to ponder problems and purposes at length, which permits imaginative ideas to arise in the mind.	Decentralized decision making causes more minds to be engaged in problem solving and thereby increases the use of imagination among personnel.
Organizational Motivation		A high ratio increases the number of personnel with a career interest in the organization and thereby augments motivation.	A long time span enables the employee to accomplish major tasks of great importance and thereby furthers motivation.	Decentralized decision making accords greater responsibilities for important work to more personnel and thereby increases motivation.

Proportion of Persons in One Unit Having Opportunity to Interact with Persons in Other Units	Quantity of Formal Rules	Specificity of Job Goals (Local vs. Global)	Advisory Content of Communications (vs. Orders)	Knowledge-based Authority (vs. Position-based)
A high proportion enlarges the exposure of personnel to activities throughout the organization and thereby increases perception.	A small quantity of rules makes personnel receptive to innovative ideas and thereby encourages perception.	A low specificity of goals causes personnel to relate to overall aims of the organization and thereby promotes a greater breadth of perception among personnel.	A high advisory content leaves more personnel with the responsibility of managing their own activities and thereby encourages greater perception.	A high knowledge orientation places a premium on awareness among personnel and thereby promotes perception in the organization.
	A small quantity of rules broadens the scope of potentially relevant data and thereby enlarges the memory in the organization.	A low specificity of goals widens the base of data relevant to individual personnel and thereby increases memory.		A high knowledge orientation forces personnel to amass data in order to advance and thereby enlarges memory.
A high proportion encourages the pooling of minds in response to problems to be solved and thereby augments reason.	A small quantity of rules exposes more procedures and practices to critical evaluation and thereby increases reason.	A low specificity of goals causes personnel to concentrate their thoughts on the ultimate objectives of the organization and thereby augments effective reason.	A high advisory content leaves more personnel with problem-solving responsibilities of their own and thereby enlarges the exercise of reason.	A high knowledge orientation furthers logical thought activity among personnel in their effort to expand their knowledge and thereby increases reason.
A high proportion tends to draw many minds into problem-solving processes and thereby enlarges the exercise of imagination.	A small quantity of rules frees the minds of personnel for creative thinking and thereby encourages imagination.		A high advisory content allows greater freedom of action among personnel and thereby encourages the use of imagination.	A high knowledge orientation encourages growth in the data base as a stimulant to new ideas and thereby promotes imagination.
A high proportion makes personnel aware of their own places in the overall functions of the organization and thereby increases motivation.	A small quantity of rules permits personnel to exercise individual preferences and thereby increases motivation.	A low specificity of goals involves personnel in the ultimate, major aims of the organization and thereby encourages higher identification and motivation.	A high advisory content promotes participatory management in the organization and thereby increases motivation.	

the change process are of three classes: specialists in technology, authorities in the human factors problems of the psychosocial subsystem, and the core change team, which is expert in managing change processes. *Task forces* represent organized groups "grafted" onto the organization temporarily so that radical change may be effected.

4. Artificial Intelligence in the Modern Organization

The modern literature has documented the widespread recent trend in American industry from the rigid, compartmentalized organization structure, frequently described as "bureaucratic," to the more fluid, coordinated form which one may term the organic structure. Specific empirical research has undertaken to relate this trend to certain measurable variables that characterize human organizations. The fundamental premise of this research is that particular adjustments in the variables yield that adaptive responsiveness of the organization to environmental influences which serves to distinguish the organic structure.

Earlier literature suggests a list of dynamic faculties of the human organism which account for its own capacity to adapt to changes in the environment. This list is not the only way to distingush man's intelligent faculties, but it is adopted here.

These faculties include reason, imagination, memory, perception, and motivation. It is the object of this section to correlate the measurable variables mentioned above with the concept of an artificial intelligence, *which simulates for an organization of men* the same five dynamic faculties which explain adaptation in the individual human being. Thus this discussion seeks to place a theoretical rationale beneath the empirical observations described in recent literature. At the same time, by elaborating the mechanism whereby the organizational change process can impart an intelligent capacity to complex organizations in modern technological societies, the discussion serves to illustrate radical change "at its best," that is, at its highest level of application. One interpretation is that the change system team (or temporary project group) in this case transfers its own intelligent capacity to the organization and leaves the latter in possession of those same faculties which make the change system itself so effective.

The matrix of Table A-1 has for a horizontal scale nine measurable variables suggested by recent literature on organizations. The vertical scale embraces the five faculties of an artificial intelligence. The entries in a given column of the matrix describe how an adjustment of the corresponding variable toward one extreme or the other at once facilitates the simulation in the organization of all five faculties of intelligence. There results a blueprint of organizational intelligence described in terms of relevant variables characteristic of the organization.

The chief virtue of Table A-1 is that it provides an empirical validation of the principle of artificial intelligence in the adaptive/responsive organization. This principle in turn allows a further specification of the organic structure beyond those features represented by the empirical variables. That is, by focusing effort on the synthesis of a reason, a memory, or whatever, it becomes possible to develop further details of the adaptive/responsive form of organization structure.

Some indication may be given of the practical significance for the organization of the five faculties associated with intelligence, although only the merest sketch is possible in this appendix. External perception involves the use of government economic surveys, industrial reports, and so on as well as the possible implementation of a corporate forecasting activity. Internal perception relies heavily upon procedures of reporting from personnel to their superiors, regularly scheduled conferences among department heads, company newsletters, and so forth. In the organization the synthesis of a memory clearly refers to a data bank and involves all the related problems of data tabulation and recording. In large organizations this memory depends upon the storage capacities of digital computers in the plant and so becomes a highly technical concept. The faculty of reason involves formal decision-making procedures and so entails the proper diffusion of responsibilities among those in authority. Complications include the possibility of overlapping or contradictory responsibilities and the need for coordination among personnel who must act jointly in determining policy decisions which extend across several functional departments. The attainment of an organizational imagination necessitates considerable freedom and flexibility of procedure. It therefore entails the recruitment of responsible, reliable individuals into the organization so that restrictive regulations and over-definition of tasks can be avoided. Finally, motivation in the organization requires that contradictions between organizational goals and the goals of individual personnel be reduced to minimal levels. Goal congruence can be promoted by a well-planned reward system and by the practice of tested human relations techniques.

Refer to the following list for an amplification of this sketch of the organization of an artificial intelligence. It must be emphasized that the five faculties of intelligence in themselves do not constitute an intelligent capacity. Only through the dynamic operation of each distinct faculty, and particularly through the interaction of the faculties, can intelligent behavior come into effect. The interaction implies a formal and intricate coordination of elements and processes. By the same token, the organization variables in the following list are merely the building blocks of an artificial intelligence. They must be painstakingly coordinated into a dynamic mechanism, formally described by the concept of human intelligence, before their full value can be realized in an organization. Thus the presence in an organization of the elements listed by no means implies the existence of a true organizational intelligence.

Organizational Design Variables

(as they contribute to organizational intelligence)

Perception

Quality control
Cost analysis
Economic forecasting
Consumer demand surveys
Internal reporting procedures
Merit rating

Government/industrial
  statistical publications
Communication patterns
Span of control
Environmental social indicators

Reason

Delegation of authority
Delegation of responsibility
Group decision procedures
Standardized computer programs
Breakeven analysis versus other
  standards for decision

Budget control
Planning techniques
Quantitative methods
Setting of goals
Interactive methods of computer
  utilization

Motivation

Independence of action
Participatory management
Disciplinary procedures
Reward procedures
Goal congruence (organization
  versus individual)

Supervisory practices
System of appeals
Flexibility of regulations
Superior/subordinate
  relationships
Salary scales

Memory

Computer storage capacities
Data encoding procedures
Data tabulation techniques
Accounting methods
Design of data files
Inventory records

Computer tape versus core
  data storage
Computer output devices
Data retrieval procedures
Organizational location of
  data

Imagination

Task definition
Formal restrictions on activity
Bureaucratic rules
Suggestion boxes
Style of leadership

Personnel selection techniques
General organizational climate
Levels of conformity
Freedom of communication
Research and development

5. Management and Organization References

Alexis, Marcus, and Wilson, Charles, *Organizational Decision Making.* Englewood Cliffs, N.J.: Prentice-Hall, 1967.

Anthony, Robert N., *Planning and Control Systems: A Framework for Analysis.* Boston: Division of Research, Harvard Graduate School of Business Administration, 1965.

Branch, Melville C., *Planning: Aspects and Applications.* New York: Wiley, 1966.

Buckley, Walter, "Society as a Complex Adaptive System," in Walter Buckley (Ed.), *Modern Systems Research for the Behavioral Scientist.* Chicago: Aldine, 1968.

Burns, Tom, and Stalker, G. M., *The Management of Innovation.* London: Tavistock, 1961.

Caplow, Theodore, *Principles of Organization.* New York: Harcourt, Brace, 1964.

Churchman, C. West, *Prediction and Optimal Decision.* Englewood Cliffs, N.J.: Prentice-Hall, 1961.

Cyert, Richard, and March, James, *A Behavioral Theory of the Firm.* Englewood Cliffs, N.J.: Prentice-Hall, 1963.

Deutsch, Karl W., "On Communication Models in the Social Sciences," *Public Opinion Quarterly,* Fall 1952.

Drucker, Peter F., "Long-Range Planning: Challenge to Management Science," *Management Science,* April 1959.

Emery, F. E., and Trist, E. L., "Socio-technical Systems," in C. West Churchman and Michael Verhulst (Eds.), *Management Sciences: Models and Techniques.* New York: Pergamon, 1960.

Fiedler, Fred E., *A Theory of Leadership Effectiveness.* New York: McGraw-Hill, 1967.

Homans, George C., *The Human Group.* New York: Harcourt, Brace, 1950.

Hower, Ralph, and Lorsch, Jay, "Organizational Inputs," in John A. Seiler (Ed.), *Systems Analysis in Organizational Behavior.* Homewood, Ill.: Irwin, 1967.

Jasinski, Frank J., "Adapting Organization to New Technology," *Harvard Business Review,* January–February 1959.

Jennings, Eugene E., *The Executive.* New York: Harper & Row, 1962.

Kast, Fremont, and Rosenzweig, James, *Organization and Management.* New York: McGraw-Hill, 1970.

Katz, Daniel, and Kahn, Robert, *The Social Psychology of Organizations.* New York: Wiley, 1966.

Landsberger, Henry A., "The Horizontal Dimension in Bureaucracy," *Administrative Science Quarterly,* December 1961.

Lawrence, Paul, and Lorsch, Jay, "Differentiation and Integration in Complex Organizations," *Administrative Science Quarterly,* June 1967.

LeBreton, Preston, and Henning, Dale, *Planning Theory.* Englewood Cliffs, N.J.: Prentice-Hall, 1961.

Leys, Wayne A. R., "The Value Framework of Decision Making," in Sidney Mailisk and Edward Van Ness (Eds.), *Concepts and Issues in Administrative Behavior.* Englewood Cliffs, N.J.: Prentice-Hall, 1962.

Litterer, Joseph A., *The Analysis of Organizations.* New York: Wiley, 1965.

Lotka, Alfred J., *Elements of Mathematical Biology.* New York: Dover, 1956.

March, James G., and Simon, Herbert A., *Organizations.* New York: Wiley, 1958.

Merton, Robert K., *Social Theory and Social Structure,* rev. ed. New York: Free Press, 1957.

Miller, David, and Starr, Martin, *Executive Decisions and Operations Research.* Englewood Cliffs, N.J.: Prentice-Hall, 1960.

—— and ———, *The Structure of Human Decisions.* Englewood Cliffs, N.J.: Prentice-Hall, 1967.

Miller, James G., "Living Systems: Basic Concepts," *Behavioral Science,* July 1965.

Pfiffner, John, and Sherwood, Frank, *Administrative Organization.* Englewood Cliffs, N.J.: Prentice-Hall, 1960.

Rice, A. K., *The Enterprise and Its Environment.* London: Tavistock, 1963.

Simon, Herbert A., *The New Science of Management Decision.* New York: Harper & Row, 1960.

Steiner, George A. (Ed.), *Managerial Long-Range Planning.* New York: McGraw-Hill, 1963.

Thompson, James D., *Organizations in Action.* New York: McGraw-Hill, 1967.

Thompson, W. W. Jr., *Operations Research Techniques.* Columbus, Ohio: Merrill, 1967.

Trist, E. L., and Bamforth, K. W., "Some Social and Psychological Consequences of the Longwall Method of Coal-getting," *Human Relations,* February 1951.

White, Ralph, and Lippett, Ronald, "Leader Behavior and Member Reaction in Three Social Climates," in Dorwin Cartwright and Alvin Zander (Eds.), *Group Dynamics: Research and Theory.* New York: Harper & Row, 1953.

Woodward, Joan, *Industrial Organization: Theory and Practice.* New York: Oxford University Press, 1965.

Additional Readings

This list is an addition to and not a substitute for the many excellent books and authors referred to in the main body of the book and in the appendix. It is designed to assist the manager who is now ready for an in-depth investigation of the many fields of expertise that affect processes of change in organizations.

Adding Change Process Techniques

Ayres, Robert U. *Technological Forecasting and Long-Range Planning.* New York: McGraw-Hill, 1969.

Box, G. E. P., and Draper, Norman R. *Evolutionary Operation.* New York: Wiley, 1969.

Cleland, David I., and King, William R. *Systems Analysis and Project Management.* New York: McGraw-Hill, 1968.

Sayles, Leonard R., and Chandler, Margaret. *Managing Large Systems: Organizations for the Future.* New York: Harper & Row, 1971.

Schon, Donald A. *Technology and Change.* New York: Dell, 1967.

Acquiring the OD Perspective

Addison-Wesley Series on Organizational Development. Reading, Mass.: Addison-Wesley, 1969, 1972.

Argyris, Chris. *Intervention Theory and Method.* Reading, Mass.: Addison-Wesley, 1970.

Blake, Robert R., and Mouton, Jane S. *Corporate Excellence Through Grid Organization Development.* Houston: Gulf Publishing Company, 1968.

Herzberg, Frederick. *Work and the Nature of Man.* Cleveland: World Publishing, 1966.
Maslow, Abraham H. *Motivation and Personality.* New York: Harper & Row, 1970.
Schein, Edgar H., and Bennis, Warren G. *Personal and Organizational Change Through Group Methods.* New York: Wiley, 1965.

Reshaping Manager Values

Baier, Kurt, and Rescher, Nicholas, eds. *Values and the Future: The Impact of Technological Change on American Values.* Glencoe, Ill.: Free Press, 1969.
Drucker, Peter F. *The Age of Discontinuity: Guidelines to Our Changing Society.* New York: Harper & Row, 1968.
McHale, John. *The Ecological Context.* New York: Braziller, 1970.
Rokeach, Milton. *The Open and Closed Mind.* New York: Basic Books, 1960.
Scott, William A. *Values and Organizations.* Skokie, Ill.: Rand McNally, 1965.
Teilhard de Chardin, P. *Man's Place in Nature.* New York: Harper & Row, 1966.
Toffler, Alvin. *Future Shock.* New York: Random House, 1970.

Building Organization Consciousness

Ashby, Ross W. *An Introduction to Cybernetics.* New York: Wiley, 1964.
Forrester, Jay W. *Industrial Dynamics.* Cambridge, Mass.: MIT Press, 1961.
Sackman, Harold. *Computers, System Science, and Evolving Society.* New York: Wiley, 1967.
Shannon, Claude E., and McCarthy, J., eds. *Automata Studies.* Princeton, N.J.: Princeton University Press, 1956.
Wiener, Norbert. *Cybernetics.* Cambridge, Mass.: MIT Press, 1961.

Understanding General Systems

Buckley, Walter, ed. *Modern Systems Research for the Behavioral Scientist.* Chicago: Aldine, 1968.
Rapoport, Anatol, ed. *General Systems Yearbooks.* Proceedings of the Society for General Systems Research. Washington, D.C.: Society for General Systems Research, published annually.
von Bertalanffy, Ludwig. *General Systems Theory.* New York: Braziller, 1968.

Describing Organizations

Katz, David, and Kahn, Robert C. *The Social Psychology of Organizations.* New York: Wiley, 1966.
Lawrence, Paul, and Lorsch, Jay. *Organization and Environment.* Boston: Division of Research, Harvard Business School, 1967.

Miller, E. J., and Rice, A. K. *Systems of Organization*. London: Tavistock Publications, 1967.

Pelz, Donald C., and Andrews, Frank M. *Scientists in Organizations*. New York: Wiley, 1966.

Steiner, Gary A. *The Creative Organization*. Chicago: University of Chicago Press. 1965.

Woodward, Joan. *Industrial Organization: Theory and Practice*. New York: Oxford University Press, 1965.

Evaluating The Futures Game

Boguslaw, Robert. *The New Utopians*. Englewood Cliffs, N.J.: Prentice-Hall, 1965.

Center for the Study of Social Policy, Stanford Research Institute. *The Changing Images of Man,* to be published.

Ellul, Jacques. *The Technological Society*. New York: Knopf, 1964.

Fuller, R. Buckminster. *Nine Chains to the Moon*. Carbondale, Ill.: Southern Illinois University Press, 1963.

Gabor, Dennis. *Inventing the Future*. New York: Knopf, 1963.

Index

Adams, John, 148
adaptation
change and, 4
organization and, 6–7
agapation score, 134–136
agreements, constraints set up by, 95
Agriculture Department, U.S., 63
Amara, Roy, 213
American Indian nations, 61
American Revolution, 147–151
amphibians, first, 15
Anderson, W. Thomas, Jr., 31
artificial intelligence
change systems and, 170–172
in modern organization, 250–252
organization variables and, 248–249
arts and culture, influence of, 22
Atomic Energy Commission, 167
Australopithecus, 15
automation, unionizing and, 21

Bacon, Francis, 149
Battelle Memorial Institute, 74
Beau Brummell (George Bryan Brummell), 216
Beer, S., 55 n.
Bennis, Warren, 55 n., 87
Bertalanffy, Ludwig von, 37, 228
Bertaux, Pierre, 139
biological organization, vs. manmade, 17
birth control, compulsory, 211
birth rate, decline in, 49
Blake, Robert R., 53
Boeing Aircraft Company, 98
Boewadt, Robert J., 31
Boulding, Kenneth, 28, 56–57, 69
Boy Scouts of America, 57
Bremer, Otto, 27
budget estimates, for change systems, 176–177
Burns, Tom, 55 n., 183

business, as social force, 26–27
business community, future and, 27
business organization
change goal formulation for, 105
image problem in, 30
radical change and, 30–32
rejection of people by, 20
value systems and, 30–31
see also organization(s)

California, University of, 61
Calvin, John, 16
Caplow, Theodore, 55 n.
career, cynicism about, 23–24
cartels, 68
Chandler, Alfred D., Jr., 173
change
by defense or national emergency, 98
by evolution, 98
executive techniques in, 83
failure in, 85–86
goals and, *see* change goal formulation
in group behavior, 93
inadvertent, 39–40
in individuals, 94–95
key issues and blocks to, 130
long-range planning and, 93
managing of, 10
measurement of, 183–198
by monopoly, 98
myths and, 18–19
need for, 46
negative, 4
organization response and, 13–15
organizations as vehicles of, 56–57
planned vs. inadvertent, 39–40
possibility of, 96–99
radical, *see* radical change
rate of, 4, 13–14, 183–198
reality and, 117–119

THE SEVEN ORGANIZATION CONCEPTS

CLASSIFICATION	SYMBOL	IMAGE	STRUCTURE	AUTHORITY PROCESSES	INTERACTION AMONG PEOPLE
I LEADER/ FOLLOWER CLUSTER		Human	Leader at center, followers at periphery	Centralized authority with subordinates equal among themselves	Master/slave relationship
II MOSAIC		Social interdependence	Loosely connected assembly of subsystems	Each subsystem relatively independent in authority	Flow of inter-action partitioned by subgroup walls
III CLOCKWORK		Mechanical	Rigid, inflexible interdependencies	Centralized authority with subordinates not equal among themselves	Rigid pattern of interaction defined by original design
IV PYRAMID BUILDERS		Geometric	Hierarchy	Hierarchical division of authority	Interactions dominated by superior/subordi-nate relationships
V CONGLOMERATES, MERGERS		Geometric (cluster of pyramids)	Assembly of hierarchies united at summits	Centralized authority over hierarchies of authority	Interactions among hierarchies flow through a common junction
VI ORGANIC ORGANIZATIONS (PLANT TYPE)		Biological unfolding, but mindless	Loose network	Dispersion of authority in accord with concept of corporate citizenship	A new but limited freedom of interaction among people at many levels
VII ORGANIC ORGANIZATIONS (HUMAN TYPE)		Biological growth with man as the model	Tight network	Broad, uniform distribution of authority which clusters as operations require	Complete freedom of interaction

GLOSSARY   PHOENIX PROCESS   destruction by fire (merger or bankruptcy), rebirth from the ashes
HIERARCHY   a pyramidal arrangement of people on levels of authority and power
INTERACTION AMONG PEOPLE   the gross pattern of interpersonal behavior which most clearly characterizes each organization class